The teaching of English in secondary schools

Assistant Masters Association

FOURTH EDITION

CAMBRIDGE
At the University Press 1973

Published by the Syndics of the Cambridge University Press
Bentley House, 200 Euston Road, London NW1 2DB
American Branch: 32 East 57th Street, New York, N.Y.10022

© Cambridge University Press 1957, 1966, 1973

ISBN: 0 521 08611 6

First published 1952
Second edition 1957
Reprinted 1959   1962
Third edition 1966
Fourth edition 1973

Printed in Great Britain
by W. Heffer & Sons Ltd., Cambridge

Contents

Members of the committee

Gilbert Bennett	Gowerton County Grammar School for Boys, Swansea
Lauri Griffith-Jones	Prince Henry's Grammar School, Evesham
Trevor Hesketh	St Helen's County Secondary School, Barnsley
Henry Lawrence	Newport High School, Monmouthshire
Anthony Pike	Ecclesfield Comprehensive School
Vivian Summers	Queen Elizabeth's School, Crediton
George Watkins	Lancaster Royal Grammar School
Michael Woods	Chesham High School
Raymond Hemington (Chairman)	Dinas Bran School, Llangollen

Messrs J. Barrett, L. Brown and K. C. Jones also served on the committee during the early stages of its work. The committee wish to thank them and the many corresponding members who helped with comments.

Preface to the fourth edition

'English as a school subject has problems that are common to all types of schools and to children of all ages.' This statement in the preface to the first edition, published in 1952, is as true today as it was then, and during the last ten years or so a wide variety of ways of solving these problems have been proposed and discussed. In the preparation of this fourth edition full account has been taken of the changes in the organisation of secondary education which have occurred during recent years, and in the teaching of English in secondary schools. It is our hope that this book will be of value to teachers in all types of secondary schools, to students who are training for the teaching profession, and to teachers of English overseas.

The Association has been fortunate in being able to bring together a group of members with wide experience who were willing to devote a large amount of time to the preparation of this book. Their approach to the task is set out in 'Please read this first' (I hope all readers and users of the book will comply with their request): to them and to those who helped them in their work, I express our grateful thanks.

A. W. S. HUTCHINGS
Secretary, Assistant Masters Association

January 1972

Acknowledgements

Thanks are due to the following for permission to reproduce copyright material: Leslie Norris and Chatto and Windus Ltd for 'The Ballad of Billy Rose' from *Finding Gold* by Leslie Norris; 'Red Piano' from *MAYA: Works 1959-1969* by Anselm Hollo, published by Cape Goliard, London, and Grossman, New York, 1970 © Anselm Hollo, 1965, 1970, 1972. The extract from *A Portrait of the Artist as a Young Man* by James Joyce, copyright © 1964 by the Estate of James Joyce. All rights reserved. Reprinted by permission of The Viking Press, Inc.; Jonathan Cape Ltd; and the Society of Authors as the literary representative of the Estate of James Joyce.

Introduction
'Please read this first'

'Never mind the introduction; let's start reading what the writer himself has to say.' This is often sound advice to give to a class about to begin a study of a piece of imaginative writing, but in the case of this book it does not apply. This book does not consist of imaginative writing, and it is written not by a writer, but by a committee of writers. To avoid any misconceptions which might arise from this plurality of authorship, we ask you to read this introduction first.

It might be argued that the only successful book written by a committee is the Authorised Version of the Bible. They had, let us say, Advantages. Even so, these have not prevented the rise of many misconceptions about it, leading on the one hand to a vain attempt to reconcile all the various points of view, and on the other, to bitter attacks on its veracity *just because* it expresses different points of view. Lest the reader should be tempted to beat himself or us with these rods, here is a brief account of how the committee set about the writing of this book.

First, needless to say, we all re-read the 1966 edition of *The Teaching of English*. We found many admirable things in it, and approached our task with a new humility. Nevertheless, we were unanimous in deciding that nothing short of complete re-writing would do. For instance, to mention one obvious point, the previous edition refers throughout to the teaching of boys. The spread of co-education has meant that by now a majority of our members teach girls as well as boys. An even more fundamental reason for a complete re-writing has been the growth of comprehensive education. Underlying the last edition was the tacit assumption that most of our members were grammar school teachers. A few taught in modern schools, it was acknowledged, so let there be a special chapter for them. It seemed to us that a treatment far more comprehensive, in both senses of the word, was patently needed in the new edition. Moreover, we had to bear in mind the phenomenon of earlier maturation, and the raising of the school-leaving age. When we added to these considerations our realisation of the vast amount of new thinking that had emerged from educational research generally, and from N.A.T.E. and Schools Council projects in particular, the case for a completely new book seemed unchallengeable.

Our first task was to draw up a list of the aspects of English teaching that we wished to deal with, and to allocate them among ourselves, in the first instance on the basis of individual interest. Our guiding principle was to be that everything in the book should be written from personal experience, and this we hold to be true of the book now in your hands.

Even in our preliminary discussions it became obvious that there were certain tender areas where we were likely to disagree, and the most important of these was in the field of language teaching. In order to help our member who had undertaken this difficult chapter, each of us wrote a paper on 'My attitude to language teaching'. This preliminary step enabled us to narrow down the area of disagreement to the question of the place of grammatical terminology, and the need or otherwise for formal grammatical teaching. We found, for instance, that the practice of some was to begin in the first year with a brief intensive course in simple grammatical terms, after which they were never mentioned except in cases of dire need. Others of us saw a point in having grammatical terms as a kind of time-saving shorthand. All of us rejected stoutly the view that it was the duty of the teacher of English to teach grammar for the benefit of the foreign language department. None of us seriously believed that the teaching of grammar would do more than marginally improve the quality of expression. Whatever our individual views, we are all light-years away from the attitude that produced such a delightful monstrosity as *Shakespeare's 'Love's Labour's Lost': Parsed and Analysed*, a treasured copy of which was on the common-room shelf of my first school — treasured, I hasten to add, as an historical exhibit, not as a teaching aid.

As the first draft of each section was completed, its author had to submit to grilling by his colleagues on the committee, and by the corresponding members. No one was expected to alter any statement of strongly-held belief, but there were many generous concessions to cogent argument. By this procedure we hope to have kept alive the individuality of the writing, while eliminating what might be considered egocentric statements. The more conservative reader may feel that many of the ideas here are visionary and impractical. Let him remember that some visionary theorists discovered America; others conceived the idea of an old age pension. We in our turn have tried to remember that visionary theorists also invented the pseudo-science of phrenology and advocated annual parliaments. It would be as unreasonable for the reader to expect, as for us to claim, that we have finally settled many of the controversies raging in education today. Are examinations an absurd hindrance to good teaching, a necessary evil, or (in moderation) a good thing in themselves? Does spelling really matter? What do we really mean by 'slipshod' pronunciation? Ought the teacher to be influenced by the social disadvantages attendant on speaking a dialect? Conversely, ought the natural possessors of Standard English to be encouraged to speak a 'good' dialect?

Our failure to agree on the answers to these questions was not surprising. What may surprise some is that we were united in dissatisfaction with written homework in the lower school. The poor conditions under which such written work had to be done by the majority of pupils were felt to militate against any possible advantages that might accrue from increased practice. Homework was too often administered as a kind of moral tonic prescribed by Dr Head, at the insistence of anxious parents. We felt that, instead, parents could best help by giving every possible encouragement to wide reading at home.

Our modest aim, then, is to stimulate thought on these contentious subjects. Indeed, the committee would not wish it to be thought that any of the chapters constitute a complete treatment of their topics. They are intended as a lead-in. Whole books, as the book lists show, are available for those wishing to pursue the various topics in greater depth. The contributors have tried wherever possible to acknowledge sources, but when ideas are 'in the air', unconscious, and therefore unacknowledged, quotation is bound to occur. We wish to apologise for such lapses. In any case, there is a sense in which the originator of a new concept should be proud that his idea has become common property. No doubt the makers of a certain patent vacuum flask can take a wry pleasure in the fact that their patent name has become, in common parlance, the generic term for all vacuum flasks!

Those who read all the chapters will find that there is some overlapping. This is inevitable. English teaching must be a unity; there is no clearly-defined boundary between one aspect of the subject and another. In some cases this overlappping has been cut down by cross-reference. In other cases we have left in a certain amount of detail, repeated in other chapters, either for the convenience of the reader, who is thus spared the necessity of too much thumbing over of pages, or where we felt it was a pity to spoil the natural flow of an argument by having part of its support in another place. Readers may also feel that at times we have stated the obvious, or laboured points known to all competent teachers of English. ('Sir, I've read it!', 'Sir! Seen it on the telly!' O words of fear!) This also is deliberate. We hope that among our readers will be many about to begin their training. As the old hands should know from bitter experience, nothing is obvious to everyone, and not everything is obvious even to the most intelligent. Having mentioned the beginner, I feel that this is a convenient place to stress something that the committee feels cannot be said too often. *Where group methods are advocated, it is with the proviso that, first of all, firm class-control must have been established. To adopt group methods prematurely is a sure recipe for disaster.*

What other readers, apart from beginners, do we hope to attract? Certainly the mature teacher. None can, or should, escape the divine discontent with his own methods which is the mark of an alert sensibility. Moreover, the book is by no means exclusively concerned with methods. There are chapters full of sheer, hard facts, which we hope should be valuable to heads of departments when ordering books and equipment. Yet perhaps the mature teacher will find his greatest use for the book in the fact that, properly used, it constitutes the nearest approach to a syllabus that good teaching will permit. The day of the rigid syllabus has gone, we hope for ever. Nevertheless, some guidelines remain essential, and it is our belief that this book provides them.

We should also be glad to find head teachers and members of governing bodies and education committees among our readers. Amid the universal clamour for more money, more teaching time and more teaching aids, to which all these persons are subjected, the clear voice of the English specialist should be heard. Dear enemies, the English department needs tools as much as the metalworkers, laboratories as much as the scientists, books more than any other department, and *floor space*; and please encourage in-service training for the English staff, and be generous with money for it. New ideas in teaching English need to be promulgated with at least as much vigour as New Mathematics and Nuffield Science.

We hope also to find readers among the staffs of departments of education and colleges of education. It is our belief that some of our ideas may increase the amount of actual practical advice that can be given to the teacher in training. We feel that every intending teacher of English should be taught to type, and to manipulate all the aids that the electronic industries are putting at his disposal; and since we hold that chalk and talk still have a valuable part to play in the English room, we should like the basic skill of writing on the board to be part of the training of the English teacher. Let there be boards all round the corridors for him to practise in his spare time, even if he only writes up the slogans so beloved of the young!

Finally we feel that all those who, for want of a more euphonious word, are styled educationists, may be interested in this report from the field. Here they may discover which of their seeds have taken root, which did not germinate, and which did not even reach the farm.

For this is above all a book written by practising teachers, all heads of department, whose combined experience covers a wide variety of schools. If you are also a practising teacher, then however idealistic, iconoclastic, or even reactionary you may find us, please remember this. We, too, have known what it is to teach forty in a room designed for twenty; to have to make the choice between suffocation with the window closed, and being deafened by a pneumatic drill with the window open; to be reading a favourite poem to a class, and to have it interrupted by a persistent cougher, or a message from the head on paper, or even over the Tannoy; we, too, have experienced that first, faint whiff of spearmint that betrays the chewer, the exhibitionist who shouts out all the answers, and the inhibitionist who never says anything. And the marking. . . ! (We have not shirked the fact that, to be effective, English teaching needs to be backed by large quantities of marked work. Is it too much to ask in return for specially generous provision of English specialists, so that classes may be smaller, and marking proportionally reduced?) Nevertheless, none of us would voluntarily do anything else for a living but teach English.

It has given me much pleasure to chair this committee. Not the least of the small incidental pleasures was to learn that there is a system of library classification known as Bliss – and another called Modified Bliss. While at work with the committee, I have felt the teaching of English to be bliss. At other times – well, modified bliss! I here record my thanks to the committee for making my task as chairman easy, and this book possible. Together we would thank all our corresponding members for their valued comments, and also the staff of the Association's headquarters for assisting us in our work.

RAYMOND HEMINGTON

1 Writing – personal and impersonal

George Watkins

It is not much use trying to prescribe a course of instruction in written English for all secondary schools. What you can do in your own particular school will depend on what kind of school it is – comprehensive, grammar, secondary modern, technical, bilateral, wealthy urban, poor urban, suburban, rural, or whatever. It will depend on the talents and interests of the staff, and on the talents and interests of the pupils. The best I can do for you is to outline some general principles and pass on some general information about successful practice.

To begin with, ask these questions: what do your pupils *want* to write, and what do they *need* to write? Anything? You have to ask these questions, because it is a dreadful waste of time and effort to force pupils to perform tasks that neither they nor anyone else want. Just consider, for instance, 'a well-constructed paragraph of 70-100 words on "The pleasures of the countryside" '. Who wants to write it? Who wants to read it? If the honest answer to both questions is 'nobody', there is not much point in asking for it.

Unless they have been actively discouraged, most young people are eager to communicate a lot of things in a variety of ways. You can fairly say that they want to communicate their own experiences by means of painting and drawing, modelling, singing and dancing, miming, speaking, and writing. Some experience – though certainly not all – is best communicated in writing, and this remains true whatever you think about our changing society in which television, tape recorders and telephones are becoming more and more plentiful. Most young people of secondary-school age can read a page much faster than anyone can speak the text to them, and a written text can be re-considered and checked in detail over and over again much more easily than any spoken recording, cue button and other gadgets notwithstanding. It is simply true that some things are best communicated in writing.

Your pupils will want to communicate some of their *personal* experiences in writing: things they have heard and seen and felt through the other senses, things they have pondered and wondered about. For some of these personal experiences, intensive writing will be the best medium: verse, prose-poems, aphorisms, epigrams, *pensées* – the forms in which the words communicate much more than their literal significance. Characteristically, this kind of writing has a high proportion of ellipsis, of broken syntax or non-syntax; it is composed more or less in linguistic patterns other than sentences. For instance:

> red piano
>
> a red piano
> he says
> a red piano
> I never saw one
> I knew a man who had a red typewriter
> he hardly ever used it
> a red piano
> would it seem lighter to carry upstairs
> than a black one?
> a red piano
> a red piano
> let us think more musical thoughts

Anselm Hollo

> Impressions
>
> Excitement – Beaming Faces – Multi-coloured Jeans and Sweaters – Away at a Gallop – Churned-up Canal Bank – Strong Winds Impede Progress – Slackening of Pace – Hot Soup; Revival – Prevailing Wind lends a hand – Cathedral Spire in sight – but on the Horizon! – 5 miles to go – Weary Feet – Blisters – The Longest Mile.
>   – Hot Baths – Bandages, Plasters – Walking Sticks – The School limps – but several Families re-housed – Success.
>
> Sixth-form pupil: impressions of a sponsored walk

Anselm Hollo's poem consists of speech items which are near sentences, or not quite sentences, full of associations but not exactly systematic in the conventional way. The sixth-form boy's prose-poem makes no pretence of being composed in sentences; it consists of headlines and significant fragments which stimulate sympathetic responses in the senses and emotions. Both would be the poorer for being composed in conventional syntax.

Characteristically, too, intensive writing contains a high proportion of active metaphors as opposed to conventional ones. Here is a simple example:

Stage décor

There we were, holding the canvas for him.
Then he ran at it.
I tell you, he ran at it
With a great big brush, full of paint.
And flung it.
Well, we saw him coming, and ducked down behind,
And heard it splat
Like twenty seven cows.
We could hear him growling on the other side.

After a bit he calmed down, and said, 'You can come out now.'
So we did.

Then he did it again.

Here there is a new perception of similarity between dissimilars —
between cow-droppings and action-painting. It is not elegant, but it is
illuminating. The metaphor is characteristically live.

Generally, in intensive writing, there is not much explanation; for
instance, of how Anselm Hollo came to hear about the red piano, or of
what stage-set the boy was painting. Things are left to speak for
themselves. Done badly, this kind of writing can all too easily be
slovenly or maundering. At its best it produces a text which is unique,
in which nothing can be altered without changing the significance of
the communication. The text is thus-and-not-otherwise. From producing
such a text a pupil gets the satisfaction of having made something
which is uniquely his own.

Extensive writing

Other kinds of personal experience are best communicated in extensive
writing — narration, description, various kinds of ratiocination.
Characteristically, this kind of writing contains a lot of explanatory
material; obviously, since the writers want to explain their experiences
at length. Consequently, it is usually composed in a full syntax of
complete sentences, with more or less elaborate systems of
subordination. The language tends to be denotative, with the words
used in their generally accepted senses, and with a high proportion of
conventional metaphors as opposed to actively original ones. Here is an
example from a script written in an English examination by a first-year
pupil:

Because burning something in water is a bit difficult, we had to use
steam.

To pass steam over burning magnesium to be left with Element X, we set up a test tube with a wad of water-soaked cotton wool in the end followed by a coil of Magnesium half-way down the test tube. Then a holed cork with a nozzle of glass tube was put in.

Then we started heating. We had to heat very strongly at first to get the magnesium to burn, when that was burning, we heated the cotton wool wad to obtain some steam to pass over the burning magnesium, the oxygen would be used up, and Element X would emerge from the nozzle. But we could not see anything. This means that Element X is either a colourless gas, or we are not producing anything.

But suddenly a burst of flame from the nozzle startled us. The flame lasted for about fifteen seconds, and then died away.

Everything is told here, nothing is suggested. Reasons and explanations are given, and even at the most exciting moment the metaphors are restricted to the conventional 'burst of flame' and 'died away'. It is excellent of its kind.

Since the writers of extensive writing are particularly anxious to inform their readers rather than to establish an instant rapport, the typography and the lay-out of the page tend to be conventional – the kind of thing most readers expect, rather than what the writer feels he must have. The texts produced by this kind of writing do often bear the marks of the writers' individuality, but it is unusual for them to be unique. What is communicated could usually be communicated just as well in other orders and other forms of words.

Your pupils have to live in society with other people, so they will want and need to make social communications, some of which are best made in writing. In this class come letters of all sorts (personal, official, business, etc; letters requiring tact and persuasiveness; letters of indignation or of sympathy, frosty ones, friendly ones and penitent ones); notes (for the milkman, for the baby-sitter, for people who were out when you called, for telephone messages, etc.); postcards and picture-postcards, invitations, acceptances and polite refusals; memoranda, minutes, and other records of activities and decisions; notices.

Characteristically, social communications are highly conventional, because, at any rate in day-to-day matters, people get on best with each other by observing the conventions. In particular there are conventional forms of beginning and ending social communications (especially letters); conventional forms of language (e.g. in invitations, acceptances, etc., and minutes); conventions of lay-out (each kind of communication has its own) and even of typography. There are, too, conventions of style that depend on the rôles and relationships of the participants. A note from mother to daughter to say that the dinner is in the oven will not be in the same style and lay-out as a note from the same girl to her headmistress to say that she has been called for an interview at short notice and will not be at school on Monday.

Your pupils need, and, I hope, want, to communicate in writing the results of their work in school. Communication of this sort includes evidence of what they have learned, and material for their own reference and revision.

Each field of study has its own conventions in this kind of communication. The conventions of syntax, style, and lay-out are quite different for a history test, a set of geography notes, an account of an experiment in chemistry, a recipe in domestic science and an essay on *Lord of the Flies*. These examples are given in terms of traditional subjects, but the general argument will still apply to integrated studies. At the moment there seems to be no single style or register peculiar to, say, humanities. Each field of study has its own conventions of form and usage in written communication.

By and large the specialist teachers must be responsible for teaching the linguistic conventions of their own specialisms. There can be no wriggling out of it by saying in a particular school that the old subject divisions no longer apply. Probably they don't, but new ones do. In secondary education no teacher can know enough to teach everything. Each of us has his field of study and his field of responsibility; whether they are traditional or emancipated, we still have them, and it is part of our business to teach the conventions that belong to them. The job cannot be dumped on to the English staff. They know the conventions of their own specialism, which is probably English literature. They cannot be expected to have more than a nodding acquaintance with the conventions of other specialisms, and in any case they usually have quite enough to occupy them in meeting the demands of their own specialism with inadequate resources and too little time. Besides, our pupils' command of language is likely to be enriched by diversity of usage. The more the merrier, as long as everybody understands that there is no one universally 'correct' kind of English, and nobody sets himself up as sole keeper of the one and only temple of 'good' English.

Techniques of communication

A lot of the work in school consists of communicating in writing the things that have been learned. As far as teachers of English are concerned, this written communication of things learned is likely to be in the form of expository essays — the kind of essays in which pupils show what they have learned about the books or other material they have been studying. The syntax of this kind of writing is, characteristically, complete, and there is a more or less elaborate system of subordination to provide for the explanations which are the essence of the work. The style is formal, though by no means necessarily impersonal. There is likely to be plentiful use of quotation, reference, reported speech, and summary, each of which requires a developed and quite sophisticated technique. Incidentally, there is no room for sentimental dodging of this fact by saying that such techniques are beyond the capacity of some pupils, and therefore all pupils should be left to write about literature and all other experience as they think best. The techniques *are* beyond the capacity of some pupils, but they are well within the capacity of the majority by the time they have reached the fifth year. A pupil who has acquired reasonable skill in them can communicate an experience in literature or life very much more effectively than he could do if he had been left to fumble about without guidance because he would be more 'spontaneous' that way. Spontaneity is probably at a premium in personal communication; technical skill is important in the communication of things learned.

The best practice for learning to write is actual writing. I am talking, of course, about communication in the written language, not about calligraphy. Pupils learn to write well by writing often, and supporting their efforts with reading. Plenty of serious material has been published in recent years to confirm this; for example:

Clegg, A. B. *The Excitement of Writing* (Chatto and Windus, 1965).
Dakin, Julian, 'More Advanced Teaching of Writing'. *Proceedings of the Edinburgh University Summer School in Applied Linguistics,* 1966.
Holbrook, David. *English for the Rejected* (C.U.P., 1964).
Newsom, J. and others. *Half Our Future* (H.M.S.O., 1963).
Whitehead, Frank. *The Disappearing Dais* (Chatto and Windus, 1966).
Wilkinson, Andrew. 'Research on Formal Grammar'. Research note in N.A.T.E. *Bulletin* vol. 1, no. 2, with bibliography.
Working Paper No. 3 – English (Schools Council) (H.M.S.O., 1965).

Both published research and the experience of many successful teachers tend to show that isolated exercises in specific linguistic techniques do less to develop skill in writing than does regular practice in composition at length. Although some teachers find it useful to let very able pupils have a short list of examples of bad usage to avoid, it is overwhelmingly true that when pupils do a lot of exercises in analysing sentences into clauses and synthesising clauses into sentences and punctuating unpunctuated texts and correcting 'common errors', they become more or less adept at doing these exercises, but are not able to transfer the skills when it comes to continuous writing. Even those who have got the exercises right are as likely as not to write strings of sentences joined by 'and', with commas scattered like currants in a bun, and split infinitives jostling unrelated participles. Pupils who have spent on continuous writing the time that might have been spent on isolated exercises still make mistakes. Not many of them get the whole thing right every time. But in the space of an academic year you can see most of them steadily acquiring confidence and competence, which is by no means true of those pupils – and it is the majority – who try to do the exercises but simply cannot understand them. Writing seems to be rather like riding a bicycle: you can't practise the leg-drive with the left leg, then the leg-drive with the right leg, then the distribution of weight, and so on, in isolation, one at a time. You have to do it all at once, or not at all. In writing the native language you have to manage syntax, lexis, orthography, punctuation, and paragraph structure all at once, or not at all. When you are learning to ride, it doesn't matter if you wobble a bit, so long as you keep going; but fail to co-ordinate, and you fall off. When you are learning to write, it doesn't matter if you make some mistakes so long as you keep going comprehensibly; but fail to co-ordinate and you fall into incoherence. So, if the analogy holds good, the best practice in learning to write is to keep on writing.

The writing situation

If the pupils are going to practise writing, they must have something to write about.

The best way to study writing is to practise it. Children only learn writing by writing, and they are best prepared to write about their own experiences . . . Writing is most likely to flourish in an atmosphere of ideas, discussion and reading . . .
from paras. 481 and 482 of Half Our Future

there must be something to write about and a reason for writing . . . Furthermore, there is in my mind no doubt that the readiness of children to write and the quality of their writing is influenced by opportunities to express their thoughts through other materials such as paint, clay, fabric and dramatic movement.
teacher quoted in The Excitement of Writing, p. 28

Pupils are unlikely to write well unless they have something they really need to communicate in a more lasting form. Only a skilled professional writer can turn his hand to anything, and write of shoes and ships and

sealing wax as the arbitrary occasion arises . . . If children have
something to say, and want it to last, they will make very great efforts
to write it in the most telling way they can – and that means that
handwriting must be legible and punctuation and spelling ought not to
pull the reader up. But a pupil wants to communicate only if he feels
he is recognised as a unique and valuable individual; how else can he
gain confidence?

Schools Council Working Paper no. 3, p. 5

Your main contribution, as a teacher of writing, is to provide, or to
help the pupils to provide, suitable situations for them to write in; to
write *in,* not *about.* Most of us must remember what it is like to be
given something to write *about*:

The candidates sit in disciplined ranks and files of desks, the question
paper face down before them, the air full of tension. At a signal from
the invigilator, the little green, pink or white slips are turned over.
There is an empty silence as the wisps and shreds of ideas and teachers'
advice disappear before the subjects now revealed. None seems possible;
'no ideas here'.
  Do you remember that feeling? Nine o'clock in the morning and an
hour to produce 600 acceptable words out of the void, driven by none
of the motives that normally bring pen to paper.

Esmor Jones, *English Examined,* N.A.T.E.

Well, perhaps Esmor Jones is being a bit less than impartial, but all the
same, what a situation to be *in*! Remember Auden's lines:

> In theory they were sound on Expectation
> Had there been situations to be in.
> Unluckily they were their situation . . .

'The Quest', I

Non-professional learners, obliged to start writing from cold, on an
arbitrary topic, are their own situation with a vengeance. Anybody who
puts them in that situation gets what he deserves when he has to read
the results.
  Pupils who have undergone an experience (not necessarily an
enjoyable one) and have become aware of it will generally be keen to
write about it if it is at all suitable for expression in writing. There are
exceptions, usually to do with the act of writing rather than with the
experience (see p. 27) but most pupils are ready enough to write about
the situations they find themselves in. What they need is to be aware of
the situation, and the awareness usually comes from talking about it.
An adult writer, moved by the play of cloud-shadows on snow-covered
hills, may well wish to record the experience without preliminary

discussion. He may be practised enough to write for his boss, without preliminary consultation, a memorandum about what is wrong with a defective batch of nuts and bolts. He may, however, want to talk the situation over with his wife, or with a knowledgeable friend, if not an accountant, before writing a letter to H.M. Inspector of Taxes about what looks like a mistake in his P.A.Y.E. coding. A pupil of secondary-school age, certainly up to sixteen, living intensely in the present, with a short memory and limited foresight, nearly always needs to have his attention drawn to his situation, and to talk about it, before he realises that he is in a situation at all, never mind that there is anything to be written about it. You can try this out by asking a class how they come to be sitting where they are, dressed as they are, at that particular moment. You will soon understand, if you did not know it before, the value of 'arousing interest', or 'providing a stimulus', or 'securing involvement', or 'introducing a starter', or whatever the current jargon of the handbooks tells you to do. But remember: talk first, write later. Be warned by Arthur J. Casebeer:

> [A class of American freshmen had written] an extemporaneous theme. Its subject was traditional: 'Who I am and why I came to Dwight College.' . . . Howe [the lecturer] picked up [one]. 'I am Arthur J. Casebeer, Jr.,' he read. 'My father is Arthur J. Casebeer and my grandfather was Arthur J. Casebeer before him. My mother is Nina Wimble Casebeer. Both of them are college graduates and my father is in insurance. I was born in St. Louis eighteen years ago and we still make our residence there.'
>
> Lionel Trilling, *Of This Time, Of That Place*

'No ideas here'. So put the pupils in a situation, and bring them to an awareness of it. The writing will follow.

What kind of situations? It all depends, as I said in the opening paragraph, on you, your pupils, your school and the environment. I cannot prescribe for you; only suggest. However, I do think that there should be some general plan whereby, in the four or five years that constitute the secondary course for the majority of pupils, assignments in the different kinds of writing which they both want and need, come round at regular intervals. It seems unlikely that, in the secondary stage, there is much cumulative 'progress' in writing; pupils do not have to perfect narrative technique before going on to descriptive technique, and descriptive technique before going on to reflective technique, and reflective technique before going on to the technique of argument. The memorandum is not the inescapable preliminary to the business letter, or the business letter to the official one. Pupils are ready to have a go at whatever kind of writing is appropriate to the situation they happen to be in. In your capacity as teacher, it is your business to arrange a variety of situations so that by the end of their four or five years the pupils have had regular practice in all the kinds of writing necessary for that *social competence* prescribed by the Newsom Report.

In school it is not always easy to arrange realistic situations for writing. You may be lucky and have a properly-equipped English room offering a double ration of floor space, easily stacked and informal furniture, sound-absorbent walls and good recording and play-back apparatus, storage for books and pictures and specimens, ciné and still projectors, dressing-up stuff, and so on. If you are, all you have to do is get on with using it. However, most of us still have to teach thirty-five pupils in oblong classrooms designed for thirty, ourselves defending the blackboard, the pupils sitting at desks or tables in rows like cut-price passengers in a jumbo jet. Most of us will have to go on doing it for the rest of our time, and it doesn't look much like real life. So most of the situations for writing will have to be 'let's pretend'. Yet real life does intrude. You yourself can bring in newspaper and magazine material and material from the local library (where the staff are only waiting to be asked to help), and the pupils will bring in collections of things to illustrate a theme (e.g. 'smallest', or 'hardest and softest', or 'home and abroad'). There are school visits and outings. Theatre companies, musicians, bigwigs, the youth employment officer, the road-safety officer, the school doctor, all disrupt the abstracted unreality. In the neighbourhood, disasters, elections, fairs, festivals and uproars take place. Families do have holidays, and keep pets, and many secondary pupils have spare-time or holiday jobs. Take advantage of the stir that exists, or that you have created. Mention the topic, talk about it yourself, play a bit of tape, or show some pictures, or read a poem, or show some specimens, just to start things going. Then let the pupils start pooling their knowledge and experience and material – in groups of five or six if it seems appropriate, or in general discussion if that seems appropriate. After that, set a deadline for the completion of the writing, and the scheme will apparently generate its own motive power. In fact, you will be kept very busy satisfying requests for advice and information, and in doing so you can boost the power without seeming to be directly involved at all.

If you don't mind shuffling the items on your programme – and you shouldn't – you can take advantage of the first-hand events of real life as they occur. Don't be afraid of opportunism; it is messy, but it has its place in the scheme of things. If you can rouse your pupils to genuine discussion of an event, or, better still, if you find them bursting to discuss it, let the discussion go on, stir it up if necessary, and use the opportunity for an assignment in writing. Don't worry if not everyone works in the same literary form or responds in the same way. On the contrary, try as far as possible to see that each pupil has the opportunity of developing the experience in his own individual way. A Guy Fawkes bonfire run out of control can stimulate poems, prose descriptions, narratives, letters to a newspaper, and (preferably hypothetical) obituaries, consoling, mocking, reporting, or just contemplating. It all depends on how it takes individuals. All you need worry about in these opportunist situations is the pupil who, having struck on a successful form or attitude, uses it over and over again to the exclusion of all others. You have to judge the right time to encourage him to leave the cosiness of the familiar and to be more adventurous both in the response and in the form in which it is expressed.

You should be able to organise other assignments in writing to coincide with and exploit the work of colleagues in other departments. The same stimulus (story, music, object, person) as your artist colleague uses for encouraging personal expression in painting will often produce intensive personal writing, too — a story like Bill Naughton's 'Spit Nolan', a poem like Julian Mitchell's 'Holiday', something like Solveig's song from Grieg's *Peer Gynt* music (with some pictures of fjords, glaciers, traditional buildings and national costume), or objects like a lump of coal that have well-known associations, or a person like a newspaper-seller on the town hall steps, well-known and easy to observe. Many of your pupils will have grown accustomed to writing in a personal way about the rabbits and fish and hamsters and other creatures that are kept in so many primary schools. Well, animals are kept and studied in secondary schools, too, though probably in a laboratory rather than in a general classroom. There is no reason why you should not exploit their presence for encouraging personal writing, and thereby serve your own turn as well as supplement the work of the biologists. It is worth while talking to the historians. The Spanish Armada, the Peterloo Massacre, the Factory and Education Acts, the Munich business of 1938, and Hiroshima, are all good stuff to collaborate on, if your colleague happens to be dealing with any of them at a time that will suit you. Talk to colleagues in other departments, too, and find out whether they will be doing anything that you can conveniently use. But keep your balance. Use the work of other departments when it is *convenient* for you. There is no need to run mad integrating everything all the time. Collaboration with other departments is not a miracle worker; it is just one of a number of useful techniques at your disposal.

Some situations have to be arranged at their own times. Towards the end of the autumn term is the obvious time for working on the conventions of the 'thank you' letter, invitations and acceptances. They have to be learned some time, and Christmas is the time when they will be most needed. It is no more than common sense to meet that need. By the same token, the conventions of business letters and letters of application have to be dealt with, and may as well be learned in the appropriate year, according to the leaving habits in your school, in preparation for the interviews with the youth employment officer. Incidentally, it is worth agreeing on standardised conventions for letters and so on. There is in fact very little uniformity of practice outside school, but, as long as everyone understands that the conventions are only conventions, it is worth trying to eliminate confusion within the school. Again, there is nothing really wrong with an assignment for personal writing on 'What I did in the holidays', provided that it does not have to be written starting from cold. After all, pupils do enjoy holidays, and can enjoy telling about them. It may seem corny to say this, but there *is* a case for having the 'holiday' assignment early in the autumn term. There must be opportunities, too, for sheer fantasy to break away from the real and earnest and rather humdrum business of crowded living in a more or less civilised society. Midsummer's Day and Hallowe'en are useful dates for encouraging flights into the strange, the weird, or the merely rum.

Yet other writing situations have to be timed to fit in with your other work in English studies. When you are studying a literary text on which notes will have to be written — then, more or less, is the time to teach the technique of note-making.

The making of notes from books (e.g. of criticism or explanation) is fairly easy to teach in terms of summary and lay-out, because the material from which the notes are made is there in permanent form. Presumably nobody nowadays degrades the learning process and wastes time by dictating notes; and at this stage it may be as well to point out that notes should be the minimum script necessary for satisfactory recall, not the maximum script to show diligence. But many pupils need to learn to take notes from speech, not just for the study of set books but for the study of practically everything else as well. Once again, it is really a matter of summary and lay-out, but the trouble is that the material is ephemeral. The teacher's words as he expounds the text, or the words of the group in discussion, cannot usually be recalled. Until recently they could not be recalled at all, and of course you do not want to record every lesson, or even very many lessons. But in lessons specifically devoted to learning how to make notes from speech, it helps the pupils if the speech (i.e. exposition and discussion) from which the notes are made is recorded and is later played back to them several times. They learn by intensive practice to distinguish the significant from the insignificant as it occurs, and to anticipate the form a discourse will take. However, the point to be made here is that note-making needs to be learned, and that it is best learned in connection with some activity in English studies that requires the making of notes.

If there is going to be a class debate, somebody will have to take the minutes, and there is the opportunity for everybody to learn the specialised technique of summary and reported speech that is necessary for minute-writing. If teams are working on projects, the situation can be fiddled so that they need to circulate information, and the conventions of writing memoranda can be picked up. When the study of a literary text requires the writing of essays, then the situation calls for instruction and practice in the conventions of the literary essay, which include (see p. 11) the presentation of quotations, the use and acknowledgement of references, the use of reported speech, and accurate summary. These are only some examples of how the timing of particular kinds of written assignment depends on the timing of other work in English. Each teacher has to arrange his own timing, according to the requirements of the school's English syllabus, and the talents of his pupils, and his own preference for taking things in one order rather than another.

Programmes and projects

Do not neglect broadcasting. The B.B.C. radio programmes 'Listening and Writing' and 'Books, Plays, Poems' provide, year after year, some of the very best material for starting discussion and writing. Much of the writing they stimulate is personal, but it does not have to be exclusively so. The material in the programmes can generally be used — at different levels of understanding — with all age-groups from first to seventh year in secondary schools. The B.B.C. have resources of trained actors, archives in sound, research workers, collections of sound effects, and so on, which no teacher can hope to rival. The very pamphlets for pupils are infinitely better, at the price, than a teacher can hope to produce on a school duplicator, The teachers' pamphlets, which you can use or ignore as you please, are usually a help to making the best use of the broadcasts. The timing of assignments based on radio programmes is easier than it used to be. Nowadays it is perfectly in order to make tape recordings of the educational broadcasts and play them to classes at convenient times for anything up to a year after the date of the broadcasts. The only trouble is that the pamphlets are not reprinted, and have to be handled carefully if they are to last.

If your school's timetable and equipment allow you to show pupils the excellent B.B.C. and I.T.V. television programmes for schools, you are in luck, though you have to adapt your work to fit in with the programmes. If you have a video-tape recorder and projector, you are doubly in luck, for you can adapt first-class material to fit in with your teaching.

Finally, if you have a local radio station, see whether it has an education officer. Many stations do, and are genuinely anxious to do all they can to meet teachers' needs.

So far I have suggested planned assignments in their own right, planned assignments arising from other work in English, assignments linked to work in other specialisms, and opportunist assignments. There remain projects – long-term tasks of learning-by-finding-out, probably undertaken by teams or groups, and incorporating pictures, cuttings, decorations and other display items as well as writing (see Chapter 11). As instruments of general education, projects are invaluable. Well-conducted, they extend the range of knowledge and curiosity of the group, and give every pupil a chance to do whatever he is good at doing: those who can write best, they do the writing; those who can draw best, they do the illustrations; those who are good with an index, they do the finding out, and so on. An assignment that is particularly relevant to English studies, and can – indeed should – come round again and again, is a class magazine or wall-display. Probably we can all do with a rest from 'The Wheel', but it is surprising how acceptable an assignment on Shakespeare's theatre can be . . . However, projects do take up a lot of time, and they sometimes tend to consolidate existing interests and skills only. It is not always easy to persuade pupils that there are better things to do than spend hours transcribing quantities of pudding-like prose from books of information. Then pupils who can draw, tend to specialise in illustration and to learn nothing much new about reading or writing. Those whose speciality is reading, tend to do the reading, and learn nothing much new about writing or illustration, or whatever. Some, of course, do develop their skill in writing, but they are likely to be proficient in it already. You can, and must, meet these objections, probably by allocating the work and organising the teams in different ways; but remember that projects, like all other kinds of assignments for writing, are valuable in their way without being the universal answer to all educational questions. They should take their place in your programme of writing, along with the other kinds of assignment.

To return to that programme: make your own programme if you possibly can, and make it flexible. And don't expect too much. Most course-books are utterly dispiriting documents, especially to young teachers, because they are so full of material, and seem to expect an output of 1,000 words of well-composed something-or-other twice a week. The compilers mean well. They hope they are giving teachers a choice of material. In fact, they usually fill young teachers with guilt-feelings because they don't seem able to get through all the work in the time, and older teachers with bitterness because they begin to think they are past it.

To be fair (or make a pretence of being fair), I must point out that some teachers find the new-style course-books useful, particularly at the beginning of their careers or when taking on an unfamiliar age-group or ability-group for the first time. But I still say that it is best to do without course-books as soon as you can, because in the end you will *have* to devise your own programme, if only by selecting from the course. So devise your own programme, with an expectation of a serious piece of written work about once a fortnight (or three weeks, or month; you know your pupils and your own work-load) (see Chapter 10). Provided that the assignments come regularly, it doesn't much matter what framework they are in — projects, opportunist tasks, assignments linked to broadcasts, to work in other departments, to other work in English, assignments linked to seasonal occurrences, assignments specified for their own sake as something to be learned. Decide what should be done and *can* be done in the year's work, make a programme of it, and try to get through it. Be prepared to shuffle the order, and be prepared to scrap it for individuals who are in deep trouble (see Chapter 14). First things first: a pupil who genuinely cannot cope, and is in distress, must be given circumstances in which he *can* cope. But try to get through the programme. The very fact of trying will smarten the pace of your teaching, and most pupils, strange as it may seem, like to get a move on. Also, of course, if your programme has been devised to meet the wants and needs of your pupils, there is a duty to get on with it unless it proves in practice to be completely out of touch with those wants and needs. Try to complete the programme.

Writing at length

Many pupils, but still probably a minority, come from their primary schools with a capacity for writing at length. They can manage 500 words without trouble if the assignment suits them. Others cannot. Yet there is nothing to stop them. Look at the performances of David Holbrook's pupils (*English for the Rejected*, pp. 135-6 (I.Q. 72), or pp. 164-5 (I.Q. 80)). Whatever you think of the performances (and remember those I.Q.s before you start passing judgement) you have to admit them as proof that pupils of very limited ability can write at length. What is needed, of course, in the case of intellectually short-winded pupils, is encouragement. It is not every task that needs to be worked out to 500 words or more. Short pieces have their virtues and should have their place in your programme. But when the circumstances are right, encourage pupils to write *all* that the situation prompts them to. Individuals will need encouragement, help, suggestions, more encouragement, and sometimes a bit of prodding and impatience. The process will take time – a lot of time at first, so that you may have to let your programme slide; not so much time later as the pupils get the habit of writing themselves out. They do eventually get the habit, and those who, in the interests of 'correctness', have been restricted to 'well-constructed paragraphs of 50-100 words' find that they have the courage and skill and confidence to communicate all that is in their minds. All they need is the initial excitement and the time to do the writing.

Perhaps I should add 'place' to 'time'. Traditionally, essay writing was for homework, and time in the classroom was reserved for things that needed the teacher's presence: clause analysis, taking it in turn to read set books aloud, identifying figures of speech, doing memory-tests in which co-operation had to be forbidden, and all that sort of thing. Probably the allocation was all right up to 1944, when pupils who were getting any secondary education at all could almost certainly count on favourable circumstances for work at home. But for the last twenty-five years there has been secondary education for all, which has meant that the majority of pupils have been able to count on nothing better than incomprehension and indifference at home, and a significant minority have had to put up with deprivation of facilities and blank hostility to homework. Now, in order to read a book, you need no more than a place to sit down with reasonable light. Modern adolescents can read without apparently being disturbed by the noise of family television. In order to write, you need light, at least a corner of a table, and some semblance of quiet. In many homes this is too much to ask, and the possibility of a dictionary and a few reference books is unthinkable. Yet in the worst-equipped classroom this minimum is available, and there is a teacher present to advise on organisation, form, lay-out, sources of information and possibilities of further development, to encourage and give confidence, to help in the production of a first-class job. There is, therefore, a lot to be said in secondary education nowadays for specifying writing in class and reading at home rather than the other way round.

Of course, deadlines have to be met, and it seems reasonable for work which has already taken shape to be finished at home if no more class time can be allowed. It is also true that some pupils prefer to write continuously at home rather than fragmentarily in the forty-minute bits of class time allowed in most schools, and there is no obvious reason why they should not. If they do not want to write in class, there is, presumably, a programme of private reading prescribed for them, and they can get on with that while the others are writing. As long as the written assignment is completed on time, and is well done, there is no need for everybody to work at the same pace or in the same place. But I still think you should consider very seriously the suggestion that nowadays, for many pupils, writing is for the classroom.

Conventions of writing

Most of the assignments for younger pupils, say in the first and second years, should probably be personal writing, both intensive and extensive. There should be no need to repeat the arguments of David Holbrook, Sir Alec Clegg and others; the point is that the conventions of social written communication (see pp. 9 and 10), on which many teachers spend, ineffectively, too much time, can be learned quite reasonably easily and quickly if the pupils see the need for them and *already have confidence and skill in handling the written language.* The confidence and skill come from practice in writing at length in a state of enjoyable excitement, and that means personal writing. Personal writing demands infinitely variable response to situations, and infinitely variable technique, because each product is, in at least some respects, unique. Pupils who are used to such variety are highly adaptable in their writing habits, and more confident than they would otherwise be in their skill in dealing with the unexpected. Being confident and adaptable, they can learn the social conventions as the need arises, taking them as nothing more difficult than new variations.

Older pupils, say in the third, fourth and fifth years, because of their growing self-consciousness, tend to be more interested in, or at least more forthcoming about, technicalities. So long as they understand the need, they are quite likely to enjoy learning the conventions. But do remember to treat them as conventions, like conventions of dress or table manners, and not as immutable laws. Make sure, too, that what you prescribe is up-to-date. Does everybody nowadays put the address in the top right-hand corner of the letter? If you yourself use printed letter-heads, where has the printer put the address? In the middle, perhaps? Have you perhaps received a letter from a big firm which saved typists' time by having everything lined up on the left-hand margin, and can you say the firm is 'wrong'? And all those full stops and commas – have you looked closely at the practice of *The Times*, the *Guardian*, the Oxford and Cambridge University Presses? How many of us really describe ourselves as 'Your affectionate father' when we write to our children? If you don't check things of this kind from time to time, and remember that they are only conventional, you may have some awkward questions to answer. And all the time, keep the personal writing going. These older pupils need the opportunity to work out their thoughts and emotions in the uniquely systematic way that writing demands, and they need to have their confidence in themselves sustained.

Confidence matters most of all. Without it there is no hope of the 'social competence' prescribed by Newsom as our goal. Your skill as a teacher will be tested in judging how far to let pupils go wrong before you interfere. They must be allowed to make mistakes – to misjudge the scale of an assignment by beginning a 300-word short story in the spacious style of a three-decker novel, and finding out the enormity of what they have undertaken, or, when committed to writing a first chapter only, cramming the whole narrative into a couple of breathless pages; to misjudge form by forcing into pedestrian verse a bit of description that calls for precise, denotative prose; to misjudge style by writing a formal communication in casual language and hearing how inappropriate it sounds; to make errors of taste by adopting a bullying tone in what should be a civil communication, and getting a polite but acid brush-off. They have to learn from these mistakes, and you have to judge how far to let each individual go wrong before he begins to lose his nerve. Before the limit is reached, you have to take preventive action, and there may be times when you virtually have to provide a pupil with what to say and how to say it. On the one hand, you save time by giving general advice and guidance before the writing begins;

on the other, you have to avoid fussing over pupils by too insistently interfering with their 'learning the hard way'. This is one aspect of education in which you are really needed, in which you can never be replaced by any teaching-machine or course-book, however well-programmed.

Another aspect in which you are indispensable is the follow-up. Somebody must read what the pupils have written, and at some stage of every assignment that has to be you. In the first instance the pupils may read and help to re-draft each other's texts – they learn more about spelling, punctuation and acceptable usage that way than from formal lessons. And, incidentally, remember that the first draft of a piece of writing is very rarely a satisfactory final draft. You yourself are very lucky and experienced if you can produce final drafts of your own work at the first attempt. If you always take pupils' first drafts as final, you are asking from pupils what you can't do yourself, and also inhibiting them from working to anything like the limits of their ability.

In the last instance, the work may go into a magazine or personal portfolio, or something of that kind. Certainly it should go somewhere that implies respect for the achievement it represents; no respect, no effort. Then at some stage between first draft and final placing the work must be read by you, the teacher. Quite possibly no other adult will ever read it, and that being so, if you do not read your pupils' work, and they know you don't, their motive for writing is virtually gone. Wouldn't *you* skimp work if you felt that the person who set you to doing it was too lazy (busy, distracted, etc.) to look at it? Haven't *you* done just this? There is no escape: the teacher must read what the pupils have written (see Chapter 10).

Marking

Correction and assessment are a different matter. It is impossible to correct every line of an assignment. There simply is not the time, and in any case there are good reasons for thinking that heavily-corrected scripts only produce despair. A palimpsest of red corrections over black original makes a pupil think that he has got everything wrong, and that ruins his confidence. In the business of correction, spare yourself a lot of unnecessary labour by keeping a sense of proportion and of priorities. First, identify and acknowledge the achievement. A writer who has produced a text has achieved *something*. Even if you don't like what he has succeeded in doing, acknowledge it, and praise it if you can. Without acknowledgement, there can be no useful discussion between teacher and pupil. In making your acknowledgement, consider content and organisation. Second, discuss how the content and organisation might be improved, if they can be. Third, deal with a few selected points of grammar, spelling, punctuation or lay-out. *Selected* points: you can't do everything at once. You can announce beforehand that you want to concentrate this time on full stops, or on spelling, or on the different ways of joining sentences (i.e. subordination and co-ordination), or you can choose one or two aspects that seem to need attention, or you can choose, say, ten lines at random and correct them intensively. Any of these methods of selective correction, or similar ones, will do. It may be best to use them all in turn. Fourth, if an assessment is required, give one. Try to relate it to past work, so that each pupil knows how he is getting on compared with what he did last week, last term, and so on.

In assessing personal writing, in particular, it is very difficult, and probably irrelevant, to make a numerical comparison of one pupil's work with another's, or with the work of the rest of the class. If you have to do it (and most of us do) for the sake of mark-lists, form-orders and so on, at least do not pretend to an arithmetical accuracy finer than your discrimination. When you have two poems, one metrical, the other accentual, one wittily contrived, the other spontaneously emotional, one conventionally correct in usage and amusingly clever in diction, the other unified by a fully-developed metaphor but rather badly spelled, how *can* you decide between 73% for one and 74% for the other? And if, at the end of term, you have to add up the marks for ten pieces of work and produce an average, what *is* the sense of expressing it as 65.723%? The best I can recommend is a simple, five-point scale corresponding to *bad, inferior, average, superior, excellent,* represented as E, D, C, B, A or 1, 2, 3, 4, 5, or 10%, 30%, 50%, 70%, 90%. Resist attempts to force you into being more specific, and if anyone pushes you too hard, let him have a try.

Some of your follow-up will almost certainly have to be in the form of written notes. A system of numbers in the text corresponding to the numbers of footnotes at the end will disfigure the script less than anything else, and give you room to write what you want. But try to discuss personally at least some pupils' work after every assignment, and try to see that over a given period – say a term – every pupil has at least one chance of personal discussion with you.

In your notes and discussions you may like to bear in mind the following points. The generally-accepted written language for social and educational purposes is organised in sentences, a proportion of which are complex. It has its conventions of form, of courtesy, of lay-out. Socially competent pupils have to be able to handle it, so within the priorities recommended above, insist on its proprieties and conventions. In personal writing, the *fact* of communication matters supremely; the manner decides itself. Both may well be unconventional, so the principle to work on is that anything goes so long as it works. If it communicates successfully, it is 'right'. If it communicates with only partial success, consider how, *in its own way*, it could be more successful.

When you have to deal with imaginative writing, bear in mind that inventiveness, in which fantasies simply follow one another, is not really imaginative at all, and is a rather easy and perhaps lazy quality. The process of invention calls for nothing more than abandonment to impulse, whereas that of imagination involves a more or less complete re-creation of experience, self-consistent within its own limits. Take this example of work by an inventive twelve-year old:

In five months time the boys had made three identical subs (i.e. submarines) which were armed with lasers and had radar scaners torpedoes and mini subs. These all had mini subs except John Jacksons which was a mini sub itself and cruised at six hundred knots per hour this was only its cruising speed it could travel for fast speed at one thousand eight hundred Knots.

The boys just suddenly left home and went to their subs and started off for the polar cap.

They reached the polar cap in two days time and came face to face with an army of mechanical whales they soon melted them and got underway again. after this incident the boys trusted nothing and went as carefully as possible. While the boys were traveling at one point they came across an eight mile thick wall of ice. In a formation shown in the diagram below we made our way through the ice. It seemed more like one hundred miles said one boy.

We suddenly cam to an awe inspiring cave . . .

Spelling, grammar and paragraphing are not at all bad, you know. But no experience is being re-created here, in the way it was by the pupil who wrote about making and testing for hydrogen. The writer of the submarine fantasy is inventing as he goes along, without reference to what has gone before or to what is to come after. Thus the boys make three identical subs and in the next sentence one of them turns out to be different. The narrator is detached for most of the time, but for a moment he joins in the action. The army of mechanical whales, which, one thinks, ought to be exciting, is conceived in one moment and slaughtered in the next, to make just one more event. The awe-inspiring cave arrives 'suddenly', as do so many of the phenomena in tales of this kind: as suddenly as the writer invents them.

There is a place for this kind of rather self-indulgent writing in your programme. Everyone is the better, every now and then, for a chance to tip the contents of his mind on to paper. It is even claimed that there can be valuable therapeutic results from pupils writing-out fantasies which they know will be free from correction and public scrutiny – i.e. will be confidential between themselves and their teacher. My personal view is that psycho-therapy by writing is not for the ordinary classroom teacher like you and me, with our meagre and probably obsolescent training in educational psychology. We can't do everything, and the great majority of our pupils will learn to write best by the process of trial-and-error, correction-and-emendation.

The original point, however, was that imaginative writing makes greater demands on the writer than does inventive writing, and that it should be·recognised when one is correcting and evaluating the work. Bear in mind, too, that really imaginative, live metaphor arises out of the needs of a situation, and is not applied afterwards as a decoration. It was stuck-on decorative metaphor that Coleridge described as 'the rag-fair finery of a meretricious muse'. It is very important to encourage pupils to write imaginatively, but you do it by encouraging them to look and listen observantly, not by prompting them to use fancy language.

Difficulties

From time to time individual pupils, or even groups, will turn sour about writing. They may get stuck, doing the same kind of thing over and over again, or may grumble about 'having nothing to write about', or produce obviously skimped and inferior work, usually late. The sourness may be in motive or technique or both. When it occurs, particularly in individuals, make sure as a matter of routine that the cause is not simply physical – say a defect of vision or hearing that has developed unnoticed. Don't just ask once; ask at intervals, and keep an unobtrusive look-out as well. Adolescents are notoriously sensitive about having to wear spectacles or hearing-aids, and may go to great lengths to hide symptoms of needing them.

Environmental factors can induce sourness, too: the beginnings of illness, troubles at home, bullying at school, sheer fatigue arising from long journeys on school buses or paper-rounds or part-time jobs. Probably the commonest cause is loss of confidence, which may come from external pressure applied (unwittingly and with the best of intentions) by other departments, from excessive worry about 'correctness', or from inappropriate assignments set by yourself.

First, do what you can to remove or alleviate the cause of the trouble, bearing in mind that what you *can* do in certain circumstances may be strictly limited. Things like physical defects, illness, worry, and fatigue may best be referred to a head or deputy-head teacher, or a house- or year-teacher; it will depend on your school and your own experience and your degree of responsibility in the school. Do what you can, but be prepared to withdraw quickly and tactfully from situations which prove to be none of your business.

If the trouble is due to simple loss of confidence, you may have to try finding a tactful way of suggesting to a colleague that it is not really very helpful to get indignant about 'bad English' unless there is some positive recommendation on how to write 'good English'; you may try reassuring the pupil, without implying or permitting unprofessional criticism of a colleague, that 'correctness' is important but not all-important, and that there are different kinds of English for different situations; or you can, for the time being, scrap your own programme of written work for the one particular pupil. Then you can set about restoring confidence.

Try small, simple assignments based on thoroughly familiar material (e.g. an account of an experiment that you know has been thoroughly learned and mastered, or of a deeply-ingrained routine like paying in dinner money). What you want is immediate and repeated success, so, in consultation with the pupil, choose the things that he *knows* he can do. Put him in situations in which he is virtually sure of success before he starts. As soon as possible, move on to small assignments of personal writing, ostensibly because it doesn't matter if they are a bit odd or go wrong. In fact, any honest effort in work of this kind will produce something that can be praised — which is what you want — and may help to exorcise or at least reveal hidden fears about illiteracy. As the pupil regains confidence from repeated small successes and the influence of personal attention, get him to write at greater length and to be more ambitious in choosing the material. Aim at bringing the pupil back into the normal run of work as soon as possible. He needs special help and consideration for a time, but it is not good for him to become permanently dependent on special treatment or to be isolated for a long time from the others in the group.

. . . on some night when a draft was 'proceeding to the Front' . . . [the Colonel] would make his stuttering little farewell speech about being a credit to the regiment . . . And then the local clergyman would exhort them to trust in their Saviour, to an accompaniment of asides and witticisms in Welsh.

'And now God go with you,' he would conclude, adding, 'I will go
with you as far as the station . . .'

Siegfried Sassoon, *Memoirs of a Fox-hunting Man*

Sassoon says he didn't see what else the colonel and the clergyman
could have done. Well, what is your position when your pupils are
starting an assignment in writing? In a sense they are 'proceeding to the
Front'. T. S. Eliot described the attempt to write as 'a raid on the
inarticulate'. Are you a company commander seasoned in this kind of
warfare, capable of advising and guiding from recent first-hand
experience, or do you have to stand aside making encouraging noises
like: 'I will go with you as far as giving out the exercise books'?

The point I want to make is that anyone who presumes to teach
writing needs to be a competent practitioner in recent practice if he is
to be credible. We can take it for granted that all teachers of writing get
plenty of practice in social written communication. I wonder how
many, after they have qualified, find or make the occasion to write
essays or dissertations or papers as the result of study. How many
seriously practise personal writing – not necessarily for general
publication, or for any publication, but even for the satisfaction of
exercising a skill? Yet a driving instructor, without aspiring to be a rally
winner, is expected to keep his driving skill in good order and to be able
to demonstrate when necessary. A science teacher needs to keep his
experimental technique up-to-date. A woodwork teacher is expected to
be skilful in using and demonstrating the tools of his craft. A teacher of
French is expected to be able to speak that language and translate into
and out of it. Why should so many teachers of writing blush and
wriggle and say 'What? Me?' when asked for some verses or other
'original contribution'? It seems no more than reasonable to expect
from a teacher of writing – not immortal literature, but respectable
craftsmanship in academic and personal writing. The difference in a
classroom between saying 'God go with you . . .' (or words to that
effect) and saying 'What I usually find is . . .' has to be experienced to
be believed. May I conclude by asking you and all our colleagues who
teach writing to examine your practice and your consciences in this
matter of craftsmanship? In this chapter you have one of my poems
and plenty of my prose to rake over if you want to. I've got a
department to run, and a family to provide for and a garden to be
neglected, and you've got one of my contributions in front of you. So
what about yours? Come on! let's see the colour of your ink and the
whites of your eyes.

2 Spoken English

Vivian Summers

The coining of the word 'oracy' by Andrew Wilkinson in 1965 marked the new status achieved by Spoken English. The word challenged comparison with 'literacy' and demanded equally serious consideration from teachers of English. While it is still very far from achieving comparability of status with literacy, a recognition of its importance continues to grow and the gap is likely to narrow because teachers are coming to see speech and writing as complementary modes of using the same language resources — acquired orally in childhood — and because communication by the spoken word has far greater importance in the modern world of radio, telephone and television than it has ever had before. For the vast majority of people, the *writing* of English is bound to be a very occasional activity, whereas the *spoken* language will occupy most of their waking hours and will have a profound effect, not only on their careers, but on every aspect of their personal lives.

It is salutary to remember that a great deal of a child's language development has taken place by the time he is five years old. It is very late in the day to begin oral work when the child enters the secondary school, and far too late when he begins a C.S.E. or G.C.E. course in the fourth year. The best infant and primary schools are well aware of this, and secondary teachers may hope to receive in increasing numbers new pupils whose talk has been well-cared-for over their school years. Even so, in the most important years (i.e. before five) the child will be dependent on his mother for his language education — unless he is fortunate enough to attend a nursery school or an alert pre-school playgroup which cares about his linguistic development.

This has direct relevance to secondary-school work — not as a ready-made excuse for our own inadequacies but as a challenge to do all we can to make the parents (and especially the mothers) of the *next* generation realise the need to talk more effectively to their young children (in ordinary conversation and story-telling) and so to open up and then broaden the path of their whole mental development and future education. Those parents are the secondary pupils in our classrooms today!

Whatever the linguistic background of the pupils, the secondary teacher has to do what he can to increase their ability to communicate in speech. The first thing is to create the right atmosphere in the classroom. This, it is true, must depend to some extent on the atmosphere of the school. It is dispiriting for the teacher of English to be told to cut out his lively discussion groups because the teacher of mathematics next door can't make himself heard. (This of course raises the question of the design of English rooms – see Chapter 9). But the process can work the other way, too: a change of atmosphere in the English rooms can have a beneficial effect on the whole school.

Certainly the first step to oracy is simply to admit that in all English lessons good talk is encouraged, not suppressed. An exchange of ideas on the subject for a composition; opinions on the merit of a poem; suggestions for interpreting a character in a play are all commonplace activities in an English class. But the teacher who is interested in speech work will be conscious of opportunities here even when 'oral work' is far from his pupils' minds. He will draw out the reticent, develop the tentative answer, not only for the sake of the matter in hand but also as part of a continuing process of oral education. If there is a good relationship between teacher and pupils, the latter will sometimes raise matters of topical interest, such as world events or items from school life. This will, on occasion, provide the teacher with an opportunity for pursuing something which is of absorbing interest to the class. It may be worth his while to postpone the lesson he has prepared in order to take advantage of it.

The more purposeful development of this is the use of group work. All kinds of opportunities for this present themselves in English lessons – planning and carrying out projects; making up plays; discussing reactions to poems and novels; exchanging ideas on topics for composition; preparing poetry recitals or choral speaking, etc. These activities are not simply 'oral' exercises but quite natural modes of procedure in which pupils will find themselves talking, simply because it is necessary for the work in hand. The value of this is manifold: on the oral side, the pupils learn to use language to express their opinions, urge their own ideas, comment on the ideas of others and listen to other points of view and assess them; if the group has to report back to the class, they learn how to change from the informality of conversation and discussion to the more formal style of the public statement. As for the work in hand, there should be an enrichment of ideas and a livelier, less 'desk-bound' attitude generally.

Moreover, if speech precedes writing there is opportunity for the pupil to gain ideas from the group, order his own thoughts, and try out forms of verbal expression in easy conversation with his fellows. As a result, when he comes to write, he will obviously be in a better position to succeed than if he is given a sheet of paper, a pen and an essay-subject — and told to write in silence. After written work, speech is again involved when the pupil discusses the composition with his group — prior to revision and possible re-writing (see also Chapter 1).

Some teachers may fear the noise and the apparent loosening of discipline that group work implies. It is encouraging to remember that nowadays hundreds of teachers use this method as a matter of course and without any disastrous decline in discipline. Naturally the size of the classroom and its proximity to other teaching rooms is relevant; but three or four groups can converse in a normal-sized teaching room. It is of course much easier if desks and chairs are movable. If the school hall or adjacent classrooms can sometimes be utilised, so much the better. Pupils unaccustomed to this sort of work may at first feel awkward, and show it by silliness or boisterousness, but when they realise this is to be a normal working technique, they are likely to respond seriously and sensibly. Best of all is to introduce the children to this when they first enter the school; then they grow up accepting it as quite normal. Teachers new to group work should be warned that careful planning and preparation are needed (see 'Please read this first', p. 4). A really absorbing topic is the first essential.

Listening

Implicit in all that is said here about speaking is the recognition of the importance of *listening*. Not only should this always be impressed on the pupils: it should be deliberately cultivated and practised. Exercises can be devised — for example, the pupils listen to a taped conversation, repeat it (in speech or writing) and then listen to the tape again to find out what a second (and third and fourth) hearing adds to the 'recall'. The ability to take one's turn in a discussion, listening carefully to another's point of view before offering one's own, is well worth developing.

There is a tendency in some quarters to think that when all these activities — spontaneous conversations, class discussions, and group work (and the presentation of poetry and drama, which will be discussed later) — are encouraged, there is no need for any more formal training in Spoken English. In fact several important areas have not been covered and it seems necessary to set aside a number of lessons per term to deal with them. There is a distinct advantage in letting the pupils know that, while their Spoken English is always important, there are definite lesson-times when the entire emphasis will be on their speech. It will counteract their feelings that they can already speak adequately and that whereas good writing can be taught in school, good speaking can't! It will also make them conscious of the range of speech situations in life, the problems attending them and ways of extending their own capacity for handling them.

Registers

Perhaps the basic requirement for oracy is the ability to communicate in a wide variety of settings: that is, to have the vocabulary, idiom and structures suitable to as many as possible of the situations likely to be met in life and to realise immediately *what is appropriate and what is not.* The word now used for this relationship is 'register', and the ability to select the appropriate register and talk effectively in it is a prime task of speech education. The pupil is already aware, if only half consciously, that the manner of talk between himself and his family is different from that between himself and his headmaster, and different again between himself and his fellows in the youth club. The teacher's aim is to make him fully aware of these differences and the reasons for them, and then to increase his flexibility in moving from one register to another – including those which he may not yet have experienced (himself and his employer is an example of this). What will become clear is that it is meaningless to talk of 'correct speech' as if one standard existed which was always to be desired. There are dozens of types of 'correct speech'. The mode of speech which is clearly 'right' in a school playground is very far from right in a bishop's palace – and, vice-versa. Indeed, it would be better to use the term 'appropriate' in place of 'correct'.

An oral English syllabus might well be built around the need for practice in various registers. It would include at one extreme the formality of the full-scale debate, and at the other extreme a study of the pupils' own slang and why they use it. In the broad area between would be many social situations: meeting strangers, talking on the telephone (where clarity and brevity are paramount), leading a deputation to a person in authority, communicating in family situations, addressing different audiences, e.g. appealing for funds at a youth club, a Rotary lunch, or in a parish church; explaining a car breakdown, first to a garage man and then to father, who did not authorise the car's use!

Another branch of communication, with its own set of registers, is the imparting of factual information. This includes talking to the class on a topic that interests the speaker, to be followed by questions and discussion; the reporting of the same incident (e.g. a bank raid) by a frightened eye-witness, by a policeman, by a press reporter, by the victim; the describing of a process, with or without actions (e.g. mending a puncture explained to a younger brother), the broadcasting of news items, using a tape recorder, etc. In every case, the audience, real or imagined, should be clearly established so that the appropriate language is used.

A place too could be found for committee work, which many pupils will encounter later in life. For instance, a form council, meeting during English lessons, could send forward proposals to the School Council or 'parliament'. Yet another activity which has been tried with success is the compiling of questionnaires on matters of local interest. The questions are put to friends and neighbours, and then reports are drawn up and presented to the class.

It will be noticed that several of these speech activities involve 'rôle-playing' and that the work has crossed the border into improvised drama (see Chapter 5). In such rôle-playing, more is achieved than practice in appropriate speech: an understanding of emotions, attitudes, and the view-points of others is also involved. For a boy to take the rôle of a father angry with his teenage son, find the appropriate language for him and enter imaginatively into his situation in order to speak his words, is to extend the boy's mind and sensitivity to the problems of others and help him to come to terms with his own family tensions.

Yet another activity proper for the oral lesson is the *imaginative use of speech*. At its simplest, we have the story-telling that can be taken with first- and second-year pupils — where the teacher supplies a stimulus in the form of a theme, a character, an opening line, a picture or a piece of music and the pupils create the story. At a more advanced stage, the pupils in pairs or groups may be given a situation (a strange meeting; finding an unfamiliar object on the road; landing on a new planet) and left to devise the conversation and bring the episode to a suitable climax. Here, again, we have entered the realms of drama — a natural and desirable progress, showing once more that English cannot be taught in separate compartments. Often valuable activities in the English class embrace literature, speech, writing and drama. For example, the reading of an episode from a novel might lead to group discussion on characters and their motives; next to the improvisation in speech and movement of an imaginary scene to do with these characters; then the scripting of the scene and finally the classroom performance of the finished playlet. One specific example of this sort of thing was given by a fourth-year class, studying *The Merchant of Venice*. They imagined that radio existed in Elizabethan England and they treated the trial scene as a *cause célèbre* which demanded full B.B.C. coverage. Thus they had reporters in Venice inside and outside the courtroom; fashion experts describing the lavish costumes; local historians giving the background to the case; interviewers talking to Shylock, Bassanio, Jessica and others; a 'live' transmission from the trial itself, and — as a post-script — a commentator on the water-front describing the unexpected return to Venice of Antonio's argosy. The whole was tape recorded.

So far we have, for the most part, been discussing teaching which has to do with improving speech communication in various practical situations. Now we must consider the aesthetic use of speech in the speaking of poetry.

Poetry speaking

At the time of writing, there is so much interest in poetry recitals, poetry and jazz, pop poets and so on that a teacher can feel happily in tune with the times when he gives his pupils the opportunity of speaking poetry aloud. It is, after all, a natural human activity to create poetry and recite it, and young children take to it as something quite unremarkable. As they enter the secondary school this spontaneous interest should be encouraged and then preserved right through their school lives. Fourth formers who have always spoken their poetry aloud take it as a matter of course; those who have never done it before are at first acutely self-conscious and awkward about it.

But what is the point of *reciting* poetry? What is gained over silent reading? Surely the listener is made more vividly aware of the music of the words and the rhythmic effects. Furthermore, the poem is interpreted by a speaker and his reactions to the poem should reveal new insights to the audience. All this may be granted as good reason for allowing pupils to listen to gramophone records and to their teacher reading aloud — but why should they themselves be encouraged to speak verse? The answer to this lies in the fact that as soon as a person undertakes to speak a poem he enters into a special relationship with it: he becomes an interpreter. That is to say, he must fully understand the poem — its sense, its imagery, its musical and rhythmical effects — and then he has to share it with his listeners, so that the poet's experience is re-created and made to live through his own understanding, personality and vocal resources. It sounds a formidable challenge, but it is by no means an improper one to set to adolescents, nor is it beyond their capabilities. Used as one of the methods for teaching poetry, it has great value in that it demands close study and appreciation and then conscious decisions on the pace, tone, emphasis, phrasing etc. necessary to communicating the poem successfully. Nor should we overlook the satisfaction a speaker gains in having experienced the poem in his voice and being.

Is it necessary to *memorise* the poem to be spoken? The answer to this would depend on how far a really finished performance is required. Certainly there should be opportunities from time to time for pupils to proceed as far as this. A class (or group) poetry recital; an inter-house competition; a term examination or contest are examples — and for these recitation from memory is desirable, because in this way the pupil can commit himself entirely to the poem and share it with his audience, unhindered by a book in hand.

Reading aloud

Every teacher knows the frustration and boredom caused by poor reading aloud in class, and if it is necessary for a pupil to read aloud, he should be carefully chosen by the teacher. All the same, the ability to read aloud is one worth cultivating. The sheer practical need for mothers (and fathers surely!) to read to their children is in itself a sufficient reason. Therefore opportunities for this should be found. Senior pupils could prepare programmes of readings for the youngest classes or for a visit to a neighbouring primary or infant school. Some senior girls help with pre-school playgroups; here is a wonderful chance to use their skill at reading aloud!

Such traditional opportunities as Bible-reading in assembly should be made use of. Some schools use their inter-com. system for regular news bulletins and this gives scope not only for reading a script but also for interviews. Whatever opportunities are found, in school or out of it, passages to be read should be carefully prepared beforehand and pupils need to be instructed in such matters as variations of pace, pitch and intonation — and the handling of dialogue. Poor readers should be given every incentive and encouragement. Some teachers have found work with a tape recorder a great help with such pupils; but whatever method is used, the teacher's help in preparation is essential.

Speech training

Management and control of the voice do not come naturally, and communication will be hindered by poorly-produced vocal tone, lazily-formed consonants and distorted vowels. The teacher of English is likely to be the only person in a position to help a child over this and he can do so effectively only if he has taken the trouble to acquire a little technical knowledge himself. (It is to be hoped that all colleges and departments of education see to it that students are equipped in this way before they are passed as qualified teachers of English.) However, a simple working knowledge of the speech organs and their function, together with an understanding of breath-control can be gained from books and personal experiment. Thereafter the teacher may, with due care, practise his pupils in simple exercises for breathing and flexibility of the jaw, lips and tongue — such as may be found in any good textbook (see book list). This sort of work will be more readily accepted by younger pupils than older ones and so it is best put in the syllabus of the first two years. Afterwards, the teacher can revive such exercises with an older class or individual pupils when there is an obvious need — especially if the pupils themselves acknowledge the need (after hearing their own tape recordings, for example).

Accent

So far nothing has been said of the vexed question of 'accent'. Is the teacher to encourage a 'received Standard English' pronunciation? Is he merely to tolerate a regional accent or is he to cherish it as something of value *per se*? People become very heated in discussions on these points. The answer surely lies in the word *communication* — which is the aim of oral English teaching. If a local accent limits the communication of a person to a comparatively small area, then surely the teacher must enable him to extend his range by helping him to a more widely accepted pronunciation. This may involve bi-lingualism. In fact, people are, in this sense, often multi-lingual. The reader may ask himself if he does not sometimes subtly modify his own pronunciation when speaking to people with different accents.

The wise teacher will avoid trying to impose a received standard accent on his pupils but will see to it that where a regional accent is of the sort to limit communication and social adaptability, the pupil is given help to modify it. A person's speech is a very personal thing, linked to feelings for his family and background, and should always be treated with respect and discretion. It is as well to remember that pupils do not usually try to talk badly! All the same, malformed vowels and sloppy consonants which are neither good 'standard' nor good 'regional' speech either, should not be accepted in the English class. The English Speaking Board, in one of its pamphlets, suggested teachers should encourage 'an acceptable pronunciation, accurate in stress and near enough to standard English to cause neither ambiguity nor embarrassment'.

We should perhaps say something here about *elocution.* It is unreasonable to condemn this art simply because some insensitive teachers of it have encouraged an insincere and highly artificial style of speaking. The cultivation of a pleasing speaking voice is surely as admirable as the development of a fine singing voice: but both are of limited value unless placed at the service of the author (and, in singing, the composer). It is not, however, a matter for an oral English class in school. Children with an interest in this direction will, like music pupils, work with a private teacher.

A teacher of English, even one with a special interest in oral work, should not attempt to remedy speech defects which need the specialised knowledge of a speech therapist. The teacher can be a great help, however, simply in noticing a defect and advising the parents that treatment is needed and how it can be obtained.

Examining Spoken English

When oral English was given a place in the C.S.E. syllabus, teachers found themselves face to face with the problem of examining it. Fears that a practical test of this sort must be less 'reliable' than its written counterpart were allayed by P. J. Hitchman (*Examining Oral English in Schools*, 1966) who pointed out that there was little difference between the reliability co-efficient of speech exams (+0.75) and those of written ones. Nevertheless the problems of what the most valid forms of spoken test are and how one should assess them continue to confront teachers. Help has been forthcoming from research in university departments and from the English Speaking Board — a body which pioneered speech examinations nearly twenty years ago and has since carried out many pilot schemes for local education authorities and C.S.E. Boards. The result has been that certain activities have emerged as the most useful for a Spoken English examination, and a combination of two or three of the following are to be found in many C.S.E. Mode 1 syllabuses:

(1) the prepared talk — either on a personal project or on a topic

chosen by the examiner from a short list presented by the
candidate;

(2) a personal interview with the examiner for reading and conversation
test;

(3) conversation on topics of either the candidate's or the examiner's
choice;

(4) group discussion;

(5) reading aloud either from an 'own choice' book or at sight;

(6) aural comprehension with written answers;

(7) assessment on course work in Spoken English.

Undoubtedly the most widely used of these is (1) — the prepared
talk — and it is easy to see why: the candidate chooses something of
real interest to himself and therefore is likely to communicate this
interest to his listeners in livelier language than if he is forced to speak
on something uncongenial. He will be encouraged to deepen his
knowledge of his subject by personal research and to illustrate it with
his own visual aids. Above all, he is placed in a *position of authority*
before the listening group. A child rarely finds himself in this situation
in school and very often he gains new self-respect when he realises that
he knows more about a subject than anyone else in the room, including
the examiner, and can hold his audience's interest. Many a pupil who is
known as an indifferent writer gains respect and attention when
revealed as an able speaker.

Some form of group discussion is often used as a companion test to
the prepared talk. It may arise from the talk itself, with the examiner
and listening group joining in the discussion, or it may be on a separate
topic prepared by the candidates.

The private interview for the whole or a part of the examination is
still employed by some C.S.E. (and G.C.E.) boards; but there is much
to be said in favour of the examination being conducted before a
listening and participating group, usually of fellow candidates, so that
there is more reality about the speech situation.

A notable rarity is the presentation of poetry, prose or drama. Only
a very few C.S.E. boards give scope for this. It is worth considering if
it should be included, at least as an optional item; certainly it should be
thought about if and when the G.C.E. and C.S.E. examinations are
combined in the future. If candidates are asked to *write about*
literature, surely some of them should be allowed to *speak* it for their
examination?

The English Speaking Board, which maintains a full range of

examinations from junior grades right through to adult vocational ones, firmly includes such interpretative work in its junior and secondary grades. Its usual examination pattern is four-fold: (1) a talk on a prepared project; (2) a reading chosen by the examiner from a book selected by the candidate; (3) a poem, prose passage or drama excerpt chosen from a wide list of prescribed pieces; (4) an impromptu exchange of ideas on one or more of the above – usually on 1. These examinations are always conducted in front of a listening group.

Many schools have found that orientating their Spoken English syllabus towards this type of four-fold testing has given a notable impulse and interest to the work of both staff and pupils. Regular examinations, whether conducted by examiners from the Board or internally by the teachers working on the same lines, have provided goals to be worked for, and the examinations themselves become 'occasions', when the results of much hard work and preparation can be shared with others in mutual enrichment.

Some teachers are worried about the time such internal examinations are likely to take up. Of course they *are* time-consuming, but the teacher has to make the policy decision as to whether or not they are worth while. Each pupil would need about ten minutes allotted to him (fifteen for older pupils). For a class of thirty children, this would mean a minimum of about five hours. One may ask if this is really too much to give up once or twice a year to such an important activity. There will be no problem in occupying the rest of the class. They are usually very ready to listen to the talks by their classmates and contribute to the question-time that follows.

If Spoken English is going to continue as a feature in school-leaving examinations, it is essential that the pupil does not face his first formal test in his fifth year, when adolescent self-consciousness may be at its peak, and the feeling of pressure and 'exam nerves' is already bad enough. This final examination should only come to a child after a whole school career of education in oracy, marked at regular intervals during the course by occasions when he is called on to show his progress by taking the central position in a group – addressing them, reading and/or reciting to them, answering their questions and joining in the discussion that arises.

The examiner

'Perhaps the greatest single factor deciding the success or failure of the test is the personality of the assessor' (P. J. Hitchman, *Examining Oral English in Schools*, page 41).

These are sobering words when one remembers that in the C.S.E. world 'we are all assessors now'. Apart from his professional knowledge as a teacher of English, allied (one would hope) with some specialist understanding of 'speech', the most important attribute of an examiner is the ability to create a good atmosphere and put the candidates at ease. He must always be encouraging and receptive, continually on the look out for ways of bringing out the best performance that the candidate is capable of. In no other examination can the examiner be so obviously on the side of the candidate. Anyone called on to examine oral work should realise that, to do a satisfactory job, he will require all the sensitivity, receptivity, tact and sheer friendliness that he can muster.

G.C.E. examinations in Spoken English

The only G.C.E. board to include Spoken English at 'O' Level (Mode I) is London University, where it is an optional addition to the English Language examination. The syllabus consists of a reading and conversation test.

The Joint Matriculation Board (Manchester) has an Optional Test in Spoken English for candidates offering general studies at 'A' Level. It is also based on conversation, preceded by either a reading or a prepared talk selected from a list of topics.

No other boards include Spoken English in their Mode I syllabus at Ordinary or Advanced Level.

The Associated Examining Board has Spoken English as a component of some of its Mode III examinations, as does the Oxford and Cambridge Schools Examination Board — though their secretary comments 'at the present time (1970) very little use is made of this provision'. The Southern Universities Joint Board has no oral English examination but states that it would favourably consider requests from their schools for one. The University of Cambridge Local Examinations Syndicate discusses the topic from time to time in the appropriate subject committee, but has no plans to introduce such tests at present.

Compared with the C.S.E. examinations, where Spoken English is nearly always included, the G.C.E. picture is depressing. But it should be noted that the boards are by no means unwilling to consider the possibility of an oral English examination. What is lacking is a vigorous demand from the schools!

Book list

Atkinson, D. and Dalton, J. *The Living Tongue* (Black, 1970).
Burniston, Christabel. *Speech of Life* (Pergamon Press, 1965).
  Creative Oral Assessment (Pergamon Press, 1968).
Casciani, J. W. *Speak for Yourselves* (Harrap, 1966).
Colson, Greta. *Voice Production and Speech* (Museum Press, 1963).
Harvey, Basil. *The Scope of Oracy* (Pergamon Press, 1968).
Hitchman, P. J. *Examining Oral English in Schools* (Methuen, 1966).
Mulcahy, Betty. *To Speak True* (on poetry speaking) (Pergamon Press, 1970).
Wilkinson, Andrew. *Spoken English* (University Education Dept., Birmingham, 1965).

Language teaching

George Watkins

3

When we started planning this book, one of the first tasks we set ourselves was for each of us to write a short paper on his attitude to language-teaching. Then we studied and discussed what each of us had written; re-defined, clarified and modified our statements; and continued to exchange ideas more or less regularly until it was no longer possible to delay the writing of this chapter. You see, we were afraid of the chapter. We knew before we began that hardly any two teachers of English agree with one another about what, if anything, should constitute language-teaching in secondary schools. We knew that experts in linguistics, experts in curriculum-development, admissions tutors in higher education, employers, and the general public all disagree with one another and with the teachers in the schools about the same thing. We were afraid of encountering among ourselves the extreme opinions and unbending attitudes that we had met among colleagues in our own and other schools; afraid, too, of revealing ourselves to each other as hopelessly traditional and reactionary, or as weakly and fatuously acquiescent in a general collapse of literacy, or even as both at the same time. In the event we found that although there were differences among us, our personal principles and practice had a lot in common. If, in this chapter, we seem to adopt a middle line, or to compromise, it is not because any of us shuffled or equivocated in committee. It is because there is a large area of agreement and sound practice to be found, in spite of the plethora of nostrums, panaceas and cure-alls for every kind of ailment from unrelated participles to gunshot wounds that is being touted and peddled round the English departments of our secondary schools, each purporting to be the only hope for the survival of our language. Teachers — real teachers, I mean, who organise lessons, mark exercises, and patrol corridors — have become so bothered with conflicting advice and so deprived of proper professional guidance that they no longer feel sure about what is expected of them, and are bewildered by a choice of material much of which they instinctively mistrust. Many have lost confidence in themselves and their practice in the teaching of English language.

Well, we, the authors of this book, every one of us earning his living in the classroom, can claim perhaps more than most to represent the teachers of English in secondary schools, and what we have to say is this: all is not lost. Quite the contrary. Things aren't what they used to be — thank God. But a famous victory for human values is in process of being won, and it is up to all of us to exploit the gains.

Grammar

It is no use trying to teach traditional 'English' grammar, since it is not a grammar of current English at all, but a description based on a false analogy with the grammar of classical Latin. Just in case you need to be convinced, look at this example:

> Bill sent John a penny.
> Penny sent John a bill.
> Penny sent Bill a john. (American slang)
> John sent a penny bill.

The words are identical in all the sentences; only the order is different. The syntactical functions of the words (subject, object, etc.) are indicated by their positions. In Latin they would be indicated by inflections, and the positions would be relatively unimportant. In fact, classical Latin is a highly-inflected language in which position does not very much matter. Modern English is a relatively uninflected language in which position is supremely important. So it is futile to try to describe the one in terms of the other. If you try to describe English structures in terms of nominative, accusative, genitive, etc., the descriptions only rarely fit the facts. If you inflict such descriptions on pupils, who can see that they do not fit the facts, they naturally become suspicious and confused. Clever ones may learn to fudge the facts so as to produce 'right' answers, but there is not much profit in that.

The properly scientific description of modern English is an enormous piece of work, daunting in its complexity. The team at University College, London, have been working on it for years, and look like being busy with it for years to come. You cannot teach all that to secondary pupils, even if you can grasp it yourself. For one thing, there isn't the time, or a tenth of the time. The number of hours available for instruction in English in the five years of secondary education between 11 and 16 can be roughly calculated as follows:

$$\frac{200 \text{ days per year} \times 40 \text{ minutes per lesson} \times 5 \text{ years}}{60}$$

It amounts to 666 hours *for all purposes,* including examinations.
Divide it out among reading, writing, and speaking, including time for
drama, library, specific literary studies, and all other vitally important
activities, and you will find it hard to justify more than 50 hours for
'grammar'. That is 10 hours per year. Not much, is it? Of course, in the
good old days when everyone was given, we are told, a firm grounding
in the rudiments of grammar, they were given a firm grounding in very
little else – and pretty deprived they most of them were, culturally. Is
it unkind to suggest that the grammar was wonderfully easy stuff to
mark? Anyway, I must now ask whether, in modern conditions, with
an allowance of 10 hours a year at most, it is worth even trying to
teach grammar. After all, R. J. Harris is quoted (see 'The only
disturbing feature' in *Use of English* for 16 March 1963) as having
found in a reliable experiment that pupils who were not taught
grammar performed better in composition than those who were, and
W. G. Heath (see 'Library-centred English: an experiment' in N.A.T.E.
Bulletin 2, January 1965) came independently to the same conclusion.

Most of us in committee thought that it was inadvisable to try to
teach grammatical description to secondary pupils. It is highly abstract
work, calling for ability to generalise, and for that reason is less
suitable for the great majority of secondary pupils than are the more
humane studies of literature and of self-expression in speech and
writing. We thought that systematic linguistic description was best
suited to undergraduate and graduate students, and might be not
unsuitable for very able sixth-form pupils who expressed interest in it.
In our experience it seemed that very few secondary pupils could
understand 'all those verbs and nouns and tenses and clauses and
comparatives' because, at their age, they simply did not have the
capacity for generalising.

Then again, we asked why anyone should need to learn even a very
attenuated description of the language – should need to be able to say,
for instance, that the difference between *to put a friend up on
Thursday night* and *to put an ornament up on the mantelpiece* lies in
to put up being a phrasal verb in the first example and *to put* being a
simple verb in the second. After all, there is not much risk of
misunderstanding.

Some of us thought that there was no need at all, for secondary
pupils. All of us thought that the teaching of descriptive grammar to
any but the most able pupils was a sure way to confuse them. Some of
us thought that it was useful for able pupils to have a working
knowledge of common linguistic terms and their application – for

instance, *sentence, subject, verb, complement, object*; *noun, adjective, adverb, pronoun, preposition*; *phrase, clause*; *active, passive*. It was claimed that such knowledge is helpful to both teachers and pupils when the very important activity of explaining pupils' mistakes is going on. When there is a common technical terminology, explanations can be neat and succinct. No doubt it all depends on what sort of class you have. If you have a class of able pupils with enquiring minds, they will probably enjoy learning the names of linguistic phenomena, and what they learn will certainly make your subsequent discussions of their mistakes go more easily. But if your pupils vary at all widely in ability, you will have to ask yourself whether the advantage to the able ones in getting first-class explanations (which they perhaps need less than anyone else) is outweighed by the time spent on bewildering and perhaps alienating the less able with abstract notions which they cannot grasp.

There is a further point. Analytical and descriptive approaches tend to *teach about language* rather than to improve pupils' ability to compose in the language. Success in learning to describe linguistic features does not automatically bring success in composition. For instance, R. J. Harris is quoted as showing that the correlation between the marks on the clause analysis section of some G.C.E. 'O' Level papers and the scores in the essay, précis and comprehension sections, was only 0.36. Scores in the arithmetic papers correlated more highly with the essay marks. And these specific observations are supported by the everyday experience of very large numbers of teachers.

So the teaching of traditional grammar is not recommended, and there are the gravest reservations about teaching even modern descriptive grammar to secondary pupils for any purpose except the intellectual value of the study itself.

In the midst of this retreat from traditional practice, you may ask what has become of the famous victory. Well, it was a victory for human values. Traditional practice relied on a false description of the language. If teachers stop filling their pupils with lies, some sort of victory for human values must surely be won. Then attention has shifted from the unquestioned learning of the names of things to the questioning of why they should be learned, if at all. It is now assumed that any language-learning, to be desirable, must be directed towards improved performance in composition. All of us in committee would here include spoken with written composition. Human values are asserted, I think, when the questions are asked: *What are we doing? What are we doing it for? Is it well-designed for its purpose?*

Can we assume, then, that language-study, to be worthwhile, must conduce to an improved performance in composition? Is it agreed that in secondary schools we are concerned, not with training linguists but with helping young people to a general education that they can live with and earn their own livings with? If it is agreed, we can go on.

There is a case for concentrating on personal writing, relying, for a long-term improvement in performance, on the correction of mistakes and the individual discussion of alternative ways of expression. It does work. Everyone in committee affirmed from his own experience that it works, and there is any amount of published evidence, particularly by Holbrook and Clegg, that it works. But the effects are slow to appear, and you have to be both patient and consistent over periods of years, not weeks, to see them. It works because the pupils learn for themselves, from their own mistakes and successes, in a variety of natural situations of their own making. You control the whole process because you provide the material, but the pupils make what they want (or what they can) of it, and take from it what they need – not what someone else says they ought to need. Even if they don't learn much, they *learn* it and can subsequently apply it.

If you put your shirt on this system – or perhaps non-system – you must accept that the follow-up to each piece of writing is of supreme importance. Personal writing is not an excuse for just letting pupils mess about. You will have a lot of reading and individual discussion to do. You will have to overcome your own fears and doubts about the propriety of not doing any 'proper English', and you will almost certainly have quite a hard time reassuring parents, other teachers, and perhaps even pupils. But the non-system does work. There is more about it in Chapter 1.

One thing is certain: if you are going to teach the language, you yourself must have a good knowledge and understanding of it. This applies to the non-system even more than it does to systems and programmes of language-teaching, because under the non-system you have to be competent to explain, or know where you can find an explanation of, any linguistic situation that may arise. You can't just keep one chapter ahead of the class. You don't know where the next mind-bender is coming from. The essence of the non-system is that the pupils pick your brains, and there must be something for them to pick. If you have not had specific training in the study of language, or if you suspect that you are badly out of date, give yourself a basic course by reading:

Abercrombie, D. *Studies in Phonetics and Linguistics* (O.U.P. 1965).

Fries, C. C. *The Structure of English* (Longman, 1957).

Hill, A. A. *Introduction to Linguistic Structures: from Sound to Sentence in English* (Harcourt, Brace & World, 1958).

Joos, M. *The Five Clocks* (Harcourt, Brace & World).

Quirk, R. *The Use of English* (Longman, 1968).

Roberts, P. *Patterns of English* (Harcourt, Brace & World).

Smith, A. H., and Quirk, R. (eds.) *The Teaching of English* (Secker & Warburg, 1959).

Wilkinson, A. M. etc. *Spoken English* (Birmingham University Educational Review, Occasional Publications No. 2, 1965).

If you can get hold of a copy, have Otto Jespersen's *Essentials of English Grammar* (Allen & Unwin, 1933) handy in the classroom. Its descriptions and examples are old-fashioned, but they are accurate, and the book is well-arranged and easy to handle. Have the *Shorter Oxford English Dictionary* on hand, as well. It costs less than the price of a set of ready-made exercises. Jespersen shows how the structures work and the *Shorter Oxford* shows how the words work, and both give plenty of examples. You won't tell many lies if you base your answers on these two.

Perhaps you want to do something more apparently positive than what I have just suggested. Do not be misled into copying the often brilliantly successful methods of the teachers of English as a second language. I know that their audio-visual programmes and drills seem to get wonderful results in remarkably short time, and their work is often genuinely impressive. But their pupils are starting from scratch. Yours already have a very considerable command of spoken English, and at eleven many of yours have a pretty good command of written English. The drills which come new to pupils who are learning English as a second language will most of the time do no more than confirm what most of your pupils already know very well. You will be spending time on things your pupils do not need, and will be boring them into the bargain.

At the beginning of their secondary education, your pupils almost certainly write more or less as they speak — informally, repetitively, without much forethought or organisation, and without much explanation. When they are talking face-to-face they do not need to explain very much, because gestures, facial expressions, and other reinforcements will do instead of explanation, and the other person can always ask questions. The informality sets up a comfortable social situation, the repetitions are hardly noticed, and tight syntactical organisation is not necessary when it is easy to abandon an unsuccessful construction and start a new one.

None of this will do very well in written English. Writer and reader are not face-to-face, but at a distance, and there can be no reinforcement. Informality can seem ill-bred. Repetition is tedious. Sketchy organisation and lack of explanation, because of the remoteness, involve failure of communication. A real and sustained imaginative effort is required of the writer, to appreciate and anticipate the reader's needs. Perhaps this is why the non-system is successful, because it gives regular practice in sustained imaginative effort. However, my intention here is to suggest that drills appropriate to the learning of Spoken English *ab initio* are of less value to native speakers of secondary-school age than are activities designed to develop existing skill in speech into a skill that includes written English.

If you feel that you must do syntactical exercises, it is probably best for you to concentrate on the four or five basic patterns of sentences. W. H. Mittins's *A Grammar of Modern English* (Methuen, 1967) gives a clear account of them, and some exercises as well. But you can make up your own exercises. It is hardly worth spending a lot of money on books of exercises that you will be using for less than ten hours a year. Consider, too, that the activity is wholly syntactical, that it is wholly concerned with sentences. If it is sentences you want, this is a good way of getting them, but it can do little or nothing to help pupils to communicate 'meaning'. It can do nothing for a pupil who has been entranced by *Twelfth Night* at Stratford but is unable to write more than 'I thought Sir Toby was very good. He made us laugh. He got drunk and made a lot of noise. He was very good'. The sentences are impeccable.

Exercises

If you want to shift the balance, you can try exercises in which the pupils still have to meet specified requirements but in which 'meaning' assumes greater importance. A favourite one is simulated proof-reading, in which the pupils get a text containing what are supposed to be compositor's errors and have to correct it. Another similar one is the restoration of faulty or damaged texts. Passages couched in the local dialect can be set for 'translation' into Standard English, for instance. If you try this, do not meddle with comic spellings purporting to represent the local pronunciation; concentrate on local words, constructions and idioms. Later, you can go to work on dialects other than the local one, and with the well-meant but not always clear instructions in pidgin-English that sometimes accompany foreign-made

articles like food-mixers, tins of boot-polish, and packets of dried food.
You can have a lot of good, clean, instructive fun with Robert Graves's
poem, '¡Wellcome to the Caves of Arta!' Other possible texts for
restoration might be documents that are supposed to have been partly
burned or torn. The age and sex of the pupils will decide whether the
completed documents lead to buried treasure, or form part of the
handbook to a secret weapon, or make up a recipe, or constitute the
guarantee to an electric toaster which has been found, all too late, to be
faulty. Yet other exercises can involve the production of notices, lists
of instructions, directions for finding the way, and so on, from material
given. The material can include sketch-maps, diagrams, scribbled
marginal notes to drawings for costumes, and other comparable aids to
the written word. You can also have texts to be presented anew in
simpler usage (as it were for the benefit of younger children) or in
more sophisticated usage (as it were for the benefit of grown-ups). The
point about exercises of these kinds is that they give pupils practice in
working to the sort of specifications they will meet in real life, and they
call for a more complete response to linguistic situations than do the
purely syntactical exercises. They are still artificial, but much less so
than the syntactical exercises. As they are usually short, they can be
corrected intensively, and the whole work can be re-drafted several
times until a high standard has been achieved.

The work I have just described can be extended and diversified with
older pupils if you give them some instruction in the study of language
according to *register, rôle,* and *style.* Then your pupils will be able to
try exercises like explaining how to play football to someone who does
not know the language of the game (how do you cope with *take a
corner, play for the offside rule, kick off*?). They can try fabricating a
correspondence between a householder (non-specialist user of the
language) and a builder (specialist user of the language of building)
about having a garage built on to the house. They can try swapping
rôles, presenting the same information as though communicated by an
employer and a shop steward, or a parent and a child, or a stranger, an
acquaintance, a friend, and a member of the family. They can try
fabricating a series of communications that work through the gradations
of style from familiar, through easy and polite, to formal — let us say
as a friendship becomes strained because one of the friends is slow about
paying back a loan of 50p (see Chapter 2).

If, as you hope, exercises of these kinds increase your pupils'
command of different kinds of language, and develop their sense of
appropriateness in the use of language, the social value of doing them

is obvious. The work calls for knowledge and linguistic sensitiveness on your part. It requires care in correction and follow-up, and is meant to lead to a lot of open-ended discussion with and among your pupils. There are, of course, no absolutely 'right' answers, only more or less acceptable, comprehensible, appropriate ones; the discussion, and the interest it arouses, matter more than the answers. Incidentally, you can afford to cheat over your time-allowance with these exercises. You can reasonably say that they shade into 'writing', and give to them some of the time you had earmarked for that.

A different development of the work described on pp. 49-50 is also possible. I mentioned re-drafting. There are grounds for thinking that pupils learn more from recognising and correcting their own mistakes than they do from repeating things they can already do correctly. One's own experience suggests, I think, that one learns more about spelling by resolving one's doubts and correcting one's mistakes with the dictionary than by writing out spelling-lists. Now, if pupils do learn from their own mistakes, re-drafting of faulty work ought to be a valuable exercise. I mean, of course, the re-drafting of pupils' *own* faulty work, rather than of other people's. But you can combine the two by having pupils work in groups of not more than six. By one organisation you can have every pupil in the class producing a piece of writing of, say, 150-200 words. Then the work of each member in a group is put up in turn for discussion and refinement, or the work can be passed round and be discussed as it circulates. The writer can accept or reject the group's advice, as he thinks best, but he re-drafts his work into an 'improved version'. It is up to you to decide how many times the work goes back into the mill before being handed to you for adjudication in its 'final version'.

By another organisation, each group works to produce just one agreed text, the work of an editorial body and a scribe. The refining process is very much like the other, but by this organisation you get only five or six 'final versions', whereas by the other you get thirty-odd. You can try both organisations, and see which suits you and your classes best. Either way, you will need to make yourself available to advise the groups and help them to resolve their difficulties when they reach impasses in their deliberations. The value of the work lies in the pupils' identifying their own and one another's mistakes, misunderstandings, difficulties and gaps in knowledge, and putting them right, in a memorable way. When they *ask* for information or advice, instead of having it thrust on them, they really want it.

Remember, however, that group-work of this kind is very demanding on both knowledge and pedagogic skill. To engage in it successfully, you *must* be sure of your control over your class, and they must be on good, co-operative terms with you (see 'Please read this first', p. 4).

When dismal jemmies want to denounce the viperous generations (i.e. your pupils) for 'being incapable of writing good, plain English like we were taught in the old days', they usually pick on spelling and punctuation to supply their diatribes with evidence. Occasionally, the better-educated jemmies will complain about split infinitives (which are found frequently in Shakespeare), unrelated participles (which occur quite frequently in Jane Austen), sentences ending with words that look like prepositions (frequent in Dryden, until he himself started a fashion by going through his own works moving them away from the ends of the sentences) and sentences beginning with connectives (frequent in Shakespeare and Milton, whose majestic structures are heroic in scale, and transcend the sentence). You can generally get rid of this second kind of nagging by referring to

> the towering dead
> With their nightingales and psalms

and by pointing out that the complaints are about peripheral matters which do not really affect your central task of improving the communication of ideas. You don't tackle a famine by giving a course of lectures on table manners, even though you have a personal preference for meals being taken at table and eaten with knife and fork.

However, when it comes to punctuation and spelling, it seems as though everybody feels fully qualified to pronounce on them authoritatively and at length. Society demands, and demands clamorously, that your pupils should be able to spell and punctuate not merely well, but — if you look at the performance of the clamourers — better than previous generations. What can you do about it? After all, these two features of language can and do affect efficiency of communication.

Punctuation

As it is the more difficult, let us take punctuation first. It is a set of conventions for representing the syntactical organisation of a written text and also for representing the variations in vocal pitch and rhythm appropriate to a spoken performance of the text. In other words, it shows how a piece of writing should 'go' in a spoken performance. Fashions in punctuation change quite rapidly. The translators of the Authorised Version of the Bible punctuated on a totally different principle from Dryden, and Dr Johnson's principle of punctuation, though related to Dryden's, differed from it in detail. Dickens's punctuation was a fantastically elaborate development of Johnson's, and just about marked the end of the line. The punctuation of a modern stylist like Evelyn Waugh is probably nearer in principle to Shakespeare's than to Dickens's. Moreover, the situation is complicated by each publishing house having its own house rules. Study side by side some comparable passages from *The Times*, the *Guardian* and the *Daily Telegraph*, and from books published by, say, the Oxford University Press, the Cambridge University Press, and Faber and Faber. You will soon see how the conventions vary from house to house, and see how ridiculous it is to hanker after a single system of 'correct' punctuation. There just isn't one. The best you can hope for is good punctuation, which is usage that shows clearly how a text should sound; and you can tell that to the know-alls. Every writer has to develop his own usage.

Certainly there are some standard practices. Full stops mark the ends of sentences, though they did not always do so. Most writers use quotes to indicate direct speech, though not all do so. Exclamation and interrogation marks are usually employed to indicate the relevant tones. But beyond that, writers suit their punctuation to what they imagine to be the sound of their own voices. For authoritative guidance in a handy form, turn to two little books, *Punctuation* and *Mind the Stop*, by G. V. Carey, formerly of the Cambridge University Press. For examples of sensitive and scrupulous punctuation of modern English, and to set your standard of practice, look at the New English Bible. It embodies the practice of the Oxford and Cambridge University Presses, and must be the most carefully-edited text of our times. Incidentally, the contents are well worth reading for their own sake, too. Exercises in punctuation can be worked as follows:

Punctuation in free writing. Here you set a piece of writing, and make clear from the beginning that you are going to pay special attention to punctuation. If you are short of time for correction, you can reasonably say that you will choose at random ten lines from each pupil's work and correct those intensively. A class that is used to the kind of pupil-teacher relationship in which personal writing prospers will understand that you can't do everything all the time, and will accept selective correction. In the follow-up you discuss the problems and mistakes of punctuation that have occurred in the work of individuals. In particular, you should find out and talk about the *decisions* that gave pupils the most trouble.

In this kind of exercise you hope that the pupils will learn from their mistakes and puzzles, and you can apply the system of 'group-therapy' described on p. 51. Remember that the pupils cannot be expected just to pick up the principles of punctuation without instruction. Sometime or other you have to tell them what the various marks are for.

Marking of unpunctuated texts. In this work, a text is prepared and duplicated. It may be completely devoid of punctuation, or shorn of certain chosen marks — full stops, for instance — in which practice is desired. The copies are then punctuated by the pupils. A traditional form of the exercise used to consist of writing the mutilated text on the blackboard, for the pupils to copy down and punctuate. I suppose you can see the intention behind the exercise: it is meant to give practice in the use of punctuation marks in a controlled situation. But the committee is unanimous in finding little or no value in such work. The pupils have to punctuate a text that was composed somewhere else, for someone else's voice, and they may not be able to 'hear' it in their imagination. Then the purpose of punctuation exercises is to improve pupils' punctuation of their *own* texts, not of someone else's. There is a risk of pupils becoming skilled at doing punctuation exercises and remaining poor at general punctuation.

Marking of texts according to sound. More preparation is needed for this work. Prepare and duplicate an unpunctuated or part-punctuated text, and this time tape a recording of the text being read aloud. You can use material recorded from B.B.C. programmes, or you can record your own voice. Explain to the class that you want a well-punctuated text as the end-product, then play the recording before you give out the duplicated papers. This ensures that the pupils' preconceptions are aural, not visual. Deal with questions, if there are any, then give out the papers and play the recording again, while the pupils follow the sound of it in their texts. Set a time-limit for the work, make yourself available for consultation, and play the recording as often as it is asked for. End with a play-back so that the class can make a final check of their versions, then collect the papers for correction.

There is no reason why — subject always to the proviso of your being firmly, if comfortably, in control — the pupils should not work in pairs or in small groups. The point about the exercise is that while pupils may not be able to *imagine* how someone else's text should 'go', they can certainly hear how it does 'go', and the material is under your control. Thus you can give instructions on, say, interrogation marks, then set an exercise of this kind which gives practice specifically in interrogation marks.

Spelling

Now for spelling. At present it is fashionable to blame bad spelling on the look-and-say method of learning to read, and also fashionable to attribute it to dyslexia. Well, look-and-say has its shortcomings, one of which is the promotion of a tendency to guess at spellings instead of working them out. But it has also been responsible for children learning to read who might not have learned by analytical/phonic methods. You can't have everything, and surely literacy with bad spelling is preferable to illiteracy, which gives no chance to spell at all. As for dyslexia, it certainly exists, but no one seems to be very sure as yet about how widespread it is, and there is no therapy for it that we in school are qualified to give.

Perhaps the best thing to do about spelling is to fuss and worry about it as little as possible. Most pupils, by the age of sixteen, have, by dint of reading and writing, learned to spell quite reasonably accurately – as accurately, let us say, as they do the arithmetic of addition and subtraction, or dance, or draw maps, or cook; well enough for everyday purposes. They do pick up spelling as they go along, and many of them become perfect at it. But it is unreasonable to expect everybody to be infallible in this one accomplishment when only a proportion of success is expected in other accomplishments. People who really need to spell in order to earn their livings seem to learn all right. The majority do not need specific instruction beyond the correction and discussion of recurrent mistakes when you find those in their work. What you must do is try to develop in your pupils a concern for correct spelling as an element in efficient communication. Once they appreciate that they must spell correctly in order to be fully understood, and appreciate the need for making themselves understandable, most of them will find the means of achieving correctness. As I point out in Chapter 1, strong motivation counts for almost everything in learning the conventions.

It is no use propounding the principles of English orthography to those who do not seem to be picking up spelling. It would be too hideously confusing and would require more time than you can give. Nor is it much use making the pupils write out lists of words that they might be expected to mis-spell. They have enough trouble already without looking for more. The best that we could suggest in committee was for you to check regularly the work of bad spellers, and get them to write out, several times each, the correct spellings of the words they have mis-spelled. It is old-fashioned, and it is uninspired, but it does seem to do some good as long as one does not make a moral issue of it. There is nothing wicked about mis-spelling a word; only a failure in communication. Writing out spellings must not be thought of as a punishment. It is a device for memorising, and must always be thought of as such. If you can think of any other trick for helping pupils to memorise the correct spellings of words they have got wrong, try it. R. H. Thouless, in *General and Social Psychology* (University Tutorial Press, 3rd ed., 1951), reports that where there is a strong wish to correct spelling mistakes, it is even worth writing out, several times, the *incorrect* spelling of a troublesome word, in the hope of exorcising it!

Even bad spellers sometimes grow up into quite good spellers when they see and feel the need to spell words correctly. They are like the grubby urchins who, in adolescence, become finicky about personal cleanliness and tidiness, and for the same sort of reasons: they want to make a decent figure in the world. Personally, I think that in spelling, as in all linguistic activity requiring care and conformity, pupils' attitudes are more important than what they are told. If they care about what they are saying to the extent of wanting to conform, they will find ways of getting to know what is expected of them. They will pick your brains and anyone else's; preferably yours, since in linguistic matters you are the expert and the professional. So your task and mine, as I see it, is first to excite interest and concern (in this case about spelling), then secondly to satisfy the concern and sustain the interest. I hope it is no anti-climax to recommend word-games like Lexicon and Scrabble, and crossword puzzles and the old-fashioned acrostics. To succeed at any of these, one has to spell correctly. If playing at them sends some of your pupils to the dictionary to check spellings, a start will have been made to the development of a desire for the social accomplishment of correct orthography. Besides, does anyone ever come away from consulting the *Shorter Oxford Dictionary*, for whatever purpose, without browsing in it?

Conclusions

So there you are, with a certain amount of rather disparate advice about language-teaching, wondering what to make of it all. In committee — that grim conclave of hard-faced, war-weary, penny-pinching heads of department — we all knew in our hearts and affirmed from our experience that Holbrook and Clegg are right: that given time, encouragement, fascinating topics, and really devoted follow-up work by well-informed teachers, the overwhelming majority of secondary pupils learn to use their written language reasonably accurately and appropriately, and some of them very well indeed, without specific exercises in linguistic detail. We were unanimous that *success* in communication must over-ride all other linguistic considerations, followed by *appropriateness*, and that, for most purposes, sentences are the most satisfactory form of written communication. We did not discuss exercises very much, because we have not a lot of faith in them, and feel that there are usually many more important things to do, such as making each other laugh or cry with stories. However, I personally have, at one time or another, tried every one of the exercises discussed in this chapter. Try them for yourself, and see whether any of them suit you or your classes. Browning wrote of his Grammarian:

> This man decided not to Live but Know —

Well . . . yes, a noble ideal. Browning admired it, and a minority of us must always try to live up to it. But I cannot help thinking that if life is going to be worth living in our old age, not to mention theirs, we must now, in secondary schools, be trying, not to train Grammarians, but rather to bring up sixteen-year-old readers, writers and speakers.

4 Poetry

Michael Woods

What is poetry 'for'? It is for the delight of sharing an experience that has been crystallised in words. This experience can be humorous, sad, joyous, gay, or on an epic plane: but to be meaningful, the experience shared must be recognisable also. This is not to mean only those experiences which pupils may be likely to have had themselves, but those which they can readily share, either by linking up with their own memories or making an effort of their imaginations. And to share, it is not necessary for them to identify: they must merely be able to recognise something which is identifiable. It is not necessary to be Kubla Khan to appreciate the poem; nor do they have to know anything about horse-riding to go galloping along from Ghent to Aix.

Yet the problem, especially for beginners, is just precisely how to bridge this gap between the mundane world of everyday and the luminous, evanescent world of the poet. Moreover, there is the problem of language; the poet doesn't just see, hear, and feel in a different way from most of us, he 'talks different' too.

Perhaps we will be lucky. Perhaps, in their primary schools, pupils will have been much exposed to poetry, and not regard it as a foreign language. Perhaps, being avid pop fans, they will have got used to seeing pop lyrics printed on the backs of record sleeves. Perhaps . . .

But the chances are that none of these things will have happened, and the 'poetry lesson' will remain the most slippery part of our timetable, a kind of exquisite hair shirt, to be viewed from our point of view with dread and trepidation and from our pupils' with utter boredom. These pages are offered to those wallowing in this particular Slough of Despond. For there is, I believe, a remedy. There are other ways of 'teaching' poetry than breaking butterflies on wheels.

The trouble with most disquisitions on 'teaching' poetry is that they too often regard it as a passive activity only. Sir reads: the class listens. Someone may ask a question. If *they* are asked a question, the response is apt to be vague, or stereotyped. ('Did you like that?' Silence.)

Sometimes you can bridge this particular chasm of uninterest by using various devices – a picture, a song, the poem in another context.

These may be helpful, they may be not. They may even detract from the intrinsic value of the poem itself. (A former colleague of mine told me of the following horrendous experience, which took place many years ago when he was still a student. He and his class were doing something heroic – maybe it was Henry V at Harfleur – when the lady lecturer who was sitting in on his lesson suddenly jumped on a chair and started waving her arms about. 'What am I?' she cried to the gaping multitudes. Nobody could supply the correct answer; as it transpired, she was supposed to be a flag.) Perhaps a piece of music may establish a mood akin to that of the poem you wish to take, or even one in contrast: this can be fine; but when you find yourself relying on the music as an end and not as a means, you may as well give up trying.

Much the better way to take the 'foreign' feeling out of poetry is to take the plunge and share it from the outset as a kind of common experience, rather than set it up as a barrier which must be overcome by fair means or foul.

Verse-making

Pupils should be encouraged, from the very beginning, to participate in verse-making for themselves – it is a process you can initiate right up to the senior end of the school, if you're lucky. And by verse-making, I mean free-verse-making. It is of course assumed you will not waste your time trying to produce effusions of the Christmas card variety, though I have seen school magazines proudly displaying such work.

Now many people shy away from this as if it were a mystery beyond their grasp, but basically it is quite simple. The first thing you need is a stimulus of some kind. Take snow. I've had many lessons from snow. The best thing you can do is walk about in it, and let it fall on your face; if you can't do this, watch it glide and settle. Here is an attempt by a first-year boy:

Flakes

The feather duster wipes the fine
powder from
the shelves of the frozen stream.
Sheets fall onto the green bed.
Unsuspecting
river, tree, and bush quiver in the
cloud fallen garden.
Then vanishing mysteriously out of
sight,
as the cold wind blows in

> winter, flakes drowsily
> fall, heavy
> then softer, soft
> as powder.
>
> Crystals clear as sugar glisten in
> the cold Winter.

While you were with them, of course, you asked them questions, the commonest being: 'What is it like?' (feel like, look like, and so on) or 'What does it remind you of?' One girl wrote of the snowflakes on this particular occasion:

> The path devoured them as they
> touched it.

The commonest images were: soap flakes, white dust, salt, icing sugar, crystals — someone said 'heavenly feathers'.

Of course, Sir has been assisting in the making of this piece of free-verse: encouraging observation, setting imaginations in the right gear, suggesting points of contact. But how much more meaningful if, while the pupils are busy writing themselves, Sir co-operates by producing his own little piece on what they have just seen or done! It cannot be over-emphasised that this element of participation, of sharing in a common language, does more than anything to make a class feel 'at one' with poetic form, to render it less inhibiting to them, and to encourage them to explore its possibilities.

The only technical rule you give them is this: 'Each time you want to say something new — even if it's only one word — begin on a new line.' Encourage them to keep their lines as short as possible, especially in the early stages. Your questions will have already introduced them to the first stage of image-making, simile. (Whether you call it simile or not is your own business. I find the term unnecessary at this stage.) Later, using the same process but omitting words like 'like' and 'as', you can go on to introduce metaphor — if the pupils haven't already found it for themselves.

Afterwards, they may read their work aloud to you, or you to them. At any rate, you talk about it. 'Was that a good picture?' 'Someone talked of *sand* there, and I don't think it quite fits. Can anybody else see what I mean?' I usually insist that fair copies are made, either verbatim from the originals or from improved versions. The best are then displayed at the back of the room: and the class knows that the best of these stands a good chance of being included in the next school magazine.

Later, of course, you may wish to go on to develop and vary both
expression and form — two sides of the same coin — but the point I
wish to make here is that this kind of activity, if consistently
encouraged, is more than just an ice-breaker. It is the creative process
itself. Sense stimuli of some kind or other are the best things to use.
These need not be exotic. You may not have any snow. But each
member of the class has a face:

> This eyebrow
> is sloping
> like
> a furry hill.
> This chin
> is curved
> like
> a boot top.
> This hair
> is high and wavy
> like
> an angry sea.
> These teeth
> are jagged and not straight
> like
> a ring of sharp rocks.
> This tongue
> is long
> like
> a whale
> and a lashing wave.

The authoress of this little piece was in the fourth stream down of a
five-stream entry secondary modern school when I met her. She was in
her first year, and so far as I know had no experience of this kind of
writing before this piece was attempted. The method used was the one
prescribed above. She based her writing, I think, on a random sample of
faces she could see around her; but notice the attempt at a pattern, and
the developing imagery of the latter part. Some of her contemporaries
in the next stream down also responded to the same sort of situation
quite successfully: boys who had difficulty in writing two lines of
normal prose dashed off a page and a half of free-verse and were quite
astonished when it was pointed out that they had probably never
written so much in their lives before.

Still safe indoors in my classroom I have used, at other times, the
so-called 'silence' of the room itself; chalk dust clouds ('like a cushion
of soft threads, plaited' wrote one girl); making the class giggle and

laugh. Some very good effects can be produced by letting drops of ink swirl round in a milk bottle full of water. Once I was able to do this in a tank I borrowed from the science lab. I also had a length of rubber tube, which I used to blow bubbles in the resulting mess. Here is one of the consequences:

Bubbles

Burgle,
burble,
gurgle,
POP!
pap!
Like a fish talking,
singing,
like a trout singing the bass chord!
Mysterious
noise.
Pop, gurgle,
pap, burble,
glog, burgle,
spitting in hatred,

POP!

This may provide you with interesting material (subsequently) if you wish to devote a lesson to sounds or patterns, but I must emphasise that no particular 'form' was prescribed for this or any of the examples in this section of the book. The only directives were those of encouragement. The 'form' and the language and the viewpoint were supplied by the creators themselves.

Simple natural objects are good to see and touch. Many of them — conkers, say, or leaves — can be brought into the classroom. But it is good to send your pupils on explorations outside if you can. Here is a detail about a tree:

The long fine branches
entangled with each other
looking like a
used Brillo pad

Fourth-year girl

or something about grass:

Grass
like straggly hair,
or tiny swords,
sometimes erect,

        sometimes tilted,
        as if tired
        after the battle
        with the wind

                               Second-year girl

or falling leaves:

        They flutter and splutter
        as they drop and plop.
        Some twirl and hurl themselves to the ground,
        twisting like helicopters and diving like rockets.
        Gliding and sliding through the air.
        They tumble and fumble
        from the roof of the trees.
        Graceful are they,
        pirouetting, curling
        as they drift to the ground.
        Dancing, prancing as they fall.
        Swirling and looping through the air.

                               First-year boy

But it need not be all trees and flowers. Puddles, especially with oil in them, are good; as are rust, mould ('Yellow eyes amidst a growing river of green moss' wrote one), mud, mist ('There is a greasy polythene bag covering the whole world today'), and pieces of clinker:

        A HUMAN BRAIN
        gone mouldy.
        Little bogie bubbles,
        ready for picking.
        Shadows all queer
        and distorted.

        Abstract sculptures
        could never match
        this work of art.

        Red moss
        dead and morbid
        Little bits
        of gunge
        all
        soft —
        What a masterpiece!

                             Fourth-year boy

In the case of 'Falling leaves' you will see how the writer has tried to capture the twirling, loping movements of the leaves by the internal rhythms of the words. Some may think the arrangement of the lines might be altered: but it is as its author left it. I have never given lessons in iambics or feet of any kind at this stage or cut up 'I wandered lonely as' into long or short bits. The most we can legitimately do is to experiment with patterns, pointing out individual needs to individual cases. The whole of my experience in this field points to the fact that the child will find its own rhythms and patterns of expressing what it wants to express: the most we can do is initiate, encourage, and correct. It is profitable to point out that such a thing as rhythm exists, and what some of its forms are: it is a waste of time to insist on perfect iambics, or 'imitations' as a substitute for the genuine article of the child's creative imagination.

Starting points

There are other starting points. In Chapter 11, 'A Thematic Approach to English Teaching', I have mentioned the opportunities offered by listening to music and engaging in dramatic work. Painting, or pictures from the colour magazines, are also useful. Many verse anthologies nowadays offer illustrations as an integral part of the material. Two such which spring immediately to mind are *Voices*, edited by Geoffrey Summerfield, and the new 'Penguin English Project', in which he also has a guiding hand. The pictures are included not only as a reinforcement to the text but also as something valuable in themselves. Some collections of pictures on their own have been published, but these are expensive for what they are, and the teacher will spend his time best in arranging his own collections of visual material. I have many such collections, labelled 'The sea', 'Shapes', 'Faces', and so on.

Some teachers like to offer a verbal challenge. 'Key rhymes', words like 'gloom' and 'doom' can be selected, thus forming a couplet or a succession of couplets. The class can supply the rest. Sometimes a definite title can be given. Sometimes you will have to teach a definite poetic 'form' in order to gain the response you require. It is no use, for instance, expecting them to gaily churn out limericks if you haven't undertaken some sort of investigation into what a limerick is, and what syllables are. Another 'form' that springs immediately to mind in this connection is Lear's 'Nonsense Alphabet', where we have pictures accompanying the verses: or, better still, the 'Nonsense Botany' where things like the Bubblia Blowpipia or the Crabbia Horrida have their illustrations but could also do with some texts to accompany the drawings.

Standard word work is not exempt, either. An examination of words like 'miniature', 'minuscule', 'petite', 'microscopic' and so on leads quite naturally to an exploration, where everybody must bring back an example. It is amazing what an enterprising child will find when put to it: a collection of dandelion petals, grains of dirt, the wings of dead insects . . . all these, of course, are gifts for creative writing.

Memory can sometimes be of use as a stimulus, but it needs careful handling. Jack Beckett, in his book *The Keen Edge*, describes how he first began to versify by taking general emotional states like being afraid, and then asked the class to remember when they last were. This is all right, up to a point. For although our pupils' verse writing will be of a personal nature there are limits to respect, and it is as well for us to remember that we are neither psychoanalysts nor, one hopes, voyeurs. It is true that many children find an emotional release in writing poetry, but I do not feel that justifies us in setting up the operation solely on that basis. The situation is rather analogous to the old chestnut of asking a child to write about its family – and then finding it hasn't got one. Children deserve, in this respect, the same discretion one would give to an adult. Teachers have a tendency to see them all too easily as cannon fodder of one kind or another, and verse-makers, if the wrong attitude is adopted, can fall into the same category. Such immediate emotional release as our pupils may gain is incidental to the exercise itself: the true release lies in creation, which transcends the world of everyday, touches it with magic perhaps, but certainly never leaves it unadorned.

For it is as well to remind ourselves here, that what we are doing is simply placing the child in situations where it can create with words. We supply the confrontation and a bit of guidance, if you like, plus a few accolades at the end: nothing more. If we have done our job well, then the confrontations will have been enjoyable and stimulating and the child's powers of observation and imaginative perception will have been strengthened thereby. The outcome of the encounter is his attempts to write about his experience in a special way, a way that attempts to recapture its newness and its wonder.

Other poets' verses

It is this sense of newness and wonder which may provide one of the strongest links between writing poetry ourselves and reading what is written by others. I like to treat the process as a kind of continuum, intermixing our own efforts with those of older, more practised hands.

The pupils in your care will probably have got used by now to reading and discussing their own work, seeing it displayed, even viewing it in cold print. It is not too great a step to extend this by introducing other work by more 'professional' poets. Not as models, be it noted: we do not imitate. We observe. These are other people's ways of dealing with things they have seen, have felt, have noticed. They are not necessarily better than our own attempts. It is to be hoped we would subject them to the same kind of scrutiny as we would our own writings: a picture here, a phrase there, some special effect, the poem's total meaning . . . does it 'come across'? Do the words help it to do this? Has reading it given us something we didn't have before? Did we enjoy it? The purpose of the comparison is to provide a link merely. We must notice that other people are trying to do the same things as ourselves.

For if it is all right for us to write our own poetry, then it must be all right for other people, too. If we are critical about ourselves, we must be critical about the work of others. There is no need to adopt a 'double standard' here — one for the adult writers and another for the people sitting in the classroom. That involves the wrong kind of patronage. A creation is a creation is a creation. No matter by whom.

Every piece of work is unique and separate and must be treated as such. If there are several pieces of work on the same theme or written around the same stimulus or subject then they are separate contributions to the development of that theme or subject. Treated in this way, the writing and reading of poetry react and interact.

Some people may like to start with the reading: I prefer the writing, as being more productive. Once you start, you may find that some or several bright ideas may have to be sacrificed on the altar of success: but they will have been worth it. By the time you have written quite a lot you may have read only a little, but the flow of the thing should be established and pieces of verse should cease to be Babylonic cuneiform for most of your pupils.

Choice of poetry for reading

You may, of course, like to begin your readings with something that has direct relevance to what you are writing. Most anthologies these days are arranged thematically, and a perusal of those mentioned at the end of this chapter should offer several useful leads. Some people, however, prefer to pick their poems at random — even to the extent of adding one per lesson, as a plum at the end. The time allotted for this can gradually be extended to include comment, so that the poetry in a sense 'takes over'. Some time will doubtless elapse before your pupils are ready to browse through anthologies on their own and pick out what they like, though perhaps this is the ideal. Maybe a group of poems by one author is what you're after: here again, the anthologies can help you.

All methods have something to commend them. But there are important provisos. The first is that you should like what you read: there are certain poems I refuse to read for this very reason. I do not like them, and it shows. The second important point is that you should try to calculate the mood or receptiveness of the class you're trying to read to. If it's April Fool's Day and they've put glue on the door, tintacks on your chair and electrified the handles of your desk you'll stand precious little chance with 'My Heart's in the Highlands' – or anything else, for that matter. More poetry lessons have come to grief over this single point than, I would say, any other. When you get to know your class and they you, it becomes easier to divine their temper – but the newcomer must be wary.

I would suggest, however, that if you try and maintain the 'continuum' suggested above, you will have less friction and faction than if you restrict your poetry lessons to (say) every other Thursday. Once poetry – the reading of it and the writing of it – becomes a regular feature of everyday classroom life, and is accepted as such without restraint by the pupils in your charge, then a lot of these peripheral worries will disappear.

Whatever you select should be, in the first instance, fairly easily identifiable (in our sense of the term) – clear cut, and definite. I favour modern poetry as a jumping-off point, and preferably without rhymes; though this is not exclusive, and some people would include much that is not written in the twentieth century. It is not a good policy, either, to underestimate your audience: don't just give them things you are sure will appeal to them but, every now and then, something they will have to stretch for.

Some authorities insist on a 'graded' scheme of poetry reading. This scheme has its drawbacks. It blinkers. You end up looking for poems 'suitable' for a particular age-group and tend to forget that, in the first place, many poems can be enjoyed on many different levels; and, secondly, what you should really try to do is to sustain or satisfy a mood for various different types of poetry. Thus I frequently take Tennyson's 'The Eagle' with Form Six as an example of compression: Form Two can also take, in another context, poems like Owen's

'Strange Meeting' and 'Dulce et Decorum Est'. Appetites must be whetted, and likings encouraged. Moreover, poems will seem to have a mood of their own: these can be fragile experiences, initially lasting half an hour or so, the duration of the first reading and what follows. But if the spell is cast successfully, the mood can be recaptured and the pupils will want to return to it.

Some poems repay (and must have) careful attention: others appeal immediately in themselves. This is a point often overlooked, not only by teachers, but also by writers of manuals who tend to treat every poem in the same way. Whitehead is rather solemn and claustrophobic on this point (*The Disappearing Dais*, Chapter 3). Talking of dealing with early classes' approaches to poetry, he says: 'A stress upon enjoyment seems to me fully justified at this initial stage, though by itself it would certainly not be enough later on.'

I cannot agree wholeheartedly, though I can see his point. Too often poems are flogged to death in an attempt to extract all the meat at one sitting. Poems, like people, need careful handling: some can be confronted direct, others have to be sidled up to. A poem may serve its purpose by illustrating a definite point you wish to make, or you may serve the purpose of the poem best by only concentrating on one particular aspect of it – its appeal as a song, say, or its narrative quality. But once our pupils stop gaining pleasure from what they write and read, we might as well stop trying to inflict poetry on them.

If I were asked to provide a new teacher with an 'all purpose' selection of poems for all moods and occasions, ones moreover which were guaranteed of a sure-fire success, I would answer that it could not be done: for a poem's potential can only be fully exploited by the person who presents it. On the other hand, it may be useful to suggest some lines of enquiry.

Nonsense poetry

Let us start with so-called 'nonsense' poetry. My own theory is that these pieces are far more 'sensible' than many people would suggest; but be that as it may, 'nonsense' verse is popular with all ages, and much of it is satirical (like a lot of the pieces in *Alice*) or written just for the fun of it (like Lear's 'Nonsense Alphabet'). Carroll and Lear are, of course, standard, and limericks have become a literary genre in their own right. It might be of interest to point out to more mature pupils (and even those not so mature, if you wish them to attempt their own 'nonsense') that it is ordinary language which is leavened by nonsense words, and not the other way around, as may be supposed. Thus, in 'Jabberwocky', for instance, you have a fairly standard tale of heroism and derring-do enlivened by such words as 'brillig', 'slithy', 'outgrabe'. Their incidence is less than that of ordinary verbs and conjunctions, for example. It has to be, or the poem wouldn't be 'nonsense' — it would be unintelligible. This may seem a somewhat academic point, but I find it is one well worth making, as people tend to dismiss this kind of verse as being 'child's play' to concoct, or just plain cranky. Of course, it is absurd: but it makes a serious point too. 'The Dong With the Luminous Nose', for instance, is really a very sad story of unrequited love.

Ways of treating these poems for performance are dealt with later in the section. Here we must concern ourselves with finding more material. The work of Hilaire Belloc should not be ignored, with classics like 'Henry King' and 'Matilda', moral stories all. There is also a very sarcastic piece called 'The Microbe', in which he attempts to debunk science. Eliot's *Practical Cats* also comes into this category (not scientific, nonsensical): my own favourites are not the much-quoted 'Macavity' or 'Skimbleshanks', but 'Growltiger's Last Stand' (shades of Tennyson's 'Revenge') and 'The Aweful Battle of the Pekes and the Pollicles', which has a rousing barking chorus almost certain to galvanise the most reluctant class. Two collections by the late Don Marquis also deserve mention here, *archy and mehitabel* and *archys life of mehitabel*. Archy is a cockroach with the soul of a poet and he works the typewriter by butting his head on the keys. The poems are full of sly humour, much of it social in content, and will enable your classes to meet memorable characters such as Freddy the Rat and Warty Bliggens the Toad. Archy's inability to manage punctuation on his machine is an added bonus.

Spike Milligan, in *A Dustbin Full of Milligan* and *Silly Verse for Kids*, has much that is amusing, if a trifle undisciplined. At times he seems like a modern-day Edward Lear. He also provides his own illustrations. Another collection which also has much to commend it is James Reeves's *Prefabulous Animiles*, illustrated by Edward Ardizzone. My own favourite from this collection is 'The Hippocrump', a truly fearsome tale, and one admirably suited for group work of various kinds. I was even able, on one such occasion, to find a set of accompanists complete with bongo drums. The works of John Betjeman, too, provide, if not nonsense, poems that are certainly humorous in content: 'Hunter Trials' is probably the classic for children, who appreciate its satire of the horsy set.

Animals in poetry

It is a short step from poems presenting animals humorous or absurd to some which wear a more serious face. There are, for instance, umpteen poems about cats: the cat seems to have a status in our literature akin to that of the sacred beasts of the Egyptians. But perhaps the most famous animal poet of modern times is D. H. Lawrence. Although his total output in this respect was comparatively small, these poems are among the finest things he ever wrote. The swooping, elliptical style perfectly captures Lawrence's own reactions to what he obviously regarded as perfect works of nature, even if they are conventionally unattractive. The most famous of these poems is, of course, 'Snake', but I have often found this curiously unrewarding to attempt. A much more direct confrontation (from the child's point of view) is provided in 'Mountain Lion', where 'her round, bright face' is sung about with a lyricism disarming in its simplicity. His masterpiece in this genre, 'Man and Bat', is a much longer poem but one which repays careful attention.

Animal poetry is a field literally vast in its scope and a selection of one or two items is bound to disappoint. However, Hardy's 'Darkling Thrush' often provides a useful contrast to Hopkins's 'The Windhover': perhaps they both reach roughly the same destination but through widely different routes. Both Hardy and Hopkins repay attention in themselves, and another Hopkins poem which I find often rewarding is 'Inversnaid', though this, concerned with a wet Scottish Landscape, does not really fit in here. Ted Hughes is another modern poet well worth looking at from many points of view, but he has also written convincingly of birds and beasts, two of his best-known pieces being 'Hawk Roosting' and 'View of a Pig'. The latter, deceptively clinical in its approach, nevertheless serves to evoke quite an emotional response to the dead animal. Robert Frost, too, is another writer who, though not writing so much specifically about creatures, still takes 'nature' as the setting for many of his pieces, which are almost conversational in style and often deal with little incidents or happenings.

Many of the anthologies, of course, will prove a boon here in selecting poems of this nature, especially light, easy stuff which treats of animals as pets or playthings. But there are some poems which view the subject in a more thoughtful light: W. W. Gibson's 'The Ponies' tells of a group of pit ponies let loose for a while during the General Strike; Elizabeth Bishop's 'The Fish' deals with a minor Moby Dick, the one that repeatedly got away; John Wain, in 'Au Jardin des Plantes', describes the boredom of an animal in captivity and allies it to some of our own social disorders. But if you still want something on the lighter side, and something that is easy to swallow to boot, you could do worse than ransack the works of Ogden Nash, for pieces like 'The Kipper', 'The Armadillo', 'The Turtle' and so on. Nash appears deceptively simple: his is the artlessness which really does conceal true art.

Another American writer who seems artless (some may even say ingenuous) is Emily Dickinson. Recently 'rediscovered', the little outpourings of this lonely woman have a simple, dreamlike quality, sometimes folksy perhaps, but often displaying a true, almost eerie, insight. Her two best-known pieces over here are 'A Narrow Fellow in the Grass' (a snake) and 'I Like to See it Lap the Miles' (some say an automobile, though it's more probably a train). Like Robert Frost, she may be said to belong to a more domestic school of poetry: she writes about the little world she knows, and it is all easily visualised. Two that I like are 'I Know Some Lonely Houses off the Road' and 'There's Been a Death in the Opposite House', The mood of these pieces is perhaps too elusive for junior forms to capture.

Poems about people

I have deliberately given a selection of poems which, apart from the nonsensical or satiric, are of a more thoughtful nature. These are pieces which would obviously repay a thoughtful, deliberative approach: a first reading which is calm yet authoritative, and a probing for whatever you wish to gain which is thorough yet never relapses into dullness. For contrast, we may take some more vigorous poems about people. Heroes and roughnecks abound. Kipling's 'Danny Deever' can be a stark and moving piece, if properly handled, likewise that old imperial war-horse 'Gunga Din'. 'The Shooting of Dan McGrew' is another classic which usually grips. Hopkins's 'Felix Randal' is another possibility, perhaps a little too obscure for some, though few can fail to rise to the marvellous alliteration of the last two lines. In a more modern age, we have such coves as 'Butch Weldy' (E. L. Masters), 'Cynddylan on a Tractor' (R. S. Thomas) and 'Timothy Winters' (Charles Causley). If the child is father to the man, there's food for thought here. Ezra Pound's 'Ballad of the Goodly Fere' presents Christ as a man's man, a view which goes down very well with older children. Michael Baldwin's 'Death on the Live Wire', though not properly a portrait, might still be included in this category. It is certainly powerful, and has been known to make fifth formers squirm.

War poems

From the people themselves, we might progress to the wars they have made. The poetry of the First World War is the richest field for anguish — and some preliminary heroics, too. It is hard to decide, for instance, which is the more harrowing: something like Julian Grenfell's 'Into Battle' ('And he is dead who will not fight . . .') or something like Siegfried Sassoon's 'Attack', with its heartrending last line: 'O Jesu, make it stop!' Poets like Isaac Rosenberg, Siegfried Sassoon, Rupert Brooke, Wilfred Owen, Robert Graves, many of whom gave their lives, write with a bitterness unmatched in the poetry of the Second War. Although well known pieces like 'Strange Meeting', 'Dulce et Decorum Est', 'Exposure', have their power, the ultimate in nausea is provided by a lesser-known piece of Wilfred Owen's, 'Mental Cases'. This ghoulish picture of shellshocked survivors, slobbering and drivelling in their wheelchairs, afraid even of the sunlight, deserves to be more widely known. For one thing, it is concerned not merely to recount the experience, but also to apportion the guilt.

By contrast, the Second World War seems almost like an outing to some exciting, far-off game. Something like 'Night Patrol' by Alan Ross tells you that it's much more of an optic adventure. Charles Causley's 'Death of an Aircraft' and Ted Hughes's 'The Casualty' describe what you'd expect, but even so, this is much more of a war of machines. Henry Reed's 'Naming of Parts' is all about the army's attempts to teach you to handle same. Keith Douglas, in 'Vergissmeinicht', does attempt some human confrontation: but there is nothing, anywhere, like the perpetual ghastliness of trench life. War is always a popular theme with young people, from the simple (and often inaccurate) heroics of the biff-bang comics to the protests about C.S. gas. What a study of war poetry can elicit, however, is how much of the response is genuine: it is easy to be 'anti war' in the cosy vacuum of your living room, but how much do they really know? How much do *we* really know? Confrontations with things like 'Mental Cases', for instance, can do much to bring spurious feelings to light. Their shock value is not to be underestimated. Also, if you wish to probe into the future a bit, there are pieces like Auden's 'Say This City' or Peter Porter's 'Your Attention Please'.

Poems of violence

With war goes violence. 'Danny Deever' and 'Dan McGrew' have already been mentioned. There are songs and ballads which have to do with

violence, like 'Frankie and Johnny' or 'The Streets of Laredo'. Some of
the older 'heroic' poetry is a justification of, or incitement to, violence:
there is Shakespeare's King Harry, but there is also Tennyson's 'The
Revenge'. Such heroism may sound a little false today. More direct
confrontations are provided in poems like Vernon Scannell's 'First
Fight'. In my school we have a popular sequence which comprises 'The
Ballad of Billy Rose' by Leslie Norris, Saul Kane's fight from 'The
Everlasting Mercy', and a poem called 'Wrestling' by John Crowe
Ransom. There are others dealing with roughly the same experience
which we might have included.

But the theme of violence itself might provide an interesting
exercise for the young teacher wishing to test his powers of poetic
assimilation. Not all violence is fisticuffs. Hardy's 'Throwing a Tree',
for instance, tells of the destruction of a two-hundred-year-old tree in
the New Forest: 'Binsey Poplars' tells of Hopkins's disgust after a
similar act of barbarism. Our interpretation of the theme governs the
poems we select to illustrate it. It should not be too difficult, for
instance, to uncover poems which deal with savagery in nature, with
accidents at work or play, with quarrels between lovers or among
members of families . . . the possibilities are legion. The *aftermath* of
violence, too, may provide a good starting point: Ted Hughes's 'The
Casualty' is a good example of this. Or being on the periphery of
violence. There is a poem by Yevtushenko called simply 'Murder!' in
which he recollects the scene, some years before, when the murdered
man's body had been found. It is a memory that haunts him always.

For those who like narrative verse, the theme can be accommodated
quite easily. Indeed, mention has already been made of this fact. But
there are more modern instances, from old chestnuts like 'Flannan
Isle' (the violent disruption of the keepers' world is the basis of the
mystery) to more warlike pieces such as 'The Nabara' or 'The Fight of
the *Jervis Bay*' or 'Incident in Hyde Park'. In fact, it is amazing just
how much of narrative poetry is taken up with violence of some kind:
on the one hand we have the old stagers, like 'The Twa Corbies', or
'Peter Grimes' or 'The Charge of the Light Brigade' or 'Sohrab and
Rustum': on the other, we have such things as Auden's 'O What is That
Sound', Masefield's two great epics 'Dauber' and 'Reynard the Fox',
little pieces like Ted Hughes's 'Two Wise Generals'. Tales of derring-do
from *Beowulf* onwards have involved physical violence of some kind.
The cynical may remark that it is the staple diet of the poetic narrator,
the only way he can hold 'old men from the chimney corner'. One of the
drawbacks of narrative verse is that people often use the 'excitement'

of the story as an excuse for having some 'poetry': it's really the poetry they want, but they haven't the courage to trust their class with a lyric. Much narrative verse, however, is neither good narrative nor good verse, so you don't get the best of any possible world at all. The 'stories', such as they are, are often better told by professional story-tellers and not by poets: with a few exceptions, the two gifts do not usually coincide. But these are things you must decide for yourself. Nobody else can decide them for you. Neither the poems mentioned above or any others for that matter are 'guaranteed' to work at 1.55 on a wet afternoon or when the class would much rather be out doing games or simply going home. One tests one's own prejudices by trial and error and finds out what goes down best, and what one can manage best.

Reading poetry aloud

Indication has already been given of one of the constant (some might say necessary) sources of enjoying poetry — that of writing it yourself. But there are others. Speaking it is one. Good reading by the teacher is essential, of course. But what about reading by the class? They will read their own work aloud, certainly. This, it is hoped, will be fostered without self-consciousness. The relevant section in Chapter 2 on 'Spoken English' may well give you some help here. But there are other, 'non-poetic' things which can be done to encourage fluent delivery. Try them from time to time with tongue-twisters. Try reading announcements in a particular tone of voice. See how many different ways there are of saying: 'Where are you going?' 'Give that book to me', and the like. Older pupils may even be revived by means of using nonsense language (see Chapter 11, 'A thematic approach to English teaching'). These activities may not be 'poetic' to some people, but they certainly help to eliminate awkwardness.

Some people like to encourage what might be called 'silent' reading of poetry. This is not to be confused with the silent reading of a novel. The idea is that pupils browse through an anthology (or, having compiled their own anthologies, use those) and select a poem or poems which they would like to read out loud to the rest of the class. I would suggest you use an anthology in which a good many poems are previously known before you attempt this.

Some schools have verse festivals and like occasions where public recitation is encouraged. For this purpose, the poem or poems may have to be learnt.

But whether a poem is being read at a public festival or to the rest of the class, the question of delivery is important. Anyone still harbouring delusions as to what poetic 'delivery' might be is requested to read the relevant chapter in *Tom Sawyer*, where the young maidens read their 'compositions' at the concert. That ought to be corrective enough for anybody: but it's amazing how habits of mouthing poetry still exist. Here again, the undertaking should be seen not as a burdensome task but as a pleasurable enrichment: the child is not to 'read' the poem in a funny alien accent (or, more often, through his nose) but to communicate what, to him, the poem means.

Try, as an experiment, reading a piece that rhymes — 'Reynard the Fox', say, or 'Dauber'. Most people will come down on the end of the line with a hearty clonk. I do not think this is what Masefield intended to happen. If a poet is skilled with this particular form of verse-writing (and Masefield was) then the couplets will frequently be made to appear as natural and easy-flowing as possible. To read them aloud in this manner involves thought and breath control. The meaning must be clear, and the punctuation scrupulously observed. A process that begins as a game may well develop into a serious exercise in technique.

For the technique varies with the poem under consideration. Reading a poem 'naturally' doesn't always imply 'naturalism'. Heroic verse has to be declaimed, and a lyric demands an intensity of feeling alien to a more reflective piece. This is a skill which can only be acquired with long and constant practice. It requires judgement as well as ability. But the effort is worth making, none the less.

Choral speech

Choral speech should not be ignored. I am not talking only of formal occasions either, where a choir has to be trained (though these occasions are valuable and important), but more informal efforts in class. Try a poem like 'I had a Hippopotamus' (itself a tongue-twister) and see how various sections of the class cope with parts of it. Or divide the class into smaller sections. Then take something like one of the witch scenes in *Macbeth*, say, or the whole of 'Jabberwocky' and work out treatments of it. Once they have got the idea, let them go away and work out something of their own. I once had a whole sequence of 'nonsense' verse (including 'The Jumblies', 'The Dong With the Luminous Nose' and 'The Pobble') tape recorded in this way, with little initial rehearsal and some ingenious sound effects (the Dong's pipe, for instance, was an old drinking straw: the borogroves going mimsy were elastic bands, plucked like jew's harps). We all enjoyed ourselves hugely. Though this particular treatment was done by a second-year group, senior classes can attempt the same sort of thing with no ill effects. A sequence of their own poems about the Ride of the Valkyries was recorded against the background of the appropriate music by some third years: one fourth-year group did a brilliant skit on 'The Ancient Mariner' complete with a pop group, and a prime minister driving the death ship.

Records

Perhaps we can slip in a word here just about records. A large stock of recorded music is always a help, and not just with the poetry allocation, either; but there is also an increasing number of records devoted exclusively to the spoken word. You can now obtain records of people like Ted Hughes, Thom Gunn, Elizabeth Jennings and Robert Graves (see the book list at the end of the chapter): but often poets are not the best interpreters of their work, and it must be remembered that your readings are aimed at young audiences, who often have not the hypocrisy of their elders to sit still politely when in fact they are bored to tears. Professional actors often do the job much better: Robert Speaight really makes the poems of Hopkins sing, for instance, on a Spoken Arts Record. Some anthologies, too, are recorded: *Voices*, for instance, has six records, the content of which is interesting if not always successful. The speaking of the verse, sad to say, often leaves a lot to be desired. But the music and sound effects are often well worth having. Ted Hughes's anthology *Here Today* is another which has been recorded.

If you are thinking of training groups for more formal choral work, perhaps one or two words need to be said. The voices in your group should be distinctive, yet capable of blending together to produce a resonant sound. Think also of the respective heights of your group members, and if you wish this difference in height to be used for any definite effect: nothing is worse than a line of serious faces like a badly-arranged coconut shy, some on long bodies and some on short. Avoid undue posturing: it is a genuine emotion you are trying to establish. The work, too, should be well rehearsed and word perfect: but that is not to stop you conducting it, as with an orchestra.

Be careful of your materials. There are some old favourites of choral speaking, like the nonsense poems of Lear and Carroll, or Vachel Lindsay's 'The Congo': all worth doing still, but a bit hackneyed none

the less. There are other things. The poems of Carl Sandburg, for
instance ('Jazz Fantasia' or 'Chicago') offer the kind of alliteration and
onomatopoeia frequently associated with choral speakaing. Yet it need
not all be bangs and thumps. Some quite unlikely things can be
presented in this way. I have performed such things as 'Danny Deever',
'Mountain Lion', 'Timothy Winters', 'Spurn Light' (J. Redwood
Anderson), 'The Story of the Flood' (John Heath Stubbs), 'Jamaican
Bus Ride' (A. S. J. Tessimond) — and these are only some of the more
obvious 'narrative' type poems. Walter de la Mare's 'To a Snowflake'
can also be attempted, as well as many offerings by John Betjeman,
James Reeves, and others. Nor should you neglect the Bible, especially
the Psalms. *Reading Aloud* by James Gibson and Raymond Wilson is a
book which may give you some ideas in this direction, and Mona
Swann's verse-speaking anthology can also be helpful in suggesting
material for the lower end of the age range, but I don't know if copies
are still in print. (See also the book list for Chapter 2 on 'Spoken
English'.)

Verse-speaking choirs, like any other choirs, should not be too large:
I find eight an optimum number. Rehearse them well, and they will
respond. Do not neglect, either, to fit appropriate actions or movements
where necessary: choral speaking is an exhilarating and delightful
experience if done well, and one of the reasons it has got a bad name
is that audiences have had to suffer too many lines of wet rags, limply
chanting. It is also an activity often neglected because teachers feel too
timid. Take the plunge. Be bloody, bold and resolute. If you are
successful, nobody will regret it.

Deeper treatment

I have saved to the end the knotty problem of poems which require a
more serious response. It is a knotty problem because it can too often
lead to the idea that poetry is some kind of perpetual obstacle race, all
poems being 'difficult' things from which understanding has to be
wrung at great cost. Too often the problem is ours because we try to
extract too much juice in one go. But if your pupils are familiar with
poetry, and do not treat it as a foreign language, are used to your
picking out key words or phrases or lines or ideas, or discussing the
substance of a poem generally, there should be no difficulty in moving
on to a little close questioning for a poem that you feel deserves it.

Let us take, for illustration, 'The Ballad of Billy Rose', by Leslie
Norris. This poem is often anthologised, but for our purposes we will
print it in full:

The Ballad of Billy Rose

Outside Bristol Rovers' Football Ground —
The date has gone from me, but not the day,
Nor how the dissenting flags in stiff array
Struck bravely out against the sky's grey round —

Near the Car Park then, past Austin and Ford,
Lagonda, Bentley, and a colourful patch
Of country coaches come in for the match,
Was where I walked, having travelled the road

From Fishponds to watch Portsmouth in the Cup.
The Third Round, I believe. And I was filled
With the old excitement which had thrilled
Me so completely when, while growing up,

I went on Saturdays to match or fight.
Not only me; for thousands of us there
Strode forward eagerly, each man aware
Of tingling memory, anticipating delight.

We all marched forward, all, except one man.
I saw him because he was paradoxically still,
A stone against the flood, face upright against us all,
Head bare, hoarse voice aloft, blind as a stone.

I knew him at once, despite his pathetic clothes;
Something in his stance, or his sturdy frame
Perhaps. I could even remember his name
Before I saw it on his blind-man's tray. Billy Rose.

And twenty forgetful years fell away at the sight.
Bare-kneed, dismayed, memory fled to the hub
Of Saturday violence, with friends to the Labour Club,
Watching the boxing on a sawdust summer night.

The boys' enclosure close to the shabby ring
Was where we stood, clenched in a resin world,
Spoke in cool voices, lounged, were artificially bored
During minor bouts. We paid threepence to go in.

Billy Rose fought there. He was top of the bill.
So brisk a fighter, so gallant, so precise!
Trim as a tree he stood for the ceremonies.
Then turned to meet George Morgan of Tirphil.

He had no chance. Courage was not enough,
Nor tight defence. Donald Davies was sick
And we threatened his cowardice with an embarrassed kick.
Ripped across both his eyes was Rose, but we were tough

And clapped him as they wrapped his blindness up
In busy towels, applauded the wave

He gave his executioners, cheered the brave
Blind man as he cleared with a jaunty hop

The top rope. I had forgotten that day
As if it were dead for ever, yet now I saw
The flowers of punched blood on the ring floor,
As bright as his name. I do not know

How long I stood with ghosts of the wild fists
And the cries of shaken boys long dead around me,
For struck to act at last, in terror and pity
I threw some frantic money, three treacherous pence –

And I cry at the memory – into his tray, and ran,
Entering the waves of the stadium like a drowning man.
Poor Billy Rose. God, he could fight,
Before my three sharp coins knocked out his sight.

This poem is much longer than the average lyric, but it has been chosen deliberately for its wide appeal and also for the scope it offers. For we can approach this poem on different levels. Some of our class might say this is a poem 'about' a fight. But is it? Look again. What are these two people doing outside Bristol Rovers football ground? Perhaps the fight is incidental. Who fought? Billy Rose. And what happened? He lost. Why? George Morgan cut his eyes so badly that he couldn't see. Well . . . Why does the man who's telling the story remember all this? Because Billy Rose is begging outside the ground. And does he feel embarrassed? Yes. What does he do? Pays him threepence and hurries on. Why is his threepence 'treacherous'? Someone might say: 'Because he's trying to make up for what he's done.' What had he done to Billy Rose? He hadn't fought him. Ah yes, but he'd *paid* to see him fight. Could we explain the last line then?

There are other points we might have raised. We might have asked, for instance, which character the class considered more 'the man' – blind Billy Rose, who accepted his defeat, or the poet, who was ashamed and ran away, and who had swaggered round at the ringside? Or we might have started with the very dramatic contrast between the surging crowds of the opening and the still boxer, 'blind as a stone' in his 'pathetic clothes'. Crowds saw him fight, once. It seems, too, they are necessary to the poet: he was one of a crowd at the ringside, and he wishes to be swallowed up 'like a drowning man' at the end.

Notice, too, we have concentrated mainly on the story – this is a *narrative* of a past experience so remembered that it becomes a present pain. I think it is as well to start with this aspect of things here. And

after all these questions, we might well read the poem again. By this
time it is probably the end of the lesson.

Later, we might look at the language. Take the scene of the fight
itself. What is 'the hub of Saturday violence'? Why is it 'the hub'? And
what about 'a sawdust summer night'? How can a night be said to be
'sawdust'? Surely, that's a peculiar thing to say? Was it a splendid place,
this 'hub of Saturday violence'? No — it's a 'shabby ring', and what's
more it's at the Labour Club. Did the boys stand close together? How
did they react at first? And what is a 'resin world'? Who or what was
'clenched'? What's the importance of the sentence: 'We paid threepence
to go in'?

Notice we have only covered two stanzas. The description of the
fight lasts for six. You might feel, with certain groups, that two stanzas
is enough: it depends on the particular point you wanted to make. You
might just have wanted to emphasise the sordid atmosphere, to notice
the build-up to the last line. You might have wanted to point out the
seeming genuineness of Donald Davies' feelings, and contrast it with
the assumed suavity of the others, and the poet's ultimate shame.
I don't believe in harrowing poems for too long, especially if the class
seems to be getting bored. In any case, the point is that one ought to
establish *by degrees* that there is a certain mode of enquiry to be
adopted in dealing with poems in this way, and this is best done little
and often, not by the occasional grand slam at one particular piece.

And then we have the tone of the poem, the poet's voice, to
consider. Is he being gay, sarcastic, or what? It is to be hoped the
teacher will have given some definite clues to this himself by his own
reading. (It is to be assumed that he will have read the poem aloud
more than once before any discussion of it takes place.) Pupils can test
the 'tone' of a piece by attempting to read various stanzas in various
tones of voice, and establishing which is the right one. 'Billy Rose' is a
bitter poem, and we ought to be able to deduce this from the memory
the incident evokes, if nothing else.

The 'question and answer' technique outlined above presupposes of
course, great participation on the part of Sir. Initially, of course, this
must be so, so that we all know where we're going. But there is no
reason why the direction of such enquiry should always remain so
exclusive. The class, ultimately, should take over at least part of this,
and one of the ways suggested is for various groups to examine various
parts or aspects of the poem under discussion. Thus, for 'Billy Rose',
one group might consider what picture he gives of the fight from the
point of view of the fighters: another, the same sequence from the

point of view of the boys. A third group might tackle the opening in the same way, trying to bring out the dramatic contrast already mentioned. A fourth set might trace the fortunes and significance of the three 'treacherous pence'. A fifth might treat of the poet's humiliation and shame: although he runs away and does little to help his former hero in any material way, they might yet decide that the poem itself is the best kind of monument the poet could give. And so on.

'The Ballad of Billy Rose' is longer than the average lyric and it is therefore suggested as convenient to deal with it in 'sections' like this. Wherever you have to come back to a poem for comment or elucidation, however, it is as well to remember that the pupils *ought* to gain more from it the second time around. Indeed, there is much to be said for the idea of dealing with certain aspects of a poem and then coming back to it some weeks or months later: this dispenses with the idea that poems are something to be grappled with once only, and the discoveries of the intervening weeks may have added more than somewhat to the pupils' growing maturity, so that they are now better able, after a suitable interval, to see more of what you want them to see.

Aim

The 'teaching' of poetry is perhaps the most esoteric and slippery of all the disciplines the English teacher has to grasp. It is certainly not the easiest. It takes considerable time for a teacher to work out an acceptable *modus vivendi* in this respect, both for himself and for his pupils. 'Teaching' poetry is a positive activity, not a passive one; the teacher's approach must be flexible, depending on his audience, his material, and his own abilities and limitations. For above all, the poem is a 'personal' thing: the poet speaks with a personal voice, and the teacher's job is to interpret it. And he finds out how best to do it by constant practice, and constant reappraisal.

It can be an exacting process, but it need never be seen as a chore. There is a great amount of fun to be had from 'teaching' poetry. It is a sad error that manuals concentrate too often on the more 'serious' type of poem and ignore the others. The result is that far too many teachers do so too, and imagine there is only one way of getting a poem across. People often meet one's attempts at informal choral verse with a wintry smile. They don't want that. They want some *poetry*. In my definition of what poetry was 'for', I used the word 'delight'. This was done deliberately. For this was the heart of the matter, the true gold at the end of the mine.

Book list

Here are some individual anthologies which we have found useful:

Allott, K. (ed.). *The Penguin Book of Contemporary Verse* (Penguin, 1960).

Baldwin, M. (ed.). *Billy the Kid* (Hutchinson, 1963).

Benton, M. G. and P. *Touchstone* (English Universities Press, 1969).

Blackburn, T. and Cunningham, W. T. (eds.). *Reach Out* (Nelson, 1969).

Crang, A. *Tunes on a Tin Whistle* (Pergamon, 1967).

Druce, R. and Tucker, M. (eds.). *Look*, 'Structural English', vol. 1, pt 1 (English Universities Press, 1968).
Around and About, 'Structural English', vol. 1, pt 2 (English Universities Press, 1968).

Evans, M. and Lawson, K. C. (eds.). *Contemporary Verse* (Longman, 1972).

Gibson, J. G. and Wilson, R. *Reading Aloud* (Macmillan, 1961).

Grisenthwaite, N. (ed.). *Pegasus* (Schofield and Sims, 1962).

Heath, R. B. (ed.). *Breakthrough* (Hamilton, 1970).

Hughes, T. (ed.). *Here Today* (Hutchinson, 1971).

Mansfield, R. and Armstrong, I. (eds.). *Every Man Will Shout* (OUP, 1964).

McGrath, J. (ed.). *The Poetry Makers* (Heinemann, 1971).

Palgrave, F. T. (ed.). *Golden Treasury* (Macmillan, 1926 or OUP, 1965).

Parsons, I. M. (ed.). *Men Who March Away* (Heinemann, 1965).

Paterson, S. C. (ed.). *Narrative Verse* (Longman, 1967).

Rose, B. W. and Jones, R. S. *Lines of Action* (Macmillan, 1961).

Serraillier, I. *The Windmill Book of Ballads* (Heinemann, 1962).

Skelton, R. (ed.). *Viewpoint* (Hutchinson, 1962).

Summerfield, G. (ed.). *Voices* (Penguin, 1970).
Junior Voices (Penguin, 1970).

Wollman, M. and Hurst, D. M. (eds.). *The Harrap Junior Book of Modern Verse* (Harrap, 1961).
and Parker, K. B. *The Harrap Book of Modern Verse* (Harrap, 1958).

Series

Reeves, J. (ed.). 'Poetry Bookshelf' (Heinemann, 1967-).

Silcock, A. 'Verse and Worse' (Faber, 1952-).

'Penguin Poets'.

'Pergamon Poets'.

B.B.C. Pamphlets for Schools also offer good material: and there has recently been a similar venture by Thames Television Ltd, well worth looking at even if you don't take the programmes.

All teachers need refreshment (mentally and emotionally) from time to time, and for this purpose is recommended *Parodies*, ed. Dwight Macdonald (Faber, 1964): *The Stuffed Owl*, by D. B. Wyndham Lewis and Charles Lee (Aldine Paperback, 1963), an anthology of 'good' bad verse: and, of course, the daddy of them all, William McGonagall, whose *Poetic Gems* (1934) and *More Poetic Gems* (1966) are published jointly by David Winter of Dundee and Gerald Duckworth of London.

Records

Argo Record Company Ltd, 113 Fulham Road, London S.W.3.
B.B.C. Radio Enterprises, London W.5.
Caedmon Records: order from John Murray (Publishers) Ltd, Records Department, 65 Clerkenwell Road, London E.C.1.
Jupiter Recordings Ltd, 140 Kensington Church Street, London W.8.

All the above (with the exception of Argo) may be obtained from Discourses, Ltd, 34 High Street, Tunbridge Wells, Kent, who also supply many other makes, as well as Jackdaw Publications.

Spoken Arts Recordings were formerly distributed in this country by McGraw Hill (Publishers) Ltd, Maidenhead, Berkshire, to whom all correspondence should be addressed.

5 Classroom drama

Lauri Griffith-Jones

If I had been writing this paper as little as five years ago I should probably have had to justify and explain and persuade to a much greater extent than I need today. There are many teachers of English (and others!) who still feel unease about the creative dramatic activity with which this chapter is chiefly concerned; but their number is diminishing so I am not writing with any barn-storming, missionary intent. What I want to do is to outline why I believe drama to be important in the teaching of English, and to show briefly an approach to it which can serve as a guide for anyone willing to have a go. I lay no claim to great originality (indeed, many of my ideas are unashamedly derivative, and I can't remember now where I first discovered them) but I do maintain that this kind of work in our teaching is not impossibly outlandish or frivolously shallow. It needs courage and imagination (and if you don't have those qualities, you should not be teaching!), a willingness to let your hair down, and a firmly-held realisation that all aspects of the teaching of our subject will be enriched.

Work in English is concerned with creativity and expertness in using our language. Therefore, of course, we base our teaching on an abundance of reading, writing and speaking – and on poetry and drama. Children learn the language as they use it and enjoy it, and this leads to a love and understanding of our literature, the experience of coming into contact with other minds, ideas and emotions. But the fullest contact is impossible unless the children's own minds, ideas and emotions have been awakened and exercised. This is what all English teaching should hold clearly in view, and it is in such a context that dramatic activity must be set. It is an essential part of our teaching – and that is why, ultimately, I prefer the teacher of English to be involved in this work rather than the drama specialist meeting the children once a week. (Ideally, of course, there should be room for both, as the specialist trained in drama, movement and dance could be a great help working in conjunction with an English department, and my comment is not intended to depreciate the value of a specialist in this direction. I do think, however, that drama is an integral part of *our* work, and I therefore prefer English specialists who have, for instance, been on drama courses to handle this aspect of our teaching *as part of the general English approach.*)

Drama is doing, yet pretending – yet with a purpose. It is a quality in all of us from birth though it is often refined out, submerged or inhibited as we grow older ('shades of the prison house begin to close upon the growing boy'). As with many of the higher animals, the activity embodies an awareness of the difference between the pretence and the reality, and often becomes an indispensable rehearsal for later life. The very young child, the babe, is basically imitative; he learns by imitation, re-creating for himself the movement, gesture, sequence or action which has caught his attention and appealed to him. This is the basis we must build on with creative drama, for the young child is immensely imaginative also, and when identifying with the world around him becomes more vividly aware of his environment through an eager, full-blooded use of his senses.

But – sadly – all this tends to dry up, and so we must use drama to perpetuate and develop this ability: we must place the child with others in situations evoking speech, and encouraging the chances and needs to speak and act. We have to live with people – some of our greatest delight, indeed, comes from living with people – but to live *fully* with them we must be aware of them and be able to communicate with them..The kind of practice these drama sessions can give is invaluable here – especially if we can overcome the idea that they tend to force children to behave in a way they have out-grown. This is no more true than to claim we coerce children into perpetuating their love of poetry as seen in their love of nursery rhymes.

Before children can be aware of others, however, they must be aware of self. Dramatic activity, in its beginnings, helps enormously here, by bringing them some understanding of their own emotions and their own body movements. Group work can then help to remove the inhibitions of the less out-giving, and lead all to clearer expressiveness and communication. Sometimes one hears the objection that we are beginning to dabble dangerously in amateur psychology when we start 'to remove the inhibitions of the less out-giving': that we must beware of offending the shy children who might well hate drama lessons if they are made to join in. This, then, might well be the moment to make three important points, and to make them boldly. The first is that the shy child is a problem for all lessons – and all subjects, indeed – not just for drama; the second is that the very nature of our subject, the good teaching of which is grounded in a live, sympathetic relationship at the human level with our class, constantly brings us face to face with the need for psychological understanding and deduction (there is no sense in denying or belittling this aspect of our job: rather we should admit it, welcome it, and prepare ourselves better for it); the third point is that this type of work should only be undertaken, anyway, when one is quite confident of one's class-control, and knows the class well enough to allow relaxation without loss of respect. There must be such an ambience before any child can concentrate on awakening that awareness I mentioned at the beginning of this paragraph.

Acting, re-acting and inter-acting

Next, of course, follows awareness of others: it is essential that we build situations in which the children can re-act and inter-act, not merely act, and situations in which they *listen*, not merely impatiently 'wait to speak next' — a common adult failing! We live *in* society, *with* people. These people condition us in so many ways, or stimulate us, or echo back to us. Response to others is important and dramatic improvisations can often show this vividly and positively.

The awakening of these two kinds of awareness, however, and the release of those emotions subsequent upon it are only completely valuable if, eventually, they are disciplined. The intellect must work upon the imagination; the children must be asked to think about what they are doing. As they move away from the intimacy of group work, the end-product of their treatment of a situation could well be seen and heard by others in the class: there must follow, then, a progression towards control and clarity — and this inculcates discipline (theirs, incidentally, not ours). If the whole class witness or participate in an experience in this thinking way, they are likely to develop greater understanding and sympathy as human beings — and this in turn will lead to a greater understanding and appreciation as literate beings, both creatively and as readers or spectators. The importance of integrating dramatic activity into all our English work, under the guidance of the teacher of English, is never more obvious. Follow-up work can include related reading, critical or creative writing and oral work (if only at the fundamental level of informed discussion). Indeed, the drama lesson could be the springboard for a sustained thematic treatment of some topic or other. Such use of the drama lesson does not invalidate the drama lesson at all — and it does offer further proof, I feel, that the teacher of English should be the one to handle it.

Drama, then, in the educational field, should be concerned with experience, expression and communication. It focuses on the growth and development of the individual, through an understanding of himself in relationship with others. It is an imaginative re-creation of all aspects of the human situation, and, therefore, all forms of human experience and expression are dealt with: all problems — social, political, religious, personal (with their complexity determined by the age and intelligence of the particular group); release and relaxation; the serious and tragic or the absurd and comic. And the aim should always be, ultimately, to put the child into another person's shoes, or into a particular situation (which must, of course, be keyed in, however remotely, to his own experience and imaginative scope) so that he can better understand that person or control that situation. We must try to help the child to discover more than he knew when he started. It is a real challenge to lively children — and offers the chance for all children to extend themselves further and to participate usefully. Even unresponsive children (again, problems not confined to drama lessons) are, at the very least, offered opportunities to waken up. Incidentally, while 13+ may probably be too late to begin this kind of activity, 11+ certainly is not, so the fact that children have not been accustomed to such an approach at primary level need not mean they are unable to respond. It is worth emphasising here that in any framework involving the existence of middle schools it is most important that there should be liaison from one stage to another to ensure a continuity of dramatic activity.

I wish to make it quite clear, however, that I want to beware of making wild claims. Drama lessons alone are not the only way of developing children's awareness or moral judgements. Obviously, thirty minutes a week cannot do that: the competition alone with outside influences such as social environment, family background, the mass media is much too great. The communication and co-operation that take place in such lessons are helpful and enriching, but they are, we must always remember, limited: they can never really help in the over-toned complexity of a personal, intimate situation. In the emotionally-charged circumstances of the private family row or the esoteric badinage of lovers, the actual words spoken are a relatively small part of the meaning of what goes on.

But what I do believe is that in these lessons the children have a chance to examine vividly some areas of experience and to understand better themselves and others; abstractions can be made concrete; confidence and speech can be developed; and, at the simplest level, there is great fun for teacher and child — and a welcome change of routine and approach. Above all, we can find great enjoyment and

benefit in doing all this because we are capitalising on what is a
perfectly fundamental part of our make-up as human beings.

Now, all schools subjects are special, but — obviously! — I believe
English is the most special. English, as I understand it, has to do with
literature, life, thought, and the glory and agony of being a human
being. It is concerned, basically, with the stimulus and nurture of the
imagination, and the development of the powers of communication.
Its purpose, also, is to awaken the self and make us more aware of
others. Drama work aims at furthering all these activities, and must take
its place as equal in status and importance to all other aspects of our
English teaching.

Some suggested approaches

It would, perhaps, be helpful at this point to be more practical.
Remember that 'drama' should mean 'people-in-action', the posing of
problems, the provoking of reactions and interactions. It is a living
experience, shared with or sparked off by others; it means 'activity'.
There are many ways of handling this activity — with music, mime,
dramatic expression exercises, group work, conventional play-acting,
static play-readings and so on. The greater the variety the better. The
only proviso that I would make is that the methods should run in
parallel not in sequence.

Preparation for each drama lesson should spill over into an earlier
lesson if you can arrange it. This not only releases more of the drama
lesson for the activity proper, but also allows the children extra time to
think about what they are going to do. This preparation is a good
example of how drama can be a lead-in to other English lessons, for we
can see how oral practice can be intensified and given purpose in the
discussion of something positive. This is not the only link possible, for
the work can be related to literary creativity also: here is actual
experience to build on profitably — a base from which a child can
explore and clarify himself and his environment. Exciting opportunities
like this should not be missed.

An outlined progression and scheme of work for the lower forms

(1) Develop expression through movement and gestures in as simple
and direct a way as possible. (Work in groups from the beginning, or
even in pairs — the smaller numbers involved cause less restraint
amongst the participants, and give the teacher more chance to study

individuals in detail.) Ask the children to show emotions like fear and surprise, with the face and/or the body. Place them in some simple situation to evoke these reactions if they do not come easily. Let the children speak or not as they wish. Lead on to rudimentary characterisation, particularly through body movements. By doing it, the children can then perceive the difference between the ways an old person and a young person board a bus; or how a clumsy and a co-ordinated person might lay a table; or how a shy and a cocky person might enter a room where a party is being held. The possibilities are endless.

(2) Introduce mimed improvisations of situations which, though still small, are more extended than what you have been doing so far: stalking; a sequence that takes place in darkness; characters in conflict of some kind; struggling through a jungle. Now is the time to start acting *with* the group, not just *in* the group. Try cumulative mimes (e.g.: one person is faced with an incredible mountain of dirty dishes, and is gradually joined by others who help). Talk them through situations so that they can mime their reactions to the events you describe happening — and don't be hesitant about making mime 'atmospheric' (e.g. the darkness sequence mentioned above could involve pursuit by something unknown and unseen, with suitable spine-chilling suggestions from you). Some teachers have questioned the value of mime, protesting that English is an articulate subject. But it is a most useful beginning to the rousing of awareness of what we do (for you should insist on progressively more exact and defined actions as the children become more experienced — whether it is a matter of pouring out a cup of tea for someone, or piloting a jumbo jet), and such discipline highlights the importance of precision, and leads eventually to their being able to speak and act more assuredly and more expressively. In other words, more articulately.

(3) The next stage could well be a mimed story, with a more clearly defined story-line and an assortment of clearly differentiated characters. In other words, shape and the necessity to convey something particular are being introduced. This kind of work should be very well organised beforehand by the teacher, and discussed in some detail with and by the class. An obvious source of such material is their current reading.

(4) So far I have been concerned almost entirely with mime. I would not prohibit speaking in these exercises if it comes naturally — unless, of course, I want to train the children specifically in the discipline of mime. When work with speech needs to be done, however, the following method might be found useful.

(i) Present the *whole* class with a familiar, but provocative situation. This should be outlined briefly — too much elaboration by the teacher or by the class in discussion could easily detract from the personal, spontaneous treatment which is so valuable and delightful. Some suggestions:

(a) The family row.

(b) Reports. Two very contrasting reports are presented to two friends by their form-masters. Then the two friends discuss their interviews with each other in the bus on the way home. The sequence is rounded off by the later confrontation with their parents.

(c) Speakers' Corner, Hyde Park.

(d) The fence white-washing episode from *Tom Sawyer*. Aim especially at bringing out the characterisation.

(e) A group of carol-singers meet, discuss their choice of programme and plan their itinerary. They then visit various families and so on. Again, bring out the attitudes of the differing groups of people, and the carol-singers' reactions to their reception.

(f) A family (or group of friends) visit a fairground.

(ii) Having given them just enough material to build on, split them up into groups, varying in size, of course, according to the project. Always vary the actual composition of these groups, too, so that the children do not become cliquish and are forced to respond to ever-changing personalities and ideas. The groups can then practise, simultaneously, the task. Not only does simultaneous group work help to remove children's inhibitions (if that's necessary!), it also gives the teacher a chance to observe where help is needed and talent exists. Needless to say, this might well be chaotic; it will certainly be noisy. This whole chapter pre-supposes certain physical conditions of space for drama, at sufficient distance from one's colleagues to prevent internal staff dissension! Fight for lesson time in the assembly hall — or the dining-hall, or the gym, or the pavilion, or the C.C.F. hut. Anywhere . . . (And fight, too, for a purpose-built English centre while you're at it. It is ludicrous and short-sighted that English, the subject of central importance in the curriculum and the only one that everybody takes all the time, should still be treated as if it could be taught anywhere without any of the facilities and equipment and specialist rooms that most other subjects now demand as their essential right.)

(iii) Each group should, after some rehearsal, present its effort before the rest of the class. A mass-discussion could follow — and the seeds of critical appreciation are being sown.

(5) A useful variant, at this juncture, would be to read a play, in class. The children's approach to the technique of reading aloud, with expression and understanding, should now be greatly improved (and remember that plays read badly are not just a waste of time but positively harmful). The play selected should be discussed as deeply as the class will tolerate, depending on their age and ability. Choose the cast several days before the reading is due — and encourage them to study their parts as much as possible. Don't be deterred by those colleagues who sneer at play-reading as being out of fashion. In the first place, it is very popular with the children themselves: it is constantly asked for when they are given freedom of choice. Popularity is not the ultimate criterion — but it should never be ignored. Secondly, however — and more importantly — it has positive, discernible assets: it helps in the study and comprehension of a text; it is an attractive way of training the voice; it develops expressiveness in communication; it aids the capacity to listen; it is a painless initiation at an elementary level into the intricacies of literary appreciation.

(6) The culmination of the year could be a simple one-act drama festival. Divide the class into groups and allot one play per group. Sit back. Leave the groups to elect their own producer and to be entirely self-governing and self-sufficient — with no help at all from the teacher. Having organised this festival, however, you must responsibly and seriously adjudicate it. If the timetable permits, a further possibility is for each form to choose its best effort, to be presented in a larger festival in which all others of the same year would be audience.

I have dealt but cursorily with this scheme of a year's work. It is not the purpose of this chapter — even if the space were available — to go into minute details and plans for each lesson (if you are hesitant about experimenting with your own notions, or find it difficult even to think of any at the beginning, there are many excellent books to help). What the scheme I have sketched in does show, I think, is how one can achieve ultimately a balance between creative drama (the subjective approach) and the theatre skills (the objective approach). Both abilities are valuable and exciting; the latter can grow out of the former; and both can stimulate growth in many other areas of our English teaching.

I have said that this could represent a year's work. The attraction of such a pattern is that it could be repeated in principle in the next year. Naturally, everything will be conducted at a deeper level. More will be demanded of the children. I find it useful at this stage to introduce some of the basic loosening-up exercises of the professional actor: they

help children with their concentration and expression – and are highly
enjoyable. Try the following:

> Take some ordinary object and ask each member of the class to
> act a mime with it in which it is anything but itself. A chair, for
> instance, could be a pram, a horse, a dancing-partner; the more
> imaginative might make it a euphonium, a beer-pump, an
> angle-poise lamp.

> Invite the children to speak a nursery-rhyme in as many varied
> ways as possible, in which the words are meaningless but the
> expression paramount. They could be a tub-thumping shop-
> steward, or a wheedling beggar, or an ardent lover, or a high-
> pressure salesman.

> Put the class in two lines facing each other in pairs. Give them a
> few seconds to think, silently, of a topic. At a given signal they
> must burst forth at their partner to try to talk him down. Stop
> them – and then ask them to relate as much as they can of what
> their partner has been saying. You can then go a step further and
> ask, next time, what the person on their right, and left, was
> saying too. It's exhausting and chaotic – but an unfailing
> destroyer of inhibitions!

Continuation into the middle school

In the middle school (i.e. the 13-14 years age-group) extend all these
ideas and practices as far as they will be accepted. As the children grow
up continuously with these methods, from the beginning, acceptance
will progress considerably. And if the teacher himself is willing to
participate, much possible resistance will be overcome. So do the mime
yourself – however inexpertly; take off your jacket and sit on the floor
with them; be Grendel's mother descending on Heorot.

Many of us, too, have found crowd-work rewarding. But *do not even
consider* this kind of free drama unless there are excellent relationships
between you and the children, so that you can allow them seemingly to
run wild though you can keep the ultimate firm rein if necessary. It
must be stressed that you must have this confidence first. Generally
speaking, the larger the crowd the better: one colleague has mentioned
even taking the whole year if the forms happen to take English
simultaneously! Obvious Shakespearian scenes suggest themselves from,
for example, *Julius Caesar, The Merchant of Venice, Henry V* – and if

you can probe into the reactions and attitudes of the children playing the crowd towards the characters of Brutus, Antony, Shylock and King Henry, guiding them to see what Shakespeare was trying to do, the lesson is reaching out into a new area of understanding and importance.

A second caveat however, must be issued: avoid encouraging excessive physical contact, violent scrambles and fighting, for these tend to be very uncontrollable and destructive activities. Forgive me if the advice is unnecessary — but it has to be said!

It does not matter if many of the situations and exercises from earlier years are repeated; they will now have deeper and wider implications. Obviously, however, more formalised drama can now be confidently introduced — enriched and more craftsmanlike because of the work in the earlier years. You might even find that there will be more play-reading than previously; this could well be encouraged in the middle school where the intellectual content of plays becomes more apparent. The exact balance will depend on your own school situation and the children's general attitude — but there is no reason to let go of the free, creative dramatic activity with which we began. My personal experience is that, while one might perhaps expect a diminution of interest and response in the fifth year because of examination pressures and adolescent development, there will be a gratifying resurgence in the sixth form, and I capitalise on it.

Dress

I suggest that boys remove their jackets, and change into gym shoes, and that the girls wear shorts, jeans or slacks, and gym shoes. This simple change will allow much more freedom of movement, create a different atmosphere for the lesson, and — in the girls' case — help to remove the embarrassment and awkwardness that skirts often bring. Also, of course, there is dressing-up. A large box or basket of simple props and costume bits is a great asset. Not only do these extras help with appearance and bring a sense of occasion to the lesson, they also appeal to the children's imagination and help the more self-conscious in their acting. The business must not be overdone (or the lesson might never start) but a basic collection of items such as the following could be enhancing and effective: cloaks; hats; scarves; long skirts; any odd lengths of material; swords; poles; brooches; crowns. Anything, really, could be of use sometime. If the art department, or some gifted colleague could make some masks for you, an enthralling new dimension is opened up. They can be very simple, but they should be clear physical and psychological types (an old man; a rustic; a haughty woman; a negro; an 'ugly duckling'; a drunkard — and so on). The children should put on a mask, study themselves in front of a mirror, and then act out a rôle suggested by their appearance — either solo or in conjunction with other masqueraders.

The use of music

A very effective way of helping children to be more free in their mimetic improvisations is the playing of music. This approach should run in parallel with the work I have outlined above, and can be used with all kinds of groups and all age-levels. It can be done also with individuals, pairs, or as a class-participation exercise. There are many actual ways of using music; you might like to consider three simple methods to begin with:

> The teacher selects beforehand a piece of music for the lesson; the class are not introduced to it. Bearing the music in mind, the teacher now practises a mood, or movement, or story, or situation with the class. The music is then played as a suitable background to the class's efforts. The advantage of this method is that the class can see how music can positively help their work; the disadvantage is that the class might be over-directed by the teacher and thus lose much of their spontaneity.

> Reverse the process. Play the music first, and then conduct a class discussion about it, aiming primarily at drawing out *their* interpretations of and reactions to it. The music is then played again (as often as you like) for the class to improvise and elaborate their original ideas.

> Play some music as before. The class listen. Then, without any prompting from the teacher at all, the class improvise against a second playing of the music. Follow this by a discussion of what they have tried to do. Polish it up.

The types of music used will depend to a large extent on funds, your own tastes, the character of your classes, and other imponderables. But cast your net wide. Go to the 'pops' as well as atmospheric or programme music of the more 'classical' genre; if you play an instrument yourself — lucky you; electronic music can be most evocative; invest in a tambour — it is simple to use and surprisingly effective. And don't forget the B.B.C. Their music-and-movement programmes are most imaginatively compiled, and can be taped for repeated use. They are aimed chiefly at younger children but, at the very least, they can give you very useful ideas to build on for yourself. You may even find that you are lucky enough to have a P.E. department willing and able to help, for there is a great emphasis on dance-drama, on music-and-movement and on educational gymnastics in the thinking of modern physical education. Contact with them could be mutually beneficial and instructive.

Play-reading and other approaches

Because I have not dwelt on this activity much, I do not want to leave the impression that I ignore or underrate it. Far from it: I have, indeed, alluded to how valuable and enjoyable it is for the children. A few remarks here, then, on this kind of lesson, and on other ways of bringing dramatic experience to our children, which can take place in the conventional classroom situation, might be helpful.

Reading a play in class can present many pitfalls for the unwary teacher. In the first place, it seems such an easy lesson — but, in actual fact, it probably needs more preparation than most. I have already mentioned the importance of casting the play beforehand so that the children have a chance to practise their parts for the greater enjoyment of themselves as speakers and the rest of the class as listeners. The play should be introduced in an earlier lesson, too, so that everyone has some acquaintance with it; every effort must be made to compensate for the lack of help normally contributed by the *visual* impact of the play. One most telling type of preparation can be in the improvised drama lesson. Work on a situation such as a political meeting, or 'Speakers' Corner' could greatly help towards a more vivid rendering of act II scene 2 of Galsworthy's *Strife*; taking children through various kinds of quarrel scenes could bring deeper understanding and more certain presentation of the row between Brutus and Cassius in *Julius Caesar*. And so on.

Ideally the plays chosen should have big casts (and mixed, too, in a co-educational school, of course) unless you are going to conduct the exercise in groups. All this helps the whole class in general and the poor or reluctant speakers in particular: preparation allays apprehension; large casts mean that their contribution, though small, can be significant; group work, as always, encourages them to shed shyness in an atmosphere of closer friendliness.

It is sometimes helpful to use radio drama for classroom

performances. A simple screen, a movable blackboard, curtains draped to conceal the performers, will serve to increase the confidence of pupils too embarrassed to face an audience. Documentaries can be prepared by the class; suitable material found in such texts as *Scott's Last Expedition* can involve simple characterisation as well as straightforward narration. It is not even always necessary to use a microphone. Pretend there is one, and preach the virtues of clear articulation.

Encourage a thoroughly prepared, acted reading. The lesson should be an event. Remember, too, that it is a reading: the children sit in desks (or, perhaps in a circle of chairs for group work) reading their scripts. I abhor the uneasy hybrid of the so-called acted reading in front of the class, book in hand; it is ineffective and unattractive.

A development of this activity which is often found worth-while is the taping of plays, by groups, for presentation to the rest of the class. These recordings require background noises, sound effects and music which could involve the whole class in some cases. Certainly all tastes can be catered for, and it is amazing how many budding electronic geniuses, complete with tape recorders and awesome ancillary equipment, you will discover amongst your pupils! There are many play collections specially designed for this, but when the class become more ambitious they could produce their own scripts: these could be dramatic adaptations from their readers — or even original. Sometimes, especially with junior forms, this kind of work (recorded or otherwise) can be done in conjunction with puppets. If you do use a tape recorder you might experience some technical difficulties for it is a rare classroom which is acoustically amenable. You can get help from various sources (see 'Hardware', Chapter 9) if you are as inept as the average teacher of English at matters scientific — or you can even ask the children themselves! One piece of advice, however: if you do buy a tape recorder, buy as good a one as you possibly can (anything cheap will eventually drive you to despair) and, particularly, buy as expensive a microphone as you can afford, to go with it.

Once again, the B.B.C. can be immensely stimulating here, for their drama programmes on radio or television are first-class, whether specially for schools or not. You should make a point of acquiring full details, which they publish annually, of all their school programmes and other literature of help to teachers: they show an impressive achievement and service on their part. (You can even be supplied with hints on how to use your tape recorder.) Similarly, excellent recordings of plays come from such companies as Argo, Caedmon and Spoken

Arts (again, see 'Hardware', Chapter 9). There is a preponderance at the moment, naturally, of Shakespeare, but more and more plays by other dramatists are now being performed.

We have moved away somewhat from the type of creative drama I outlined at the start of this chapter, but this is only further proof that drama is not a water-tight compartment of a subject: rather, it is a springboard, or a link. It is necessary, too, to consider the occasions when space is not available and colleagues are contiguous! There are many simple mime exercises which could be performed in a classroom at desks. Practice in conversation involving pairs in situations which are real or imaginary, formal or informal, consultative or inquisitive — although overlapping with oral work — forms a valid part of dramatic activities. Choral verse-speaking, with all the necessary expression that implies, allied to a simple, synchronized dramatisation of the story, can be conducted without being disruptive to your own or a neighbouring class.

The school play

Although the original brief for this chapter did not cover the publicly-performed school play, it often happens that the English teacher is the one chiefly concerned with it, so a few remarks might be apposite.

The climate must be right. Theatre and acting must be a large part of the life of the school. Not only must there be a regular programme of drama lessons, but also opportunities for the children to see plays well performed. Not only should there be play-reading lessons, but also a flourishing play-reading society as an extra-curricular activity for the enthusiasts. Organise theatre-trips and cinema visits; bring touring companies to the school; start a school film society; establish links with local repertory companies, most of whom have founded proper contacts with schools — or if not, would welcome your direct involvement. Having generated all this interest, use it. Try making films of your own. Run as many dramatic societies as you can find interested colleagues to do so — or specially qualified parents, or friends of the school. In my school, we have four: a first-form society which meets weekly, to learn the trade; and junior, middle school and senior societies which each present a full-length play to the public every year. We are lucky to have enough zealous members of staff to run them but it is only by setting ambitious objectives that anything is achieved.

Some schools believe in the school play being a highly polished job, as professional as it can be, with a cast of consistently high standard

and therefore — almost certainly — small. Others believe in engaging as
many of the school as possible: they might, for example, publicly
perform a pantomime linking together drama, music, movement, art,
craft, science — and involving half the children and staff! This is
splendidly wholehearted and unashamed. If one wants the best of both
worlds, the senior society (in conjunction, maybe, with staff, if
necessary?) could provide the more sophisticated play with the smaller,
highly-talented cast; the middle and junior levels could be embroiled in
plays like *The Caucasian Chalk Circle* with their casts of hundreds.

The type of play you choose will decide your method of production.
I find that seniors prefer to be treated like the adults they are, and
respond to the challenge and stimulus of intensive rehearsals over a
short period of time. With a full day's rehearsal at weekends, most plays
can be prepared for performance in about a month. With younger
children and larger casts, one might well take longer and treat the whole
venture as a term's work. Beware, though, of inducing staleness or
indifference. All this depends, of course, on gathering round you a team
of ardent backstage and front-of-house helpers. You cannot — indeed,
should not — do everything yourself; you must aim at delegation of
responsibility to the children, under the aegis of a member of staff, in
as many areas of production as possible — stage crew, electricians,
dressers, wardrobe, make-up, set construction and painting, properties,
box office, front-of-house arrangements, publicity . . . and so on.

But whatever play you choose, make it challenging, make it extend
you and your company. If drama is part of the life-blood of English in
your school, there are few heights you cannot attempt to scale. In any
case, do not underestimate the quality, ability and sensitivity of your
pupils. That they can always amaze us with their potential is one of the
delights and rewards of our job. We must never be satisfied just with
what is possible or convenient.

My quotation, in conclusion, from 'Andrea del Sarto', might well
serve to characterise the whole attitude I have tried to urge in this
paper:

> Ah, but a man's reach should exceed his grasp,
> Or what's a heaven for?

Book list

Book lists can be very indeterminate and unsatisfactory, but I hope the
following titles might be of some assistance, if only for those who
merely want something to start with, somewhere!

Plays for classroom reading and acting

Mixed classes, 11-13 age-group
Adland, D. E. *Group Approach to Drama* (5 books) (Longman, 1970).
Ball, I. and Macwilliam, M. *May We Recommend* (13 graded books) (Longman, 1959).
Cain, T. *Ten Ten-Minute Plays* (U.L.P., 1938).
    Ten More Ten-Minute Plays (U.L.P., 1949).
Denley, F. M. *The Man who Painted his Wife's Nose*, etc. (U.L.P., 1957).
Milne, A. A. *Toad of Toad Hall* (Methuen, 1970).
Mitchell, F. and Garrow, E. W. *Ten Graded Plays* (U.L.P., 1939).
Mitchell, F. *The Fool of the Family*, etc. (U.L.P., 1960).
Molière, J. B. P. de, ed. Hannan, B. *The Reluctant Doctor* (Heinemann, 1963).
Stuart-Jarvis, C. E. *Read, Act, Talk and Write* (6 books) (Blond, 1963).
Taylor, H. S. *A Shorter Shakespeare* (12 plays) (Ginn).
    Noah (Use of English Pamphlet).

Mixed classes, 13-14 age-group
Arden, J. *The Business of Good Government* (Methuen, 1963).
Cobby, M. *Calling All Playmakers* (4 graded books) (Pitman).
Goldoni, C. *The Servant of Two Masters* (Heinemann, 1961).
Grant, D., Holt, B. and Mitson, R. *From Classroom to Stage*: Three New Plays (Longman, 1966).
Wood, E. R. *Seven Short Plays* (Heinemann, 1956).
Wood, E. R. (ed.). *The Windmill Book of One-Act Plays* (a series) (Heinemann).
    Eight One-Act Plays (Nelson, 1961).

Mixed classes, 14-15 age-group
Barrie, Sir J. M. *The Admirable Crichton* (U.L.P., 1967).
Bradley, A. (ed.). *Worth a Hearing* (Blackie, 1967).
Campton, D. *Laughter and Fear* (9 one-act plays) (Blackie, 1969).
Galsworthy, J. *Strife* (Duckworth, 1964).
Marland, M. (ed.). *Conflicting Generations: Five Television Plays* (Longman, 1968).
    Student Drama Series (Blackie).
Rattigan, T. *The Winslow Boy* (Pan, 1967).
Roberts, G. K. *Drama in Court* (Arnold, 1967).
Shaffer, P. *The Royal Hunt of the Sun* (Pan, 1969).
Wilder, T. *The Matchmaker* (Penguin, 1970).

Mixed classes, 15-16 age-group
Ardrey, R. *Thunder Rock* (Heinemann, 1966).
Barton, J. *The Hollow Crown* (Harrap, 1962).
Bolt, R. *A Man for All Seasons* (Heinemann, 1967).
Brighouse, H. *Hobson's Choice* (Heinemann, 1964).
Durban, A. (ed.). *New Directions* (five One-act Plays) (Hutchinson, 1961).
Obey, A. *Noah* (Heinemann, 1967).

O'Casey, S. *Juno and the Paycock* (Macmillan, 1948).
Patrick, J. *The Teahouse of the August Moon* (Heinemann, 1955).
Thomas, D. *Under Milk Wood* (Dent, 1962).
Wesker, A. 'Trilogy' (Penguin, 1969).
Wilde, O. *The Importance of Being Earnest* (Heinemann, 1949).
Wilder, T. *Our Town* (Penguin, 1970).

(The age-group divisions are obviously not rigid; there is no attempt to select from Shaw or Shakespeare — apart from the Ginn abridged versions for Juniors; there should be enough variety in such a selection to please most.)

Books for oral/dramatic work

Casciani, J. W. *Speak for Yourselves* (Harrap, 1966).
Hudson, J. and Slade, P. *A Chance for Everyone* (graded series) (Cassell, 1966).
Percival, A. and Bryan, B. *Talking About* (Methuen, 1967).

Books for staff

Adland, D. E. *The Group Approach to Drama* (Teachers' book) (Longman).
Bamford, T. W. *Practical Make up for the Stage* (Pitman, 1966).
Chilver, P. *Staging a School Play* (Batsford, 1967).
Clarke, R. F. *The Growth and Nature of Drama* (C.U.P., 1965).
Cobby, M. *Calling all Playmakers* (Teachers' book) (Pitman, O/P).
Courtney, R. *On Teaching Drama: Handbook for Teachers in Schools* (Cassell, 1965).
    The School Play (Cassell, 1966).
Hamilton, P. *Amateur Stage Handbook* (Pitman, 1957).
Hudson, J. and Slade, P. *A Chance for Everyone* (Teachers' book) (Cassell, 1968).
Slade, P. *Child Drama* (U.L.P., 1954).

Also of interest: *Amateur Stage* (quarterly magazine); *Drama* (a monthly magazine from the British Drama League); 'Drama in Education (*English in Education*, vol. I, no. 3, Autumn 1967), published for N.A.T.E. by Bodley Head and containing a very full and useful book list; *Higher Education Journal* (Summer 1970), N.U.T. publication with a special feature on 'The Teaching of Drama'.

Addresses

There are three organisations which could be helpful in a variety of ways.
    (1) The British Drama League, 9-10 Fitzroy Square, London W1P 6AE. Not only does the B.D.L. publish *Drama*, and run a most extensive advisory service, it also has a huge lending library of plays, in complete reading or acting sets, which can be hired very reasonably.

(2) The British Film Institute, 81 Dean Street, London W.1. Similarly, the B.F.I. supplies all members with regular free publications which are invaluable for anyone interested in cinema, and is always most helpful with its advice. It has a special educational section, and even has booklets on such matters as running a film-society.

(3) The National Youth Theatre, 81 Eccleston Square, London S.W.1. If drama becomes (or is) a driving interest in your school, the N.Y.T. gives splendid opportunities to those eager and talented children who would like to taste the excitements of working to near-professional standards and conditions. Backstage personnel are equally in demand as actors and actresses – and the N.Y.T. always emphasises that it does not set out to be a nursery or forcing-house for the professional theatre.

Music

(Some suggestions for music to be used with drama – or even for creative writing, too.)

Many teachers use 'pop' EP's for this purpose – and this is an excellent practice, for the immediacy of the appeal is obvious. There is no point in appending a list of this kind here because of their ephemeral attraction and their short life in the catalogues. However, a cheap source of these is, of course, the children themselves, and also the juke-box companies who change their selections regularly and are often happy to sell off their discards cheaply.

The list given here is a collection of atmospheric, evocative music, more of the classical genre. All of it exists on cheap labels (apart from the obvious record firms, there are other companies named in 'Hardware', Chapter 9), and all of it has been recommended after use by teachers themselves. Obviously, such a list is very arbitrary and personal – but no other apology is needed for it! Remember that actual recorded quality does not really matter, and that you can always assemble your own collection of taped items (which are often more easy and flexible to use).

Bartok, Concerto for Orchestra (especially 'Elegy').
Beethoven, Symphony No. 7 (especially 'Scherzo' and 'Finale').
Berlioz, *Symphonie Fantastique.*
Bizet, *L'Arlesienne*, suites 1 and 2.
    Carmen.
    The Fair Maid of Perth.
    Les Jeux d'Enfants.
Borodin, Polovtsian Dances (from *Prince Igor*).
Brahms, Hungarian Dances.
Chabrier, Suite Pastorale.
Debussy, *Iberia* and *La Mer.*
Delius, *Brigg Fair* and *On hearing the first cuckoo in Spring.*
Dukas, *The Sorcerer's Apprentice.*
Elgar, *Enigma Variations.*
    Introduction and Allegro for Strings.
    Serenade for Strings.

Gershwin, *American in Paris.*
   Piano Concerto.
   Rhapsody in Blue.
Glinka, *Russlan and Ludmilla* — overture.
Grieg, *Peer Gynt.*
Holst, *The Planets.*
Ibert, 'Divertissement'.
Kabalevsky, *Colas Breugnon* — overture.
Mendelssohn, *Hebrides* Overture.
   Midsummer Night's Dream.
Moussorgsky, *Night on the Bare Mountain.*
   Pictures at an Exhibition.
Prokoviev, *Peter and the Wolf.*
Ravel, La Valse.
Rimski-Korsakov, *Scheherazade.*
Rossini, *La Boutique Fantasque.*
Saint-Saens, *Carnival of the Animals.*
   Danse Macabre.
Scarlatti, *Good-humoured Ladies.*
Shostakovitch, Symphony No. 10 (especially 'Scherzo').
Sibelius, *Finlandia.*
Smetana, Ma Vlast.
Stravinsky, *Rite of Spring.*
Tchaikovsky, *Hamlet* — overture.
   Casse-Noisette.
   Marche Slave.
   Romeo and Juliet — overture.
   Symphony No. 6.
Vaughan Williams, *Thomas Tallis fantasia.*
Vivaldi, *The Four Seasons.*
Wagner, 'The Ride of the Valkyries'.
   Tannhauser Overture.
Walton, *Façade.*

Extensive reading

Lauri Griffith-Jones

This is to be a severely practical chapter, concerning itself with certain basic principles of approach in the first part which is to be no more, virtually, than an introduction to the reading lists in the second part.

There should be no need to stress the importance of reading. If only from the quantitative standpoint, successful stimulation and guidance of the reading habit can have more effect on our pupils than any other aspect of our teaching of English: many of these pupils of ours may not again dip into poetry, or go to the theatre, or write, or even converse, very much — but all except the irremediably illiterate should be able to cope with and enjoy reading to some degree. What we must do then, quite simply, is to prepare the ground from which this interest will grow, strongly and fruitfully.

At school, therefore, your object must be to bring your pupils into contact with as many books and writers as possible, and to make that contact as varied, challenging and entertaining as possible. And I mean *many* books. This is where the bulk of your allowance should be spent. Every form should be enticed to read if it is reluctant, or fed if it is voracious — as often as possible and in as many ways as possible. Reading-matter should be as wide in scope and type as you can manage — fiction and non-fiction; serious and humorous; difficult and easy; established children's classic and bizarre modern novelty. Even at the risk of having made that itemisation sound like Polonius describing the Players' repertory, I am urging you to abjure conservatism in the choice offered to your pupils. Take a chance whenever you can; stick your neck out — in fact, do *not* be like Polonius, when he counselled cold caution to son and daughter both.

When we receive our first-year intake into the secondary school, it is almost certain that the children will have been taught to read by various methods, and that they will be at varying stages in the extent and skill of their reading. It is imperative that we find out, without delay, the speed and depth at which they read, *and* their ability to read aloud, if only to discover those who will need special care. This will necessitate, initially, some preliminary testing of their comprehension, a careful check on their individual reading rates, and simple, unashamed reading-round-the-class to discover their oral expertise and understanding. Particularly with the less able, some of F. J. Schonell's books on the diagnosis and testing of English skills (published by Macmillan and Oliver and Boyd) may prove useful. These things done, they can be launched into an organised reading programme which should be as rich and attractive as you can afford.

Once again, I must emphasise bulk. Books should be circulated and changed as freely and as frequently as is practicable. Familiarity breeds contempt, and there is nothing calculated more to turn children off books than to have to endure the dispiriting dullness of having only one a term (or a half-term) which they have to eke out like rationed water in a desert. This is no way to persuade them of the wonder and excitement of reading, which must be extensive as well as intensive.

Ideally, then, each form should have a hard core of full sets of two or three books a term which are mandatory reading, backed by a collection of about thirty or forty extra single titles, to which they progress when the compulsory minimum has been read. No children move on to their next book until they have written a review of the book just finished. The two groups of books — basic and supplementary — are changed every term.

A little amplification will show the many advantages of such a system.

The hard core of readers serves a three-fold purpose. Firstly, it helps us to ensure that certain books which we think really worth-while are read (and we should not — in the name of supposedly enlightened liberalism — weakly evade the responsibility of deciding what *is* worth-while). Secondly, such a pattern ensures that, at any stage in our pupils' career, we know they will have read certain specific books, and this can be a most useful reference and basis for any discussion — profound or preparatory — on literature. Thirdly, it supplies us with the opportunity to lead our pupils into the habits and joys of intensive reading.

This last advantage is, perhaps, the most important and opens up many avenues, some of which you may like to explore. Class-readers of this kind can be used for comprehension work — both oral and written. A progressively deepening awareness of literary judgements can be fostered by discussion (with individuals, by groups, or in the full class) of characters, plot and even style. Naturally, the depth to which criticism of this kind is taken will be geared to the capacity of the pupils, but it is a feasible and useful practice. Summary of, or reports on, certain sections of the book can develop the technique of factual writing. Imaginative writing can be stirred into being: write one more

chapter to follow the last — or one to precede the first; assume the
identity of one of the main characters in a completely different
situation; describe the events from the point-of-view of one of the minor
characters (à la *Rosencrantz and Guildenstern are Dead*). Episodes can
be used for creative drama work; groups can present dramatised
readings. Individuals can give prepared talks — and the teacher, himself,
should participate here, too, demonstrating not only his involvement
but also presenting the pupils a model for their own efforts. In such
ways a sense of criticism can be unobtrusively and painlessly born — for
what else is this elusive critical faculty than the ability to get alongside
an author and his work in ways such as these?

The benefit of an approach like this will be seen in their reviews.
These are a useful check for us on the pace of their reading, the depth
of their understanding, and the quality of their writing — but they must
not be a burden. Limit them to a very short account of the book — its
story and most interesting characters — and some elementary remarks
to clarify, for them and us, their opinions. As they become older and
more experienced, the amount spent on opinion should increase. At the
beginning our demands on them should be restricted to simple
comments on whether the author wrote in an easy or difficult way; on
classifying what kind of book it was (war-story, fantasy, adventure,
thriller and so on; comic or serious; science-fiction or history); on the
credibility of it; on how it compares with other similar books read; on
why certain characters did or did not attract them . . . I find it useful,
in addition, to ask for a simple but honest grading at the end of each
review: 'A' means every superlative conceivable; 'B' means reasonably
enjoyable — most books will be in this category; and 'C' means it's been
an utter waste of time! I also give them a separate exercise-book for
reviews (different in appearance from the normal English issue — and
stronger, for it has to be kept for some years) because it helps to give a
sense of importance to the activity. In such simple ways, their
impressions of a book are being given shape and definition — for them
and us; they are developing standards of criticism and comparative
judgement; they are being given a chance to be proud of their
achievement; and they are writing with a purpose, not *in vacuo*.

These reviews, of course, will vary enormously according to the
ability of the pupil — from the jejune to the gigantic — but I believe
they are worth doing even if they are skeletal, inaccurate and
imperceptive to a degree. At the very least, they will be reading-records,
will have helped imprint the book on the pupils' memories, and will
have obliged them to think about the book — if only a little — after

having read it. They should be kept for all that they read from the supplementary books, too, and it is with these books that we should lead our pupils into the joys of extensive, as opposed to intensive, reading.

Many English departments meet difficulty in finding money for these extra readers. This should not be a deterrent. It may be easier than you think to build up a personal library for each form on a voluntary basis. Almost all children can be persuaded — indeed, will be delighted — to donate paperbacks they have themselves enjoyed to a central pool from which all the form draw. Naturally, these contributions must be vetted by us first — but, afterwards, nothing but benefit can accrue: the children have their own collection of some thirty or forty books for the cost of one; we are closely in touch with their reading interests and trends; and we can have no better opportunity of follow-up work than asking the pupils to introduce and justify their contribution.

In such ways we can provide the material for reading, and, if this material is varied, imaginative and plentiful, the major part of our campaign of enticement has been carried out. But there are other ways, too, of encouraging, guiding and establishing the reading habit. The most important is the weekly silent-reading period. I believe this should be compulsory and sacrosanct, for, with the majority of our pupils, this will be, quite literally, the only time in the week when they can sit down in quiet with a book. Most homes are not able to supply the necessary conditions of uninterrupted peace, and many parents are quite unconvinced that books are work, anyway: there's usually 'more important' housework or gardening or shopping to do; the television's on in the only available room; there's no tradition of reading, as we understand it, at all. These may seem harsh criticisms, but as statements of fact I believe they are justified. Undoubtedly there are many parents who support us splendidly and sympathetically and intelligently — but there are many, many more who have to be educated (at parents' meetings and such occasions) to accept and, indeed, encourage their children's need to develop the reading habit. Meanwhile — and in addition — we can offer those children a half-hour island of peace in each stormy week when they know that their sitting down with a book will be noticed and approved. So ignore the jibes of those colleagues who call out, 'Off to another silent-reading period, then?' each time you leave the common-room. At the least, you are giving those children moments which many of them may never have a chance to savour again after they leave school; at the most, you are sowing the seeds for the richest of harvests. In actual fact, of course, this kind of period should never be one in which you just catch up on your marking. Rather, it can be an opportunity to talk to children individually — about a particular problem they may have; about the book they are reading or reviewing; about some poetry they have written. And so on . . . If this becomes too distracting for the rest of the class, you can use the time to check their reviews and reading-logs, or even to sit down, yourself, with a book. Let the kids know that the old man still reads, too.

I have mentioned reading at home, and I should like to state here that I believe that only very rarely should homework for junior forms be written. Reading is what we should be encouraging them to do at home; writing, we should have a more direct link with and control over in class-time. Even in the third and fourth years much of the homework should be reading, and written homework, when set, should always be significant and motivated — not because it happens to be on the timetable for that night. If the school's tentacles must reach into the private lives and leisure of our pupils, let us make sure that what we ask is enjoyable or purposeful — or both. A simple, explicit rule could be that English homework for all forms will *always* be reading unless they are informed to the contrary. A check must be kept, however, and the simplest way of doing this is to insist that pupils keep a reading-log in which they enter, each homework-night, the title of the book they are reading and the exact pages they have read (e.g. *Jim Davis*, pp. 24-35). The foolish ones might try to cheat at the beginning but they will find it too complicated to keep up, and you then have, also, an extra useful guide to their reading habits.

Apart from providing suitable conditions in class, and using homework time for reading, there are other means you might like to consider to keep this interest alive. Familiarity with the library (see Chapter 8, 'The library') will open up new treasure-houses of literature to excite our pupils. We should always try to keep the books attractive (after all, we are salesmen of a kind, and five minutes now and then with some sellotape can work wonders). Popularity polls and graphs could be published. Simple charts on the form-room notice-boards on which the pupils tick the books they have read give them encouragement and pleasure — apart from helping us to trace books from time to time!

Enticement to read should not, however, be confined to the classroom. Interest should be generated, and maintained, on a school-wide basis, too. Here, to conclude these introductory remarks, are a few practical suggestions:

Book exhibitions. These are well worth organising, at least annually. Local booksellers will often be found eager and willing to co-operate; publishers like Penguin have their own excellent travelling displays. A most attractive and enterprising scheme is organised by Books for Students Ltd, Langham Trading Estate, Catteshall Lane, Godalming, Surrey. This is an exclusively paperback exhibition which can either be on a selling or an ordering basis. In the first, books are bought at the time; in the second, books are on show only, but can be ordered – and these orders are dealt with most efficiently. For a school, I feel the second type is more valuable as, obviously, it is possible to display more titles. The firm, incidentally, is willing to tailor the actual content and duration of the exhibition to the school's wishes, and also gives to the school a moderate percentage of the total sales. Invite the parents along one evening to such an exhibition, and you will be surprised at the number who will buy books for their children – and even for the school!

A school bookshop. This needs more organising, but it can be run smoothly and effectively by senior pupils under the aegis of a member of staff. Both Books for Students Ltd and W. H. Smith, the book-sellers, run very attractive, simple schemes for schools. Briefly, they are willing to supply enough paperbacks to open a shop in the school, on a sale-or-return basis, changing the stock at regular intervals if you so wish, and offering the school 10% on all sales. The former organisation is also helpful with the free supply of display-stands and racks. In this way, you can both feed and guide the pupils' reading tastes – and quietly supplement the library grant, or some such other worthy cause.

Book clubs. An interesting venture in this field is 'Scoop Club', which is a paperback club sponsored by Scholastic Publications Ltd, Brockhampton Lane, Kineton, Warwickshire. This club can, again, be run adequately with a senior pupil as secretary. A supply of news-sheets is sent to the school monthly – enough to put one in each form-room if you wish – giving the latest selection available with details of price, content, and often editorial comments, for each book. The secretary collects the individual orders and the money, and despatches the completed order-form in a post-paid envelope. There is no statutory minimum order required and the school does not receive any direct financial benefit, but the secretary may receive some free copies if the school order is large enough.

An internal scheme can be operated with particular success at a sixth-form level – an important stage, when most of this group will no longer be under our direct influence. Each sixth-former subscribes, say,

15p-25p a term, and a committee of sixth-formers, under the chairmanship of a member of staff, then selects paperbacks to buy with the money. All the books are then kept as a separate sixth-form library for private issue to subscribers. In this way, the members have available to them a large number of books on the same pattern as the personal form-library collection I mentioned earlier.

All these ideas are designed to capitalise on and foster that delight in books we should always regard as one of our primary aims and one of our most valuable legacies to our pupils.

Book lists

The two book lists which follow claim no more than to consist of titles which many of us have found in practice to be successful. Obviously, not all of these suggestions will be successful for all of us, but you can be assured that they have been tested in the field by those who recommended them, and not found wanting. We hope they will be of practical use to you in establishing or supplementing your own reading schemes, even though we are conscious of the fact that such recommendations will be far from complete; must be very arbitrary; will amuse some, horrify others, and, perhaps, even render others apoplectic with anger and incredulity. I present no apologies: the object is to get them reading — and the glorious rewards can be reaped later.

There has been some attempt to classify — by age, ability and sex. These distinctions are by no means inviolate or unalterable; I daresay the classification of every title and author could be challenged and proved wrong by many of us. It must be borne in mind that these lists are very much amalgams of suggestions from many types of school — country mixed grammar, highly selective boys', straightforward secondary modern, large city comprehensive, and so on. We are all aware, within our own school situations, that contradictions will arise anyway: parallel forms can be diametrically opposed to each other in their preferences. So much seems to depend on imponderables — the mood of the class; a chance remark of the teacher; something else they may be doing or reading or have seen on T.V. Such charming uncertainty is another cogent reason for supplying variety and bulk.

Some general explanatory notes

 (1) The lists are in alphabetical order, no other.
 (2) They contain fiction and non-fiction.
 (3) The coding in the two right-hand columns represents:
   (i) academic/reading ability — 1 = able; 2 = average; 3 = reluctant;
   (ii) preferences by sex — B = more popular with boys; G = more popular with girls; M = popular with both.
   (These codings are hesitantly given: books can be read and enjoyed at more than one level; apart from the obvious instances of where differentiation might appear, there is often considerable overlapping of interests of the sexes.)

(4) Some titles are deliberately included in both lists (though perhaps differently coded) to demonstrate this double-appeal. Examples:
    (i) Enid Bagnold's *National Velvet* is coded differently in each section (junior: 1 – M; middle school: 1, 2 – G);
    (ii) Ian Serraillier can be read in both age-ranges by different ability groups.

(5) Generally speaking, it is advisable to avoid purchasing paperbacks for class-use whenever possible: ultimately, it's false economy – even though it may be necessary initially. Nevertheless, some paperback publishers are given occasionally – and, of course, many titles appear in both kinds of binding.

(6) If paperbacks are necessary, I would recommend Armada, Knight (Hodder), Peacock, Puffin and Top-Liners (Pan/MacMillan) as they are aiming specifically at children's interests and capabilities.

(7) Many Public Libraries and N.A.T.E. study-groups produce most useful lists of recommended reading. They are up-to-date, and often contain reviews by practising teachers – worth enquiring about

(8) The committee thought out-of-print books worth including because they have been used successfully; you might find other suitable titles by the same writers; and publishers might be moved to re-instate them.

Books suitable for the first two years (11-13)

Author	Title	Publisher	Ability		Sex
Abrahall, C. H.	*Prelude*	O.U.P., 1959	1, 2		M
Adamson, J.	*Born Free*	Collins	1, 2		G
Ainsworth, W. H.	*Windsor Castle*	Nelson, O/P	1		M
Allingham, M.	*Coroner's Pidgin*	Heinemann	1		M
Ardizzone, E.	*Tim to the Rescue* (one of a series)	O.U.P.		3	M
Armstrong, R.	*The Big Sea*	Combridge, B'ham, 1970	1, 2		B
Armstrong, R.	*Sea Change*	Dent, 1962	1, 2		B
Armstrong, R.	*The Horseshoe Reef*	Dent, 1961	1, 2		M
Avery, H.	*The Dormitory Flag*	Nelson, O/P	1		B
Bagnold, E.	*Alice and Thomas and Jane*	Heinemann, 1930		3	M
Bagnold, E.	*National Velvet*	Heinemann, 1954	1		M
Baldwin, M.	*Grandad with Snails*	Hutchinson, 1971	1, 2		M
Barne, K.	*She Shall Have Music*	Dent, 1962	1, 2		G'
Bate, N.	*Who Built the Dam?*	Macmillan, 1959		3	B
Batten, H. M.	*The Singing Forest*	Heinemann, 1960	1		M
Bayley, V.	*Paris Adventure*	Dent, 1962	1, 2		G
Bennett, A.	*Grand Babylon Hotel*	Longman	1		M
Berna, P.	*A Hundred Million Francs*	Bodley Hd, 1957	1, 2		M
Blathwayt, J.	*Jo's Neighbour*	Lutterworth, 1958		3	B
Blyton, E.	*Well Done, Secret Seven*	Brockhampton, 1968	2, 3		G
	'Booster' Books	Heinemann	2, 3		M
Bosanquet, M.	*Canada Ride*	U.L.P., O/P	1, 2		M
Brazil, A.	*The School in the Forest*	Collins, 1970	1, 2		G

Author	Title	Publisher	Ability	Sex
Brickhill, P.	*The Dambusters*	Pan, 1969	1	B
Briggs, P.	*North with the Pintail*	Hutchinson, 1962	1, 2	M
Broster, D. K.	*The Flight of the Heron*	Heinemann, 1952	1	M
Chesterton, G. K.	*The Incredulity of Father Brown*	Penguin, 1970	1	M
Chilton, I.	*The String of Time*	Macmillan, 1968	1, 2	M
Clarke, P.	*James and the Robbers*	Hamilton, 1959	3	M
Cockett, M.	*Bouncing Ball*	Hamilton, 1958	3	M
Conan Doyle, A.	*The Return of Sherlock Holmes*	Murray, 1917	1	M
Conan Doyle, A.	*The Lost World*	Murray, 1960	1	M
Cooper, J. F.	*The Deerslayer*	Collier-Macmillan, 1962	1	M
Cooper, J. F.	*The Last of the Mohicans*	Nelson	1	M
Craigie, D.	*The Little Parrot*	Parrish, 1959 O/P	3	M
Day, C.	*Life with Father*	Chatto, 1969	1, 2	M
Day Lewis, C.	*The Otterbury Incident*	Heinemann, 1950	1, 2	M
Delderfield, R.	*The Adventures of Ben Gunn*	U.L.P., 1963	1	B
Denes, G.	'John and Jennifer' Series	Nelson	3	M
Dumas, A.	*The Three Musketeers*	Collins	1	M
Durrell, G.	*The Bafut Beagles*	Allen & Unwin, 1958	1	M
Enright, E.	*Thimble Summer*	Heinemann, 1958	1	G
Forester, C. S.	*Mr Midshipman Hornblower*	Longman, 1969	1, 2	M
Fox-Smith, C.	*The Ship Aground*	O.U.P., 1958	1, 2	B
Fuller, R.	*Savage Gold*	Hutchinson, 1960	1, 2	M
Fuller, R.	*With my little Eye*	Penguin, 1963	1	M
Gallico, P.	*The Small Miracle*	Joseph, 1955	2, 3	M
Garnett, E.	*The Family from One-End Street*	Penguin, 1971	1, 2	G
Gilchrist, D.	*Castle Commando*	Oliver and Boyd, 1962 O/P	1	B
Godden, R.	*The Mousewife*	Macmillan, 1951	3	G
Godfrey, M.	*South for Gold*	Heinemann, 1968	1	M
	'The Good Luck' Series	Nelson	3	G
Grice, F.	*The Bonny Pit-Laddie*	O.U.P.	1, 2	M
Griffiths, H.	*The Horse in the Clouds*	Hutchinson, 1961	1	M
Guareschi, G.	*The Little World of Don Camillo*	Penguin, 1970	1	M
Guillot, R.	*Kpo the Leopard*	Heinemann, 1963	1, 2	M
'Herge'.	*Tintin and the Blue Oranges*	Methuen, 1967	2, 3	M
Hildick, E. W.	*Birdy Jones*	Macmillan, 1968	1, 2, 3	M
Hildick, E. W.	*Birdy and the Group*	Macmillan, 1968	1, 2, 3	M
Hildick, E. W.	*Louie's Lot*	Macmillan, 1968	1, 2, 3	M
Hodges, C. W.	*Columbus Sails*	Longman, 1953	1	M
Hodges, C. W.	*The Namesake: A Story of King Alfred*	Longman, 1967	1	M
Hope, A.	*The Prisoner of Zenda*	Dent, 1950	1	M
Hope, L. L.	'The Bobbsey Twins' Series	World Distrib.	3	G
Household, G.	*The Spanish Cave*	Longman, 1966	1	M
Jansson, T.	*The Finn Family Moomintroll*	Penguin, 1970	1, 2, 3	M

Author	Title	Publisher	Ability	Sex
Johns, W. E.	*Biggles* (and series)	Brockhampton	1, 2	B
Kastner, E.	*Emil and the Detectives*	Penguin, 1971	1, 2	M
Kent, M.	*The Twins at the Seaside*	Harrap, 1943 O/P	3	G
King, C.	*Stig of the Dump*	Penguin, 1970	1, 2	M
	The 'Ladybird' Series	Wills and Hepworth	3	M
Lederer, W. J.	*Timothy's Song*	Lutterworth, 1966	3	M
Lewis, C. S.	*The Lion, the Witch and the Wardrobe*	Penguin, 1970	1	M
Lewis, C. S.	*Out of the Silent Planet*	Longman, 1966	1	M
Leyland, E. (ed.)	*The Boy's Book of Adventure*	Evans, 1950	3	B
London, J.	*The Call of the Wild*	Blackie, 1968	1	M
London, J.	*White Fang*	Blackie, 1968	1	M
Lowe, A. M.	*Adrift in the Stratosphere*	Blackie, O/P	1, 2	B
Maddock, R.	*A Dragon in the Garden*	Macmillan, 1968	2	M
Marshall, J. V.	*Walkabout*	Penguin, 1969	1	M
Masefield, J.	*Jim Davis*	Longman	1, 2	B
Masefield, J.	*Martin Hyde*	Longman	1, 2	B
Mason, A. E. W.	*Fire Over England*	U.L.P., 1949	1	M
Maxwell, G.	*Ring of Bright Water*	Pan, 1969	1	M
Morrow, H.	*The Splendid Journey*	Heinemann, 1950	1	M
Naughton, B.	*The Goalkeeper's Revenge and Other Stories*	Penguin, 1970	1	B
Norton, M.	*The Borrowers* (and series)	Dent	1, 2	M
Orczy, Baroness	*The League of the Scarlet Pimpernel*	Cassell, 1968	1	M
Palmer, G. and Lloyd, N.	*The Obstinate Ghost and Other Ghostly Tales*	Hamlyn, 1968	2	M
Patchett, M. E.	*The Mysterious Pool*	Hamilton, 1958	3	G
Pope, R.	*The Drum*	Macmillan, 1968	1, 2	M
Rawlings, M. K.	*The Yearling*	Penguin, 1971	1	G
Ringner-Lundgren, E. R.	*Little Trulsa's Secret*	Methuen, 1967	3	G
Robinson, G. B.	*The Mate and the Midshipman*	Cassell, 1966	1	B
Serraillier, I.	*The Ivory Horn*	Heinemann, 1962	1	M
Smith, Dodie	*One Hundred and One Dalmations*	Penguin, 1969	2	M
Spain, N.	*The Tiger Who Went to the Moon*	Parrish, 1956	3	G
Spring, H.	*Darkie and Co.*	O.U.P., 1958	1	M
Spyri, J.	*Heidi*	Dent, 1940	1	G
Steinbeck, J.	*The Red Pony*	Heinemann, 1968	1, 2, 3	M
Stevenson, R. L.	*Kidnapped*	Nelson, 1931	1	B
Streatfeild, N.	*The Circus is Coming*	Dent, 1947	1, 2	M
Streatfeild, N.	*Curtain Up*	Dent, 1963	1, 2	M
Stucley, E.	*Magnolia Buildings*	Bodley Head, 1960	1, 2	M
Styles, S.	*Midshipman Quinn*	Faber, 1956	1	B
Sutcliff, R.	*Sword at Sunset*	Longman, 1967	1	M
Taylor, R.	*Andy and the Royal Review* (one of a series)	Hamilton, 1963	3	B

Author	Title	Publisher	Ability		Sex
Tolkien, J. R. R.	*The Hobbit*	Longman, 1969	1		M
Townsend, J. R.	*Gumble's Yard*	Hutchinson, 1964	1, 2		M
Travers, P. L.	*Mary Poppins from A to Z*	Collins, 1968		3	G
Trease, G.	*No Boats on Bannermere*	Heinemann, 1949	1		M
Treece, H.	*The Hounds of the King*	Longman, 1965	1, 2		M
Trevor, M.	*The Treasure Hunt*	Hamilton, 1957		3	M
Tring, A. S.	*Frankie and the Green Umbrella*	Hamilton, 1957 O/P		3	M
Tschiffely, A. F.	*Tschiffely's Ride*	U.L.P., O/P	1		B
Turnbull, E. L.	'Traditional Tales' Series 1-4	O.U.P., 1953 O/P		3	M
Turner, E.	*Night Nurse and Other Stories*	Ward Lock, 1967		3	G
Twain, M.	*Tom Sawyer* and *Huckleberry Finn*	Dent, 1963	1		M
Verne, J.	*Five Weeks in a Balloon*	Allen and Unwin, 1958	1		M
Williamson, H.	*Tarka the Otter*	Longman, 1969	1		M

Notes on 11-13 age-group list

(1) The traditional favourites, the established children's classics, should not be ignored, either. The following books can still captivate young readers of average ability or above:
Alice in Wonderland. Carroll, L. (various publishers).
Black Beauty. Sewell, A. (various publishers).
The King of the Golden River. Ruskin, J. (Kaye and Ward, 1971).
King Solomon's Mines. Haggard, H. Rider (various publishers).
Little Women. Alcott, L. M. (various publishers).
Moonfleet. Falkner, J. M. (Arnold, 1946).
The Rose and the Ring. Thackeray, W. M. (Nelson).
The Secret Garden. Burnett, F. H. (Heinemann).
Treasure Island. Stevenson, R. L. (various publishers).
The Wind in the Willows. Grahame, K. (Methuen, 1968).
A worthy top ten!

(2) Reliable, popular authors, for the same ability groups, are John Buchan, John Masefield, Ian Serraillier, R.L.S., Noel Streatfeild, Rosemary Sutcliff, Henry Treece, Jules Verne.

(3) This is the age of myths, legends and folk-lore. Nelson produce a whole series of folk tales on various areas of the country — splendid stuff. J. H. Walsh, for Longman, wrote several excellent collections of myths. Rex Warner's *Men and Gods* (Heinemann, 1951) is worth trying, as are E. V. Rieu's translations of Homer, for the very able.

(4) There is interest, too, in animal stories and biographies of great figures like Joan of Arc and Madame Curie.

(5) Finally, we should investigate the use of abridged classics: there is nothing shameful in introducing our pupils to works of Dickens in this way, or to Ballantyne's *Coral Island*, Swift's *Gulliver's Travels,* Defoe's *Robinson Crusoe,* or Wyss's *The Swiss Family Robinson.* Three

publishers who do this well are Methuen (Venture Library), U.L.P. (Pilot Books) and Blackie (The Kennett Library) — and there are others, too, interested in supplying this kind of material.

Books suitable for the third and fourth years (13-15)

Author	Title	Publisher	Ability	Sex
Allingham, M.	*The Tiger in the Smoke*	Heinemann, 1966	1	M
Arnothy, C.	*I am Fifteen, and I Do Not Want to Die*	Fontana, 1968	1	M
Attenborough, D.	*Zoo Quest for a Dragon*	U.L.P., 1965	1, 2	M
Bagnold, E.	*National Velvet*	Heinemann, 1954	1, 2	G
Balchin, N.	*A Sort of Traitors*	Pan, 1969	1	M
Balchin, N.	*The Small Back Room*	Hutchinson, 1963	1	M
Baldwin, P.	*Susan Kendall, Student Nurse*	Victory pubs., 1960	3	G
Barne, K.	*Admiral's Walk*	Dent, 1960	1, 2	M
Beaty, D.	*The Proving Flight*	Chatto Educ., 1964	1	M
Behan, B.	*Borstal Boy*	Hutchinson, 1967	1, 2	M
	'Booster' Books	Heinemann	3	M
Boyers, B.	*The Ann and Jenny* series	Ginn	3	G
Braithwaite, E. R.	*To Sir, with Love*	Bodley Head, 1959	1, 2	M
Brontë, C.	*Jane Eyre*	O.U.P., 1969	1	G
Broster, D. K.	*The Flight of the Heron*	Heinemann, 1952	1, 2	M
Buchan, J.	*The Thirty-nine Steps*	Longman	1, 2	M
Burnford, S.	*The Incredible Journey*	Hodder, 1969	1, 2	M
Calman, M.	*The Go Readers* series	Blond Educ., 1964	3	B
Canning, J. (ed.)	*Fifty Great Horror Stories*	Odhams, 1969	2, 3	M
Carruth, J.	*The Jane Carruth Books*	Odhams	3	B
Carter, B.	*Speed Six*	Longman, 1968	3	B
Cervantes, M. de	*The Exploits of Don Quixote* (ed. J. Reeves)	Blackie, 1953 O/P	1	B
Chalk, W. C. H.	*Old Ugly* (a Booster Book)	Heinemann, 1967	2, 3	M
Chesterton, G. K.	*Father Brown*	O.U.P., 1955	1	M
Chichester, F.	*Along the Clipper Way*	U.L.P., 1967	1, 2	B
Christopher, J.	*The Death of Grass*	Penguin, 1970	1	B
Clarke, A. C.	*A Fall of Moondust*	U.L.P., 1964	1, 2	B
Cleary, B.	*Fifteen*	Penguin, 1970	1	G
Conan Doyle, A.	*The Sherlock Holmes stories*	Murray	1, 2	M
Crane, S.	*The Red Badge of Courage and Other Stories*	O.U.P., 1969	1	M
Cumming, P.	*The Flying Horseman*	Dent, 1964	1	M
De Jong, M.	*The House of Sixty Fathers*	Penguin, 1971	1, 2	M
Deverson, H. J.	*The Map that Came to Life*	O.U.P., 1967	3	M
Durrell, G.	*My Family and Other Animals*	Penguin, 1969	1, 2	M
Enright, E.	*The Four Storey Mistake*	Penguin, 1967	1, 2	G
Enright, E.	*The Saturdays*	Penguin, 1970	1, 2	M
Exell, S. K.	*In Siamese Service*	Cassell, 1968	1	M
Field, S.	*A New Life for Carol*	Ward Lock, 1967	3	G

Author	Title	Publisher	Ability	Sex
Fleming, I.	*Goldfinger* (and other James Bond books)	Pan	1, 2, 3	M
Forester, C. S.	*Mr. Midshipman Hornblower*	Longman, 1969	1, 2	M
Fuller, R.	*Savage Gold*	Hutchinson, 1970	1, 2	M
Fuller, R.	*With my Little Eye*	Penguin, 1963	1, 2	M
Gallico, P.	*The Small Miracle*	Joseph, 1955	2, 3	M
Garner, A.	*Elidor*	Penguin, 1969	1, 2	M
Garner, A.	*The Moon of Gomrath*	Penguin, 1969	2	M
Garner, A.	*The Owl Service*	Penguin, 1969	1, 2	M
Garner, A.	*The Weirdstone of Brisingamen*	Penguin, 1969	2	M
George, J.	*My Side of the Mountain*	Penguin, 1970	1, 2	M
Gilchrist, D.	*Castle Commando*	Oliver & Boyd, 1962 O/P	1, 2, 3	B
Golding, W.	*Lord of the Flies*	Faber, 1954	1	M
Green, F. L.	*Odd Man Out*	Blackie, 1967	1	M
Grimble, A.	*A Pattern of Islands*	Murray, 1952	1	M
Hanley, C.	*The Taste of Too Much*	Blackie, 1967	1	M
'Herge'.	*Tintin and the Blue Oranges*	Methuen, 1967	3	M
Heyerdahl, T.	*The Kon-Tiki Expedition*	Penguin, 1969	1	M
Hildick, E. W.	*Jim Starling and the Spotted Dog*	Blond, 1967	2, 3	B
Hilton, J.	*Goodbye, Mister Chips*	U.L.P., 1952	1, 2	M
Hines, B.	*A Kestrel for a Knave*	Pergamon, 1969	1, 2	M
Hope, A.	*The Prisoner of Zenda*	Dent, 1950	1, 2	M
Hope, A.	*Rupert of Hentzau*	Dent, 1963	1	M
Household, G.	*Rogue Male*	Heinemann, 1963	1	B
Household, G.	*The Spanish Cave*	Longman, 1966	2	M
Hughes, R.	*A High Wind in Jamaica*	Penguin, 1971	1	M
Hughes, R.	*In Hazard*	Chatto and Windus, 1954	1	M
Hunt, I.	*Across Five Aprils*	Heinemann, 1969	1	M
Hunt, J.	*The Ascent of Everest*	U.L.P., 1954	1, 2	B
Innes, H.	*Air Bridge*	Collins, 1965	1, 2	B
Innes, H.	*Campbell's Kingdom*	Collins, 1964	1, 2	B
Innes, M.	*The Journeying Boy*	Gollancz, 1970	1	M
Jerome, J. K.	*Three Men in a Boat*	Collins, 1957	1, 2	M
Johnson, D. M.	*The Hanging Tree and Four Other Stories*	Hutchinson, 1961	1	M
Juster, N.	*The Dot and the Line*	Nelson, 1964	1	M
Juster, N.	*The Phantom Tollbooth*	Penguin, 1965	1, 2	M
	The 'Ladybird' Series	Wills & Hepworth	3	M
Lamorisse, A.	*The Red Balloon*	Allen and Unwin, 1957	2, 3	M
Lewis, C. S.	*Out of the Silent Planet*	Longman, 1966	1	M
Lines, K. (ed.)	'The Faber Storybooks'	Faber, 1961	2, 3	M
Mackenzie, C.	*Whisky Galore*	Chatto Educ., 1963	1, 2	M
Maclean, A.	*The Guns of Navarone*	Collins, 1964	1, 2	B
Mankowitz, W.	*A Kid for Two Farthings*	Heinemann, 1958	1, 2	M
Martin, R.	*The Mystery of the Missing Passenger*	Nelson, 1964	3	B

Author	Title	Publisher	Ability	Sex
Martin, R.	*Tony and the Secret Money*	Benn, 1964	3	B
Masefield, J.	*Bird of Dawning*	Heinemann, 1956	1	M
May, A. le	*The Searchers*	Collins, 1965	1	M
Orczy, Baroness	*The Scarlet Pimpernel*	U.L.P., 1937	1, 2	M
Orwell, G.	*Animal Farm*	Longman, 1965	1, 2	M
Orwell, G.	*Nineteen Eighty-four*	Penguin, 1970	1	M
Palmer, G. and Lloyd, N.	*The Obstinate Ghost and Other Ghostly Tales*	Hamlyn, 1968	2, 3	M
Palmer, G. and Lloyd, N.	*Ghost Stories Round the World*	Odhams, 1965	2, 3	M
Preussler, O.	*The Little Ghost*	Abelard-Schuman, 1967	2, 3	M
Raftery, G.	*The Stallion Snow Cloud*	Longman, 1968	1, 2	M
Sarton, M.	*Joanna and Ulysses*	Blackie, 1967	1	M
Saville, M.	*Susan, Bill and the Wolf Dog* (and other M. Saville books)	Nelson, 1954	2, 3	M
Schaefer, J.	*Shane*	Heinemann, 1957	1	M
Serraillier, I.	*Beowulf the Warrior*	O.U.P., 1954	1, 2	M
Shute, N.	*A Town Like Alice*	Pan, 1968	1, 2	M
Shute, N.	*No Highway*	Heinemann, 1953	1	M
Sillitoe, A.	*The Loneliness of the Long Distance Runner*	Longman, 1966	1	B
Sperry, A.	*The Boy who was Afraid*	Heinemann, 1952	1, 2, 3	M
Steinbeck, J.	*The Pearl*	Heinemann, 1954	1, 2	M
Steinbeck, J.	*The Red Pony*	Heinemann, 1961	1, 2	M
Stewart, J. I. M.	*The Man Who Won the Pools*	Gollancz, 1961	1	M
Stratton-Porter, G.	*The Girl of the Limberlost*	U.L.P., 1951	1, 2	G
Sutcliff, R.	*The Rider of the White Horse*	Hodder, 1967	1, 2	M
Sutcliff, R.	*A Sword at Sunset*	Longman, 1967	1, 2	M
Tate, J.	*Sam and Me*	Macmillan, 1970	1, 2, 3	G
Tate, J.	The Joan Tate Books	Heinemann	3	G
Tey, J.	*Daughter of Time*	Heinemann, 1959	1	M
Tey, J.	*The Franchise Affair*	Nelson, 1965	1	G
Tolkien, J. R. R.	*The Hobbit*	Longman, 1969	1, 2	M
Trease, G.	*No Boats on Bannermere*	Heinemann, 1952	2	M
Treviño, E. B.	*I, Juan de Pareja*	Heinemann, 1968	1	M
Tschiffely, A. E.	*Tschiffely's Ride*	U.L.P., O/P	1, 2	B
Van der Post, L.	*The Lost World of the Kalahari*	Penguin, 1964	1	M
Van der Post, L.	*Venture to the Interior*	Penguin, 1971	1	M
Waterhouse, K.	*There is a Happy Land*	Longman, 1968	1	M
Webster, J.	*Daddy long-legs*	U.L.P., 1952	1, 2	G
Wells, H. G.	*The First Men in the Moon*	Collins, 1956	1, 2	B
White, T. H.	*The Sword in the Stone*	Collins, 1964	1	M
Williams, J. H.	*Elephant Bill*	Heinemann, 1957	1, 2	B
Wyndham, J.	*The Day of the Triffids*	Penguin, 1970	1	M
Wyndham, J.	*The Kraken Wakes*	Penguin, 1970	1	M
Wyndham, J.	*The Seeds of Time*	Penguin, 1969	1	M

Notes on 13-15 age-group list

(1) The variety of books decreases rapidly as the slow and reluctant readers become older, as they seem to take much more interest in non-fiction.

(2) For average and able readers, I feel I need give much less guidance because, in my experience, their interests now begin to range so widely that selection and categorisation become superfluous. Try anything!

(3) Both reader-groups, mentioned above, are attracted to real-life stories, and the abler readers delight in such books as:

Autobiography of a Super-tramp. Davies, W. H. (Allen and Unwin, 1951).
Cider with Rosie. Lee, L. (Chatto Educ., 1963).
The Colditz Story. Reid, P. R. (U.L.P., 1957).
Desperate Voyage. Caldwell, J. (Heinemann, 1957).
The Diary of Anne Frank. (Hutchinson, 1960).
Goodbye to All That. Graves, R. (Cassell, 1966).
Living Dangerously. Spencer Chapman, F. (Chatto Educ., 1954).
No Picnic on Mount Kenya. Benuzzi, F. (Longman).
South with Scott. Evans, E. R. G. R. (Collins, 1962).
Three Singles to Adventure. Durrell, G. (Heinemann, 1962).
South Col. Noyce, W. (Heinemann, 1956).

(4) Historical novels, too, now begin to come into their own – as do modern short stories and science-fiction generally. The latter two genres can be happily supplied in such collections as *Stories from Science Fiction* (Nelson, 1966), *Aspects of Science Fiction* (Murray, 1959), *Second Orbit* (Murray, 1965) (all edited by G. D. Doherty), and *Connoisseur's Science Fiction* (Penguin, 1964), edited by T. Boardman. Consequently, popular writers are such as Baroness Orczy, Georgette Heyer, Margaret Irwin, Daphne du Maurier, Nevil Shute, H. G. Wells, John Wyndham and A. C. Clarke.

Publishers and series

I find myself relying very heavily on the following: Allen and Unwin (Windsor); Edward Arnold; Blackie (Teenage Bookshelf, Kennett Library); Bodley Head; Cassell (Red Lion Readers); Chatto and Windus (Queen's Classics); Collins (Modern Authors); Dent (Literature of Yesterday and Today); Faber (Educational Edition); Rupert Hart-Davis (School Edition); Heinemann (Modern Novel, Windmill); Hutchinson (Unicorn); Longman (Heritage of Literature, Imprint, Modern Classics, Pleasure in Reading); Macmillan; Methuen (Beaver Books, Venture Library); Murray (Albemarle, Scholars' Library); Nelson (Reading Today, Schools Classics, Teaching of English); Oliver and Boyd (Coromandel); Oxford University Press (Children's Authors, World's Classics); Pergamon; University of London Press (Pilot).

There you are.
That's it.
You could buy the lot for £120.
Take the plunge!

7 Intensive reading

George Watkins

Reading is a sharing of experience. When you read privately, the author, by means of his text, shares his experience with you. When you read aloud, the author's experience is shared not only with you but also with your audience. If you read aloud well, your audience may enjoy a fuller share of the original experience than they would have done by reading the text privately. Also, if a number of people all read the same text privately, then discuss it, they stand a good chance of enriching one another's share of the original experience – particularly if one of them is a trained reader, and a person of considerable culture, who has previously made a study of the text. If, then, it is desirable for pupils to extend and enrich their imaginative experience – and you will hardly say that it isn't – there is an obvious case for the study of prescribed texts, since that kind of study amounts to all the pupils in a group reading the same text privately, hearing it brought to life by the performance, live or recorded, of selected passages, and discussing it under the expert guidance of their teacher. For those secondary pupils who can read reasonably fluently – say forty per cent or even more – the study of set texts is an efficient way of developing the capacity for imaginative experience.

Yet in our profession one learns to dread the moment, after one has been introduced as a teacher of English, when the new acquaintance starts to tell in sickening detail how his delight in Shakespeare was ruined for life by having to do *Macbeth* for an examination. Throughout the community there is, or there is made out to be, a tremendous resentment of the study of prescribed texts, and the process is nearly always referred to as 'doing'. Whatever is the matter?

Well, stupid questions beget stupid answers, and provoke stubborn responses. Everyone can quote instances of obtuse, insensitive, or downright irrelevant questions set on prescribed texts by the examining boards. How can it be otherwise? Boards who examine forty or fifty thousand candidates at a sitting are obliged to use rough-and-ready methods, and the study of prescribed texts, as I hinted above, is a subtle business. Then it has to be admitted that teachers in their thousands have studied not the prescribed texts but the past question-papers, imposing EngLit on their pupils instead of studying English literature. Finally, you have to accept that *Macbeth* is a strange and disturbing work – and so are *Julius Caesar* and *Pygmalion* and *The Importance of Being Earnest* and *Lord of the Flies* and *Typhoon* and *The Destructors* and *Here Today* and selections from the poems of R. S. Thomas and Dylan Thomas and Auden and Louis MacNeice and so on. Those fifteen-year-olds whose main desire is to settle yet more cosily into the backgrounds from which they have never emerged are bound to resent having thrust into their comfortable habits of platitudinous thought an experience of wild, homicidal ambition, of awkward notions about the class-structure of society, of highly cultivated wit, of the reality of infantile barbarism, of the questioning of received notions about heroism, of the tragi-comedy of delinquency, of the singing and irony and the appalling vision of the poets. They are bound to resent the intrusion, just as they resent having to stir themselves for P.E. But the P.E. staff have ways of turning the resentment into participation and enjoyment, and so have we. Most of the objections to set books are due to bad examination questions and to teaching directed at those bad questions; that is all.

At one time undergraduates used to describe themselves as 'reading with' this or that tutor, and it was not a bad description. They used to read together, and what they read was prescribed texts. Surely there is no reason why secondary pupils should not 'read with' their teacher. If there is a suitable examination, or even a mildly unsuitable one, at the end of the process, that is harmless enough – provided always that it is the reading that matters and the examination that merely follows. Direct the reading towards the examination, and the results will serve you right; but read together, sharing the experience, enlightening each other, and you will get something worth having. Afterwards, the pupils can take advantage of the examination to display what they have discovered in the course of the reading; but if there is no examination the work will have been none the less worth doing. Briefly, if your study of prescribed texts is to be any good, you *must* keep your mind off examinations and on the texts. Keep your mind on the texts and a good time can be had by all.

In organising work on prescribed texts, remember that there is not time to do everything, and remember that, while it is right for you to stretch your pupils' experience, the limits of their curiosity are bound to be narrower than your own. You have to do what you can, rather than all you would like to do. So select a limited number of important characteristics that your pupils will be able to appreciate without too much difficulty. For instance, the ironies of *Scoop*, and perhaps the hilarious solemnities of its set-pieces like the description of Boot Magna, or the descent of the *deus ex machina* on to the roof of the Pension Dressler. Or the ironies of *Animal Farm*, and the way in which its events represent events in the U.S.S.R. between 1917 and 1945. Or the ironies of *Julius Caesar*, and the way in which Caesar's influence pervades the play. Or the variety of interests, the persistent human sympathy, the fascinating sounds, and the sheer good fun, not to mention the ironies, of *Here Today*.

Irony

I keep mentioning irony because there is hardly one worth-while work of literature which does not have its ironies. In reading together you can hardly go wrong if you all sharpen your attention to listen for the irony. After all, an awareness of irony is one of the characteristics of maturity, and literary irony can perhaps help young people to become aware of the ironies of life. It can perhaps help them to learn something about the adult world without getting too badly hurt.

In my experience, very few secondary pupils can recognise irony when they see it on the printed page. Future honours graduates can, at the age of sixteen, read privately the account of Lord Copper's personal interview with William Boot in *Scoop* and yet be totally unaware that anyone's leg is being pulled. They can, and do, read the closing pages of *Animal Farm* without the ghost of a notion that anyone's ideals have been betrayed. It takes a lot of practice, which means a lot of reading together, to bring secondary pupils to a ready and confident perception of irony; but the effort is fully justified by the commonsense − that is to say, the *social competence* (see Newsom) − which it helps to develop.

If only for the sake of the irony, you should see to it that your pupils *hear* a good deal of any prescribed text that you may be reading together. The traditional practice of taking turns round the class to read aloud from a novel is not recommended, nor is the other traditional practice of sharing out parts in a set play and just reading it aloud at first sight. The unrehearsed performances are inevitably so poor, and the intensity of the experience so small, that the time spent in these ways cannot be justified. Worse, the pupils are quickly bored, and the text gets 'done' in the wrong sense. There is more about this in 'Classroom drama' (see Chapter 5).

It is probably best for the pupils to read the text privately at first, reading as quickly as possible and not stopping for explanations. This will give them only a rough-and-ready, perhaps even a garbled, notion of what they have read, but they will have undergone a unified and reasonably coherent experience, which is what matters. Explanations take time, and if you start with them you give the impression that they count for more than the story itself.

Sound

Next comes the sound. Records, or, if you are lucky, video-tape, are probably best for plays, if only because it is the business of professional actors to perform plays. Obviously you all go to see a live performance, or perhaps a film, if there is a chance; but that may not occur just at the moment you want to begin work on the text, so you cannot depend on it. If there is no money for records, and you cannot borrow them, you will simply have to do some rehearsals and perform the play yourselves. There is no need for consistency in casting; the parts in a five-act play can be allocated to each of five groups, who get up an act apiece. If you cannot have the stage because it is wanted for school dinners, or if there is no stage, try working with a toy theatre. Alternatively, do a properly prepared play-reading of the kind recommended in 'Classroom drama'. Somehow or other, see to it that the play is *heard*, that the printed words are recognised as representing sound, and make sure that the experience is as compact as possible. Don't spread out the performance over one lesson a week for six or seven weeks.

The sound of poems matters at least as much as the sound of plays — perhaps more so, because the performance of poems is almost exclusively a matter of sound, and there are other considerations to do with plays. There may well be records of your prescribed poems, and the performances may be very good. In those circumstances all you have to do is play them. But professional actors are not always the best readers of non-dramatic verse, and some recorded performances are less than sensitive. So you may have to read aloud some, or all, of the prescribed poems yourself. That poses problems, too, because you cannot respond with equal enthusiasm to every poem in an anthology, and it is unlikely that all of them will suit your voice and manner. You can ask some of the pupils to prepare readings of some of the poems, then. Pick good performers and give them enough warning so that they can practise. Let them consult you about meaning and interpretation, and you may be surprised at the excellence of the outcome. For the sound of poetry you have to choose judiciously among recorded voices, your own voice, and the voices of pupils.

When it comes to prose fiction, it is unlikely that you will be able to use recorded material. You may just be lucky, but the chances are not good. So it will have to be your own voice most of the time, though you may be able to use pupils' prepared performances in the way I have suggested for poetry. You can't perform the whole novel, or the whole book of stories. You have to select, and, following the professional example of the B.B.C. in *Books, Plays, Poems* and *Listening and Writing*, you will do best to select readings that last about twenty minutes each. You will need to provide some continuity between the readings, but not much, because the pupils should have read privately in advance, and should know roughly what is going on. Your task is not so much to narrate events as to present the sound implied by the text. It is probably in the reading aloud of prose fiction that one's professional skill as a mountebank is exercised to its fullest extent. Watch *Jackanory* on B.B.C. TV to see how it can be done.

Background

Before the performance of the text, perhaps even before the preliminary private reading, you may have to give your pupils some background information. A very brief outline of the course of the Russian Revolution is obviously a help to someone coming to *Animal Farm* for the first time. A quick explanation of what happened in *Richard II*, with special emphasis on Richard's 'curse' on Bolingbroke, helps inexperienced readers to see what much of the fuss is about in *1 Henry IV*. An anthology of the poetry of the 1930s calls for some awareness of the slump, and the rise of fascism. But background information at this stage should be kept to a minimum. All you need is enough to provide a context; it must not amount to enough to interfere with or postpone the experience of the work of art. One lesson is plenty, and may be too much. Experience must come first; discussion, analysis, annotation and all that, can follow.

When they do follow — that is, when you are all feeling reasonably familiar with the words of the text and their sound — a certain amount of direct instruction or lecturing may be desirable. It is hardly an exciting procedure, but it is quick and quite efficient if everyone's curiosity has been aroused by previous experience. The point is that some items of information are going to be needed by everyone, and a 'talk' is a convenient way of communicating them. If Miss Prism is to be appreciated, there has to be some explanation of the standing of the governess in a well-to-do, late-Victorian family. If the pig-dance in *Lord of the Flies* is to make any sense, someone must talk about totemism in primitive societies. In a rural school it may be necessary to explain the disadvantages of slum children in cities, to get the best out of 'Timothy Winters', just as some information about life on the Welsh hill farms is necessary in a city school to make much out of 'Cynddylan on a Tractor'. You may have to read a portion of the Scriptures to put pupils in touch with poems like 'Story of the Flood' or 'Ballad of the Bread Man'. When everyone needs the information, a talk or a lecture is an economical way of making it available. Twenty minutes is probably a maximum. Note-taking can go on simultaneously, or can follow, according to need and circumstances. It does not have to take place at all unless a large measure of recall is going to be required.

Discussion

Much of the work on a text, however, must take the form of discussion and of question-and-answer. No discussion, no sharing. And it is crucially important that a large part of the discussion should be devoted to pupils' questions and the answers provided by other pupils or by yourself. As far as possible the pupils must ask the questions, because, unless they formulate the questions, they cannot even know what it is they don't know. Until a pupil has been moved to ask why you read the description of dinner at Lord Copper's mansion in a tone of bottomless contempt, there isn't a hope of his seeing the point of the episode. It is no use your asking him; he has no terms of reference. The meal probably sounds to him like a 'right good do', the sort of thing you get at

> . . . banquet-halls up yards, and bunting-dressed
> Coach-party annexes . . .

Nor is it much use your telling him; he will only make a note of it. But if he asks, you can be sure that he has discovered in himself a wish to know, and you can be almost equally sure that he will remember the answer, whether it comes from you, or from the other pupils pooling their ideas, or, perhaps best of all, from himself as a result of discussion. Remember, too, that in the final count it is not the knowledge (in this case about the dining habits of eccentric press-barons), but the attitude of mind, the curiosity and its satisfaction, that is educationally important.

Readiness to ask questions — that is, readiness to recognise a need for information — cannot be suddenly switched on at the beginning of the fourth year, or whenever it is that you want to begin studying prescribed texts. It derives from the regular practice of *consultative speech* (see M. Joos, *The Five Clocks,* Harcourt, Brace & World) which begins in the pre-school years, is continued in the primary schools, and should be continued in the secondary schools. As I said earlier, there is value in the situation in which the pupils are sat down and obliged to acquiesce in the *formal discourse* (again, see *The Five Clocks*) of their teacher; that procedure certainly 'gets through the work', but it is more suitable for presenting facts than for sharing the experience of literature. Sharing necessarily involves give-and-take in as many directions as there are sharers. The habit of sharing takes a long time to develop; the habit of sharing literary experience develops out of the unscripted part of the work in Spoken English.

Notes

If notes are to be taken, remember their purpose. They are not an end in themselves; they are no more than aids to recall — that is, they are reminders or remembrancers. Pencilled notes in the margins of texts seem to me disgusting, and they spoil the books for the next users. Verbatim transcriptions are altogether too much. All the pupils are going to need is enough to remind them, at revision-time, of what was agreed when the text was performed and discussed. If the notes are tidily and spaciously laid out, the reminders will be all the more useful. My own pupils find it convenient to make their notes on one side of a double page only, so that second thoughts, amendments, and amplifications can later be written on the blank page without spoiling the original notes. As teacher, one's hardest task in this aspect of the work is usually to persuade the pupils to *select* the material of their notes. Left to themselves, most of them will tend to put down everything for fear of missing anything.

Essays

Your study of prescribed texts may call for essays. The requirements will be so various that I do not propose to try to classify them here. Anyway, most teachers of English have had a predominantly literary training, so it is a near-certainty that you will know perfectly well what you want. May I simply put in a word about getting what you want?

When you set essays, be careful about abstractions, and make sure that your pupils fully understand what you want. I myself have always had extreme difficulty in grasping notions like *character, plot, structure, imagery, diction,* and, more recently and most obscure of all, *effectiveness.* P. N. Furbank in *Critical Quarterly* for winter 1967 made me feel easier at not being alone in finding the notion of imagery a puzzle. Donald Davie in *Purity of Diction in English Verse* (Chatto, 1952) made diction seem less nebulous. Esmor Jones in his two-page 'Appendix A: A Note on Examiners' English' in the N.A.T.E. booklet *English Examined,* convinced me that in the setting of many written tasks in schools there is a silly conspiracy of the more-or-less learned to assert their intellectual superiority and to intimidate the pupils by using what he calls 'English in cap and gown' — to set questions like, 'With close reference to the text, evaluate the character of Henchard and discuss its effectiveness'. Before you perpetrate a thing like that, do just ask yourself whether you know what you want, whether your pupils know what you want, and whether it might not be easier for all concerned to: 'Say what sort of man you think Henchard is, and go on to argue about whether you approve of him.'

At this point it is worth insisting that, whichever way you phrase the question, the answer, to be useful, must be based upon specific examples taken from the text, and must be honestly argued. In the present instance of the question on *The Mayor of Casterbridge*, it will not do for a pupil to make out Henchard as a mild, forgiving, saintly sort of person, but it does not matter very much whether he describes him as a brutal, dangerous man made interesting by occasional fits of generosity, or as a warm-hearted man given to unpremeditated and disastrous fits of self-assertion. Within these commonsense limits, it is not the opinion that counts, but the quality of the argument. Thus 'I think Henchard is a brute' amounts to nothing. Opinions are cheap; you can buy them second-hand in books of ready-made G.C.E. revision notes. 'I think Henchard is a brute for selling his wife' is better than nothing. Particular examples quoted in support of opinions do at least suggest that the pupil is familiar with his text. 'I think Henchard is a brute. For example, he gets drunk at Weydon Priors fair and sells his wife. This leaves her destitute, with a young child to look after and, as far as Henchard is concerned, no one to help or protect her. Whatever the excuse, the wife-selling is a brutal act' — this begins to be an answer. Explanations which say how the particular example bears on the generalised opinion show that the pupil is not merely familiar with his text, but has seen the point of it. Need I do more than say that the purpose of literary study is to help pupils to see the point of what they read, and is *not* to fill them up with opinions or encourage them to flaunt such articles?

Anthologies

Finally, a suggestion for the study of anthologies by experienced teachers who are on good terms with their classes. The procedure is not recommended for beginners, nor for recalcitrant classes, nor for classes which have not already acquired the habit of hearing and discussing poetry freely. In favourable circumstances it is highly invigorating and it induces the sharing of literary experience to a marked degree.

Take items (i.e. the poems or excerpts or whatever they may be) in groups of about twenty at a time. Have the items read cursorily in private, then organise the pupils — or let them organise themselves — into teams or sub-committees of not more than four members. Numbers need not be uniform, and there is every reason for friends to work together, but remember that six seems to be the largest number of persons who can all participate in a free exchange of ideas. Each team should accept responsibility for two or three items. Since the class already has a rough notion of them, from its preliminary reading, the items can be allocated by a kind of auction. The idea is that as far as possible teams should work on the items they like best. Occasionally it proves impossible to sell an item, and when that happens you can take responsibility for it yourself, thereby showing that you are really sharing the study with your pupils.

Another possibility, which sounds attractive although I have not tried it myself, is to make oneself the nucleus of a group which on that account becomes willing to tackle a difficult item that it was previously afraid of. If you do that, you will, I think, have to accept the give-and-take of the group's deliberations, then change rôles so as to become the independent expert when other groups need your advice.

When the bidding is over, each team should find from among its members a spokesman and a reader for each item it has bought. Almost certainly the jobs will be shared around, because, in my experience, no team enjoys carrying passengers. However, there may be occasions when you feel it proper to put pressure on one or two self-effacing pupils to take their turn as spokesmen for their groups. Then give a few days and some class-time for the teams to work out an agreed reading and an agreed statement or exposition for each item. The discussion will be animated and may become heated, but there is no need for it to be noisy. Your task at this stage is to go round from group to group giving advice and references and cross-references when they are asked for. Try to avoid volunteering them; the young people must work out their own answers to their own questions, and have the opportunity to make mistakes. They will keep you busy.

Then at the agreed times the teams should present their agreed reading and report their agreed statements, and open question-times should follow. There will be misreadings and misunderstandings, and that is part of the purpose of the procedure, because the mistakes will be aired and will be cleared up in the ensuing discussions. Try to let the questions go on until they reach a natural end; let the participants talk themselves out.

At the end, in the rôle of expert, contribute any necessary technical information such as the conventions of the sonnet, or those of Anglo-Saxon riddling verses, or the operation of metrical or accentual devices. In the same rôle you can tactfully make good omissions and restore imbalances of interpretation. I do mean tactfully. A lot of hard bargaining goes on in the teams. The results of their deliberations should be treated with respect, even when they are wrong. Don't, in the early stages, just because you cannot bear to see a fine poem misunderstood, or because you think it is good for discipline for you always to have the last word — don't, I say, put your hobnailed foot in it by intruding and 'correcting' a team's agreed statement. The rest of the class, who will probably be wanting to take notes from it, will quickly enough spot that there is something wrong with the statement if the matter comes within their range of experience, and will ensure that the mistake is cleared up. If it does not, you, when your turn comes, can offer your contribution to the pool of ideas. Skilled committee-man, trained rhetorician, and accomplished barn-stormer that you are, and ostensibly giving an expert, professional opinion, you should be able to see that the 'right interpretation' gets its chance. If it fails to gain acceptance in the end, you can comfort yourself with the reflection that it would never have been accepted anyway, not even if you have given way to that last infirmity of ignoble minds, the duplication and handing out of a set of notes and a model answer.

As I remarked in passing, notes of the teams' statements and the amendments which follow can be taken by the class if required. If recapitulations or résumés are called for, let the spokesmen give them. It is good practice for them, and it is their statements which are being handled.

An advantage of the procedure I have outlined is that in the course of studying an anthology a wide variety of voices is heard. There is something to listen to. Perhaps the greatest advantage is that the pupils commit themselves to performance and interpretation of a text *before* the teacher imposes his, so that they genuinely learn by trial-and-error. It is also very difficult for anyone to avoid making an honest contribution to the deliberations of his team, and therefore to the class's pool of ideas, from which everyone draws freely in return. The small teams seem to generate their own interest, to develop a corporate confidence in their own judgement, and to try hard to engage everybody's interest in the items of their choice. It is all very exciting and, strange as this may seem, it is if anything rather quicker than ordinary formal instruction. If you think of it that way, you can process more poems per hour by this procedure than by standing there and dictating notes. It is perfectly satisfactory preparation for examinations. But above all it constitutes that sharing of experience which I take to be the object of the study of prescribed texts.

The library

8

Anthony Pike

How often do we see advertisements in *The Times Educational Supplement* for teachers of English with the extra incentive 'An interest in library work and organisation could well be an advantage'? One such advertisement continued 'New entrants are invited to apply'. It is rare that other subject teachers have this extra carrot dangled before them. So the English department and the school library seem inseparable; perhaps this is not too disastrous a marriage. But, as some schools are prepared to give this very taxing job to a beginner, some words on library organisation in general seem to be in order in a book on the teaching of English.

The Newsom Report stated that 'The Library ought to be the power-house of words and ideas' (Paragraph 469). The same report goes on to say that 'The Library, fully equipped and used, has much to offer'. The key words are those between the commas; how should a library be fully equipped and in what way can it be fully used? The word 'library' can cover any collection of books from specially designed rooms for seniors and juniors to a locked cupboard in a classroom. Some schools have class libraries only, which, although valuable adjuncts to the main library, can, at worst, be a collection of tattered volumes used to keep a class quiet on some occasion. In the course of this chapter it will be assumed that all libraries are properly housed and well equipped; any other must not be tolerated by teacher-librarians. To return to Newsom for a moment, only 26% of the schools in the survey had a proper, self-contained library.

When a new library is planned, the teacher-librarian should be consulted in detail about his needs so that the Authority will not spend money on providing facilities that are not needed. It is a great shame that this consultation rarely takes place. Apart from the obvious requirements of durability, that so often are allied to ugliness, the library should make the pupil feel that the room he is entering is rather different from the rest in the school. An insistence on talking quietly is an essential rule. This sense of occasion is lost in a poorly-adapted classroom, or in a library that has makeshift shelving and 'school' type cupboards. A minor point: although a well-stocked library looks impressive, it has no room for expansion.

Direction indication must be as helpful as possible, although, as stated later on, the pupils must know how to use a catalogue and look for books purposefully. It is likely that a school librarian will have to choose between the Cheltenham and Dewey classifications; more recent ones such as the Bliss are not likely to be considered yet. Although the Cheltenham system was devised for a school — hence its name — the Dewey Decimal Classification is used widely in this country. If this is employed, the standard headings 500 PURE SCIENCE and 600 APPLIED SCIENCE are of little help to a boy looking for a book on rabbits. He will be successful in 600, but what will lead him there? Shelf labels are necessary but are only useful if the destination is nigh. A surprising feature of pupils' lack of knowledge is that many do not know what 'fiction' means.

It is the catalogue that ensures efficiency; without it a library is just a collection of books. The three main types, listed in importance to the child, are the Subject, the Classified and the Author. The first lists all subjects in alphabetical order making full use of cross references. For example, an entry 'Hats' is likely to send the borrower to the section 'Costume — Hats', rather than list all the millinery section at that point. Detailed help on this catalogue can be found in Sear's *List of Subject Headings*. The Classified catalogue lists all the books in the order in which they appear on the shelves, and is extremely useful for stock-taking. It has value for the more sophisticated borrower. The Author catalogue is self-explanatory and has rather limited use, especially in the non-fiction section. The actual layout of the cards — typewritten not handwritten — should give information helpful to the pupil and not be an academic exercise for the librarian. All the card needs is the classification number, accession number, author, title — with perhaps a little information about the scope of the book.

Classification
821
ELIOT, Thomas Stearns

SELECTED POEMS

A selection by the author
269 ← Accession number

The other details that would be necessary for re-ordering, such as publisher and price, can go into the librarian's detailed stock-book, the

accession register. This, too, is more conveniently kept as a card index
than the usual leather-bound Dickensian ledger.

Proud librarians may dream that their ideal library is one where
books are never removed from the room. This is a museum, not a
library, a display, not a living entity. Books will and must be borrowed,
so a simple borrowing system must be devised, especially one that can
run efficiently without expert supervision. Most public libraries issue
borrowing tickets and it may seem the best way to train the children to
use these. There are some difficulties, apart from the cost. Tickets can
easily be lost, become dog-eared in the course of a few days, be given
to or taken by other children, although these drawbacks can be avoided
by keeping the tickets always in the library. The two main advantages
are the ease of locating borrowers and the prevention of stock-piling;
the child can borrow only the same number of books as he has tickets.

The other alternatives are borrowing slips or borrowing cards. The
former consists of a form with one or two interleaved carbons and has
to be filled in in detail by the borrower. Three separate sheets are then
available for filing under Author, Borrower and Return Dates.

AUTHOR	DATE BORROWED
TITLE	RETURN DATE
BORROWER	FORM

The cost is quite high and many pupils are not very skilled at filling in
the slips correctly. Borrowing cards do require some preparation before
the book is placed on the shelf, but will result in a smoother borrowing
system. Each book has a cardboard slip with the relevant details placed
in the front. There is a space underneath for the child to write his name
and form (see diagram overleaf). The card is then placed in a suitable
receptacle for filling by the library assistants. A reminder, popular with
most pupils, is the provision of a self-inking stamp so that the return
date can be put on a label in the book.

I have not dealt with the borrowing book system as this is clumsy
and inefficient, although it is adequate for a small collection. A librarian
must be prepared to lose books without trace, or find some that go
missing for a long time. It is perhaps cold comfort to say that this does
mean that the books have proved to be popular.

DURRELL, Gerald		
The Overloaded Ark		
Date	Borrower	Form

The gadgetry of the library will fascinate and can bankrupt the unwary librarian. From the many delights of the catalogue from such firms as Libraco, Librex and Don Gresswell the essentials are protective backing, stationery for the filing and borrowing system, scissors, glue, rubber stamps, book labels, Sellotape with its all-important dispenser, display equipment and an embossing-tape machine. All details of the suppliers can be found in Chapter 9 on 'Hardware'.

There are many sound books on the organisation of the school library, and some have been listed in the bibliography, but the best teacher is experience. Firstly, the teacher will need a manual of whatever classification system he intends to adopt. It is likely that he will adapt whatever guide he chooses for his own use.

The best way to keep in touch with the school library world is to be a member of the School Library Association, Premier House, Southampton Row, London, W.C.1. This body publishes a quarterly magazine, *School Librarian*, and, in conjunction with the Library Association, is responsible for the organisation of the examination for the Certificate for Teacher Librarians. This examination has been criticised as being too remote from school life, and, to be mercenary, it makes no difference to a teacher's salary. But meeting other teacher-librarians on any course organised as a preparation for this test is invaluable. 'How would you use the school library and all its facilities to encourage reluctant readers?' and 'What is the purpose of the catalogue?' are two recent examination questions. If a librarian could answer these from his own experience, as the examiners expect, he must have proved his worth.

There are also more intensive courses such as the one-year course at University College, London, that leads to a Certificate in Teacher-Librarianship. This course is approved by the Library Association.

If a book is followed from its arrival in school to its appearance on the shelf, some idea can be given of the work that a librarian and his assistants must do. Whatever system of classification has been adopted, it will have been moulded to fit the school. Simplicity is all important; it might be possible to place every book in a subdivision in a small library. To give an example, any school library will have books on railways. Having decided, from the Dewey classification whether it should be under 'Communications' (385) or 'Engineering' (625) is there to be any subdividing into 625.1 'Railroads' and 625.2 'Rolling Stock'? It is better to leave all 'Railway' books under 625. As with cataloguing, help for the pupils is more important than following librarian-like whims. As it is expected that this book is being read by teachers of English, some have been or will be faced with the apparently unclassifiable science book. A sympathetic science staff will work out a system to help their students find books easily.

The details of the book will be entered in the accession register and three identical catalogue cards typed. Some form of protective backing helps to keep books in good condition. The classification number should be under this backing as it can easily become detached even if done with the otherwise excellent embossing tape. The book will then have the necessary pocket, slip and return-date label stuck inside. A rubber stamp that indicates that a book belongs to the library and not to a department saves problems at stock-taking time. A new book should then be put on special display for a while and a list of new accessions placed in the staff-room.

All this, with the addition of the daily filing, will take up a great deal of the teacher-librarian's time, especially if he is more teacher than librarian. Yet another plea for ancillary help is not out of place. If libraries are to be the 'power-house' mentioned earlier, there must be an adult present full-time to administer and advise. But even having a full-time librarian with clerical assistance, help from the pupils is necessary and desirable. Usually there will be no shortage of volunteers for this. In a single library in a secondary school, lunch-time supervision can be provided by the older children whilst the younger ones perform simpler tasks. It is better if the juniors can have their own library and run it themselves under the supervision of a member of staff. They can usually cope with the care of the stock and the borrowing system, and will be ready to prepare special displays to tempt readers. The older pupils, especially in a senior library, can deal with most problems. It is a very useful training ground for anyone wanting to enter the library service. Efficient running will be ensured by giving the children sections to look after and set tasks to perform. If a library does not run smoothly without teacher interference, it is the fault of the organiser, not the pupils.

The choice of suitable stock is a wide topic and will be dealt with but generally here. One piece of advice is specific; the library is for the school, not for the English department. Help from various heads of departments for book recommendations must be sought, and advice followed, but it is sometimes politic to check that the teacher concerned has actually seen the book he mentions. Careless buying is a great danger, and, with the pitiful grants that most librarians have, can be disastrous. The publishers produce elaborate catalogues and send representatives, but they are unwilling to supply inspection copies of library books. Many local authorities have a permanent exhibition where books can be studied before requisitioning. In this way the thin, expensive volume can be avoided, and that particular disappointment, the glossy reprint full of out-of-date information.

Young readers seem to prefer fiction to non-fiction. The older ones may use the library more as an information source and not solely as a provider of imaginative reading. In this latter they are likely to be better served by their local library. At this point it is worth mentioning the ways in which the town or county library can help the school; they will provide special books direct to the school on loan, and, more important perhaps, will supply a good selection of frequently-changed fiction, or even a collection the librarian has chosen himself. It is no shame to make some concessions to popular taste in junior fiction; if the children come in for an over-popular book they may be persuaded to borrow another that is of greater worth.

In all sections a good supply of standard works should be kept. To keep up-to-date with the new books consult *The Times Literary Supplement* for the most recent and thorough reviews; those in the quarterlies directed at schools are often late in appearing. Frequent visits to bookshops also keep a librarian abreast of new publications. Is it unnecessary to say that a librarian must be a great reader and buyer of books? Most librarians are not permitted access to large amounts of cash so they will not be able to take advantage of book sales and second-hand bargains. Even if official policy frowns on the handing over of large sums, have a petty-cash fund, if possible. This can be fed by selling old books and magazines, or by bulk-buying of some periodicals that can be sold at a small profit.

Schools that have a junior and senior library will meet the problem of the child who is too old to use the junior department but finds the books there more to his taste. The best way round this is to duplicate books that are known to prove popular with the less able in the senior section. The idea of marking books as suitable for sixth form or remedial is pernicious; books are for all to sample and evaluate, the children soon find if a volume is of any use or not.

The hardest-worked books will be the encyclopaedias and dictionaries. It is important to have as many of these as can be afforded. The number of younger children who will take a single volume and just sit and browse is high. One book that has proved, in my experience, to be very popular was the one-volume edition of the *Shorter Oxford Dictionary*. Whether it was the sheer size or the search for forbidden words that produced the large supporters' club was never clear.

As many newspapers and periodicals as can be afforded must be provided, it is helpful to find out from the children what they would like to see and work on from that. A co-operative staff will be willing to give the library back numbers of magazines and so save the school expense and clear spaces in littered homes. There is considerable debate on which newspapers should be available; should it just be *The Times* and the *Guardian* or should there be space for the *Daily Mirror* as well? That is left for the librarian to resolve, but remember, most will have the *Daily Mirror* and the *Daily Express* at home anyway. Most hobbies have their own publication, but it is often found that the girls are not too well served. Lists are provided by the School Library Association, but a visit to a large library will enable a keen librarian to find possible titles. It is worth making sure that full advantage is taken of the free magazines offered by industry; they can be very impressive. As mentioned earlier, old copies can be sold, but many will find their way into the hands of children preparing folders on various topics. It is worth mentioning here the necessity of special magazine covers. Although expensive, they do protect the copies.

The library, an important station on the head's tour of the school, can be the centre of other activities. The librarian will be assumed by all to know about books — indeed it is to be hoped that he does — and so may find himself dealing with such matters as advising on books for prizes. One important rôle that he can play is that of archivist, the English teacher becoming historian for a while. In a library can be stored and displayed all items from papers and magazines dealing with the history of the school and the area. The library office, an essential room in the complex, could well be the press-cutting agency for the school. The gradual building up of a resource centre will test the librarian's power of discernment, but there is a golden rule: never refuse any gift, be it book, paper, photograph, poster, programme. There could easily be something of great worth among the chaff. Books offered may sometimes seem to be the sweepings of an attic, but inside there may be lurking some article that is valuable for the archivist. An interesting chapter on this appears in Michael Marland's *Towards the New Fifth* (Longman, 1969).

I have attempted to give some hints, drawn from experience, on how a librarian can set about his task. He must integrate the library into the life of the school as much as he can, but in this chapter we are concerned with its use by teachers of English. With the development of schools of 2,000 plus, the librarian may well find that he does little or no classroom teaching. This seems an attractive idea, producing smooth library organisation but will it help with its integration into the curriculum? The librarian will have a class once a week and so take some time to know the pupils. The full-time librarian will find it difficult to know what work each class is doing in English and may wish to branch off on his own. This is not such a good idea and, with a full-time librarian, the class's teacher of English should always be present too. Two teachers dealing with work and enquiries would be of great value. Teachers feel strongly that the librarian must be a teacher and not a professional librarian; time will give us the answer to this one.

On their first visit to the library the children will need some instruction on how the library is organised, and this would be given by the librarian, in the presence of the class's teacher of English. Therefore the first few lessons would deal with classification, cataloguing, the borrowing system, and how to look after a book. The instruction must be simple, and this is another good reason for starting the first and second years in a junior library. They must learn that all non-fiction books are classified numerically and are listed alphabetically in the Subject index. Knowledge can be consolidated by practical tests. After the groundwork has been laid, the library period can become freer. As an example of practical work, a boy could be asked what interests him. He replies, 'Trains'. Firstly, he looks in the Subject catalogue; it may say 'Trains, *see* Railways'. He then looks under 'Railways' and finds all the books on this topic are together. He notes the classification number, follows the shelf numbering until he reaches the correct section. With helpful signposting this could be easy. Described like this, the process may seem laborious, but it is necessary. How does the reader look for a book in a public library? Later tests could consist in seeing how quickly a pupil can find a book, or answer the vague question, 'I want a book about making things'. Looking for fiction in the Author catalogue is good practice in becoming accustomed to alphabetical order.

For those who are horrified at such things happening in a library lesson, and one that is called English as well, be content that this is only the beginning of the time in the library, and it need take up only a small part of each period.

The borrowing system must be explained in detail and children will be allowed to borrow books and return them in the lesson as well as at lunch-time and after school. A library must not be a 'useful' classroom for other subjects or even a sixth-form private-study room.

As all the instruction outlined above will not take up much time, what is to be the purpose and method in the library thereafter? At times, and with certain classes, 'Get a book and read' will work, but this seems a lazy approach, and, although the children will be quiet and appear to be working, they are not really well-occupied. With many classes the children will just not get a book and read. The librarian will want to encourage them and must help. This is another reason why it helps to have the class's teacher there too. A book trolley with books to tempt the class, or ones that have been mentioned in lesson time should be placed in strategic positions. A reading list can be given out at the start of the term, and the children be asked to write simple reviews on some of the books on the list and on any they have added from their own reading (see Chapter 6). Quite interesting lessons, with examples from a book or books could be given by the pupils. This does not have to be confined to fiction. The rabbit boy, mentioned earlier, could have some of the rabbit books with him and advise the others which he found most useful and why.

As it is likely that most classes will be working on a certain theme in their English lessons, work for the library period suggests itself. A reading list, relevant to this topic, will have been provided together with suggestions for research. The children will no doubt relish the chance to work without any other class being present.

A way to introduce a class to a book or an author or a type of novel is to read extracts to them; this is useful for classes of unwilling readers. It has, though, been found that some classes of intending leavers were entranced only by books on drugs and unmarried mothers. The more relaxed nature of the library, with, it is to be hoped, more comfortable seating than the usual classroom, is more conducive to interested listening. The danger is that all may want to borrow the book at once, so have reinforcements. This leads on to a consideration of the function of the classroom library that is dealt with in Chapter 6, 'Reading'.

In the future it does seem that the library is likely to be completely separate from any department and under the jurisdiction of a full-time librarian. Student teachers will be given the opportunity to specialise in librarianship in school, perhaps taking a special course after a few years' teaching.

The library will be a centre for more and more research by the children and will have special displays from all aspects of school life. It must be available during the evening as well as during the day and maintain a closer relationship with the public libraries. Finally, the library is not for the bookish and the academic; it is for all children.

Book list

Chambers, M. *Introduction to the Dewey Decimal Classification for British Schools* (2nd ed., S.L.A., 1968).
Darton, J. H. *Children's Books in England* (2nd ed., C.U.P., 1960).
Department of Education and Science. *The School Library* (Pamphlet 21) (rev. ed., 1967).
Fisher, M. *Intent on Reading* (2nd ed., Brockhampton, 1964).
Ford, B. *Young Writers, Young Readers* (Hutchinson, 1963).
Lancelyn Green, Roger. *Tellers of Tales* (Ward, 1969).
Marland, M. *Towards the New Fifth* (Longman, 1969).
School Library Association. *Modern Adult Fiction for School and College Libraries* (2nd ed., 1960).
  Periodicals (2nd ed., 1961).
  Eleven to Fifteen. A basic book list of non-fiction for secondary school libraries (3rd ed., 1963).
  Cataloguing rules (3rd ed., 1966).
  Books of references suitable for school libraries (2nd ed., 1968).
Stott, C. A. *School Libraries. A short Manual* (2nd ed., S.L.A., 1966).
Trease, G. *Tales out of School* (2nd ed., Heinemann, 1964).

The Department of Education and Science produces a very useful pamphlet of recommended books and periodicals. It contains, also, information on certain children's bookshops.

Hardware and other teaching aids

9

Trevor Hesketh

Much of the information in the chapter has been culled from catalogues, trade representatives, exhibitions, literature and personal visits, while comparatively little is based on personal experience in schools, with the equipment mentioned, for it is not expected that any school will be fortunate enough to have (or to be lumbered with) more than a small proportion of the materials listed.

The fact that a firm or product is mentioned is not necessarily a recommendation from either ourselves or the A.M.A., and it is left to the individual teacher to seek further information and to compare products and prices. Representatives of firms are very willing to come to schools to demonstrate their products, and there is no obligation to purchase. Our only advice is that schools should purchase the best quality materials which they can afford.

Introduction

'Teachers will press for easier access to books, films, pictures, taped radio and T.V. programmes – for the right to spend money on their hire and purchase' – *Humanities and the Young School Leaver – an approach through English* (Schools Council, 1968).

It is becoming increasingly apparent that equipment, and other aids for the teacher, are as necessary for the teaching of English as for any other subject. In fact, audio-visual aids have long been an integral part of the teaching of sciences, certain of the humanities, music and modern languages, while English departments have suffered the indignity and inconvenience of sharing or borrowing such equipment and often of having to change rooms to do so. It is essential that the present-day English department has its own equipment in its own English teaching centre. Heads of departments should stress their needs to head teachers, architects and education committees. Second best should no longer be tolerated.

Teaching aids must, of necessity, be subservient to the teacher; they do not replace the teacher. Our system of education demands personal rather than impersonal contact. The time *may* come when the teaching machine eliminates the trained teacher, who may be substituted by a technician, or indeed when education in the home via television reduces the time the pupil spends in school. We are, however, in this chapter, dealing with the immediate future and not with conjecture.

How do we define 'hardware' or 'teaching aids'? They are any equipment or materials, which help the pupil to gain experience leading to understanding, by bringing into use some or all of the senses. Some aids assist the pupil to develop his innate abilities by working at his own pace. Others act as stimuli to develop the pupil's interests, and to aid expression. The use of teaching aids makes the teacher's life harder; organisation and preparation are necessary, and well-designed storage space essential. The servicing of equipment, preferably every term, is to be recommended. In a large school, a technician in charge of audio-visual equipment is important, while peripatetic technicians could visit smaller schools.

The biggest problem with hardware is the cost. Much of the equipment to be suggested is very expensive, and the normal capitation allowance of an English department would purchase only small quantities of such aids. Many local authorities, realising their value, are making special allowances for teaching aids, in much the same way as furniture is purchased. Some new schools are being equipped from the outset. What about the less fortunate schools? It is up to the heads of such schools, in consultation with their heads of department, to decide what teaching aids would be of educational value, to what use they would be put, and whether the aids would give reward for the financial outlay.

Such equipment could be purchased from less official sources, such as parent-teachers' associations, school funds, from 'sponsored' walks or swims, dramatic productions and other fund-raising schemes. Some of the equipment, which would not be in constant use, could be shared with other departments or with adjacent schools. This is not ideal, but 'half a loaf is better than none'. In addition, many teachers' centres form pools of equipment, which may be available to schools in their areas.

Another idea, which would need the willing co-operation of science and handicrafts departments, would be to make one's own equipment from kits or parts purchased locally. If, in the English departments, we are going to present lively new approaches to our pupils, the purchase of some equipment is a basic essential.

Furniture, library equipment and display boards

The furnishing of an English department, whether it be one room or a
suite of rooms, is of primary importance. Much thought, of late, has
been given to the subject, and various ideas have been put forward.
Ideally the English complex should consist of rooms large enough
for class teaching, with easily movable furniture; smaller rooms for
group discussions, tutorials or seminars; space for dramatic activities;
reading rooms; the library; storage space; a small recording studio;
audio-visual aids rooms with a technician's room; an activities room and
an office for the head of department, and his secretary (see diagram).
Architects, concerned with designing new schools, should be urged to
study these recommendations.

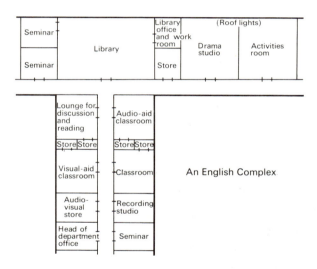

An English Complex

John Malone, who helped to design an English complex for a
Wiltshire comprehensive school, presses the need for a relaxed
atmosphere for both formal and informal work. Display space on the
walls is essential (not too much glass, please, architects!) and also
shelving for exhibits, sculpture, models and books. He suggests tables
and chairs, rather than desks — movable to permit groups of three or
four pupils, and also circular or crescent-shaped tables for larger groups.
Chairs should be lightweight stacking chairs, but a number of easy
chairs is essential for informal work and for reading.

Mr Malone insists on carpeted floors throughout (surely no more
expensive than thermo-plastic tiles) to deaden the sound and to create

the right atmosphere in the department. The carpets would also assist in recording work. He sums up the minimum basic equipment as: tape recorders, record players (mains and portable), overhead projector, film-strip projector, blackout and numerous power points.

Several firms deal in school furniture — Office Equipment Co. supplies suitable well-designed chairs, office desks and easy chairs. Morley's of Brixton have chairs, tables and cupboards, while Remploy Ltd will provide any item of furniture and offer advice to teachers.

The furnishing of a library is highly specialised and several firms deal with shelving, catalogue cabinets, magazine racks and librarians' desks. Remploy, Balmforth, Librex and Libraco are some of the firms which do this. For example, Remploy market the Lundia Fullspace Storage System, which incorporates mobile bookracks on tracks, enabling storage to be effected in a small space, and even a classroom/ school library to be a feasible project.

Prefabricated shelf units, in wood or metal, are sometimes more successful than built-in units, as the shelves are interchangeable from one unit to another. Shelf equipment, book supports, labelholders, etc. are obtainable from Librex, Libraco and Don Gresswell.

Blackboards and chalk are no longer *essential* in the classroom. The overhead projector (q.v.) has partly eliminated the need for these, but for those who still favour boards, the Q-board (by Tildawn) is the most sophisticated medium. Q-board is a clear glass-like board, on which one can write with a pencil or thicker instruments. An internal light-sandwich illuminates the writing, creating a focal point in the classroom. White, dark or coloured letters are possible.

Hellerman supplies framed White Writing Boards, with a scratch-proof surface. Writing is done by coloured felt water-markers, easily cleaned off with a damp cloth. Incidentally the white board could serve as a projection screen in an English room. E.S.A., however, supply Marker Boards in silver grey, to avoid the glare of the white. One can make one's own board, however, by covering a piece of hardboard with white Fablon or Contact, self-adhesive plastic (Arnold or Woolworth). In some schools, green boards with yellow markers have proved effective.

Other forms of board which fascinate pupils are Colorboards, Teazlegraphs and Magnetic boards (Arnold). Colorboards are white non-glare boards, which can be drawn on with wax crayons or water-based markers; Teazlegraphs may be used to fasten almost anything to a backcloth. Squares of material covered with tiny nylon hooks, are fastened to the objects to be displayed. The item will then adhere, for as long as required, to the Teazlegraph board or backcloth. Magnetic display boards enable plastic letters, signs and symbols to be fixed to a metal board, by tiny magnets (Arnold and Librex).

The Arnold Winged Lecture System is a cabinet, with opening doors, on a stand, enabling Colorboard, Magnetic board and Teazlegraph to be mounted in the same display.

Many firms supply static or mobile display stands, basically made of pegboard or wire. Wire fittings and plastic lettering may be inserted in the holes, forming useful and adaptable displays for books, objects and pupils' work (E.S.A., Librex, Don Gresswell, Invicta).

In addition to the main library, or, in less fortunate schools, in lieu of a library, mobile book trolleys are necessary. Several firms produce these including Galt, Hope and Arnold. Incidentally, other furniture may be necessary in a library including steps or Kik-steps (Librex); pamphlet and magazine boxes (Don Gresswell); filing cabinets for pictures and records (Office Equipment Co.); magazine display racks, preferably with perspex partitions to prevent magazine wilt (Librex); and gondola type displays suitable for landings or other shelving for storage (Versatile).

The Force Ten Mobile Resource Centre is a metal trolley which transports audio-visual equipment and has several built-in power sockets, but only one mains lead is necessary (Tarry's).

Purnell produces the Purpac holder in three sizes. It stores pictures in a flat and upright position and enables the pictures to be displayed without pinning them to the wall.

E. J. Arnold supplies a useful booth for tape recording or for teaching machines. They also provide screens and room-dividers.

Addresses

E. J. Arnold and Son Ltd, Butterley Street, Leeds 10.
Balmforth Engineering Ltd, Library Shelving Division, Luton, Beds.
    LU1 1TE.
The Educational Supply Association Ltd, School Materials Division,
    P.O. Box 22, Harlow, Essex.
James Galt and Co. Ltd, Brookfield Road, Cheadle, Cheshire.
Don Gresswell Ltd, Bridge House, Grange Park, London N.21.
Esmond Hellerman Ltd, Hellerman House, Windmill Lane, Sunbury-on-
    Thames, Middlesex, TW16 7EW.
Thomas Hope and Sankey Hudson Ltd, Ashton Mill, Chapeltown
    Street, Manchester M1 2NH.
Invicta Plastics Ltd, Educational Aids Division, Oadby, Leicester.
Libraco Ltd, Lombard Wall, Woolwich Road, Charlton, London S.E.7.

Librex Educational Co., Meadow Lane, London Road, Nottingham
NG2 3HS.
Morley's of Brixton Ltd, (Contracts Division), 472-488 Brixton Road,
London S.W.9.
Office Equipment Co., 363-373 St James's Road, London S.E.1.
Purnell Educational, 1-5 Portpool Lane, London E.C.1.
Remploy Ltd, Remploy House, 415 Edgware Road, Cricklewood,
London N.W.2.
Tarry's Electrical, 7 and 11 Greenwich High Road, London S.E.10.
Tildawn Electronics Ltd, The Square, Feckenham, Redditch,
Worcs.
Versatile Fittings (W.H.S.) Ltd, Bicester Road, Aylesbury, Bucks.

Stationery and writing implements

The English department should be supplied with large quantities of
stationery, to enable the work done to be as adaptable and versatile as
possible. Exercise books, of various thicknesses, with broad and narrow
rulings and also blank and ruled pages, should be stocked. Loose-leaf
files, despite the difficulties with tearing punch holes, are useful for
some work, but the workholder, a manilla folder, will take foolscap or
the metric sizes of paper, adequately. Tracing paper, card,
duplicating paper and blotting paper are essential too. In addition
coloured pencils, pencils, erasers, rulers, pencil sharpeners, drawing
pins, paper-clips, staplers and adhesives should be available.

The problem of writing instruments is one which becomes
increasingly difficult as new media appear on the market. The day of
the 'school pen' – with its wooden handle (and usually crossed nib) is
past. Today, because handwriting is so personal, the child is often
expected to provide his own writing implement, although some schools
issue them to individuals.

The fountain pen, with its variety of nibs – italic, fine, medium,
broad or left hand – has replaced the 'school pen'. The problem of
inkwells and gritty school ink is solved by the use of cartridges. Writing
with fountain pens is rather slow, but the handwriting shows character,
variety and sometimes copperplate neatness. There is no doubt that the
quality of a child's work is often reflected in the quality of his
handwriting, and so the use of a good instrument is to be encouraged.

However, one must keep abreast of the times, and, for note-making,
and general work, the ball-point pen has already proved its value, for
writing at speed. We are now faced with the fibre-, felt- or nylon-tipped
pen, which, because, up to now, it has tended to write too thickly, has
been frowned upon for handwriting. These pens can write very finely

or coarsely, and may be used for sketches, headings and for writing on other materials as well as on paper. Slow learners often show more control with a ball-point pen, but, for 'best' work the fountain pen is to be preferred. Perhaps there should be a departmental or even a school policy on writing implements.

Some firms specialise in pens for class use – Stephens make a very reasonably priced Inkline Fountain Pen; Platignum's School Cartridge Pen is available with twenty-four interchangeable nib units. Their school ball-points and fibre-tip penline writers are very well designed. Many local authorities supply stationery and writing equipment direct to schools, but the firms mentioned below offer a wide range of such supplies.

Addresses

E. J. Arnold and Son Ltd, Butterley Street, Leeds 10.
Esmond Hellerman Ltd, Hellerman House, Windmill Lane, Sunbury-on-Thames, Middlesex, TW16 7EW.
Thomas Hope and Sankey Hudson Ltd, Ashton Mill, Chapeltown Street, Manchester, M1 2NH.
Ofrex Limited, Ofrex House, Stephen Street, London W.1.
Philip and Tacey Ltd, 69-79 Fulham High Street, London S.W.6.
Platignum Schools Division, Six Hills Way, Stevenage, Herts.
The Stephen Group of Companies, Educational Division, Drayton Park, London N.5.
Thompson and Creighton (Ball Points), 202 Heaten Road, Newcastle-upon-Tyne, NE6 5JJ.

Visual kits

The kits are designed for use by the individual pupil, enabling him to work at his own pace and to progress to more difficult work as the occasion demands. Kits are valuable with slow learners as confidence is gained by success in basic skills, and the pupil feels that, in doing individual work, he has not been overlooked in the class. On the other hand, some kits are suitable for the more advanced student.

Science Research Associates Ltd, supply several series of kits. Their 'Reading Laboratory 1: Word Games (5 to 13 years)' and 'Reading Laboratory Series (12 to 18 years)' are cards, which help in developing basic reading skills. The former works through phonics, the latter develops reading habits, study techniques, comprehension and vocabulary. To strengthen independent reading skills, S.R.A. produce the 'Pilot Library Series (10-16 years)' – each library contains seventy-two books, abridged versions or complete short stories, spanning a number of reading ages. 'Reading for Understanding (9-18 years)' contains 400 lesson cards, providing pupils with practice material for comprehension; a placement test determines the pupil's starting level. For developing spelling and related word skills, the S.R.A. Spelling Work Power Laboratory Series and 'Vocabulab III' may prove useful, and for developing techniques of composition, the S.R.A. have an 'Organising and Reporting Skills Kit' and a 'Basic Composition Series'.

The Schools Council Programme in Linguistics and English Teaching, initiated by Nuffield, and then organised by Prof. Halliday at University College, London, has produced teaching 'units' called *Language in Use* for secondary school pupils (pub. Ed. Arnold).

E. J. Arnold supply individual comprehension cards — 'Harrison's Work Cards' and Platignum's 'First steps in Handwriting' help with pupils who find difficulty with control.

The natural development of card kits is to link them with tapes, film strips and slides. The Educational Supply Association has the 'Clifton Audio-Visual Reading Programme' (and, also, a 'Writing Programme' for children and adults with reading problems) comprising cards, tapes and work books. *Encyclopaedia Britannica* Avipaks, for younger secondary pupils, contain cards, slides, puppet plays and tape recordings to stimulate creative writing. 'Interplay', an audio-visual English scheme, by John Watts, is published by Longman.

Addresses

E. J. Arnold and Son Ltd, Butterley Street, Leeds 10.
Educational Supply Association Ltd, Pinnacles, Harlow, Essex.
Encyclopaedia Britannica International, Dorland House, 18-20 Regent
    Street, London S.W.1.
Longman Group Ltd, Longman House, Burnt Mill, Harlow, Essex.
Science Research Associates Ltd, Reading Road, Henley-on-Thames,
    Oxon, RG9 1EW.

Wall charts, diagrams and illustrations

It has been said, in the past, that English is a difficult subject to be illustrated by way of wall charts. However, nothing is further from the truth and an attractive room appeals to pupils, while colourful wall displays act as stimuli to written and oral work.

Several firms specialise in the production of wall charts. Pictorial Charts Educational Trust has charts illustrating 'The History of

Literature', 'The Changing Theatre', 'Analysing Advertising', 'The Newspaper' and 'Communication by Letter'. They also publish discussion charts, designed to promote a vigorous response from pupils. The charts are accompanied by teaching notes. *The Sunday Times* has published 'Shakespeare' charts, and Chatto and Windus produce 'Your England' by Inglis, and other charts.

Photographs, as a means of stimulating creative writing, may be purchased from Aerofilms Ltd; Platignum has some useful 'Handwriting' wall charts and the Educational Supply Association publish the Lee and Barron 'Phonetics' charts. 'Visigraph Aids to Reading' are charts to help the slow learner (Invicta), while Educational Productions supply wall charts, which would be useful for integrated studies. Embassies, oil firms and other industrial organisations are often very generous in their provision of wall charts, and other literature for schools, while National Savings posters sometimes include materials suitable for the English department.

Oxford University Press has a touring exhibition, which can be borrowed by schools, illustrating 'How a Book is Made'. More of such exhibitions would be welcome in schools.

Pupils' own works, of course, may form wall displays; prose, free-verse, good styles of handwriting being appropriate. Some teachers, however, find it invidious to display the work of one or two pupils, and prefer to show the work of an entire class. Other teachers encourage pupils to form their own wall displays, based on hobbies, visits or personal research. Card mounts make for an attractive display; rubber solution or dry-mounting with an iron or a press being useful for fixing the material.

To give a more professional finish to home-made wall charts, Letraset instant lettering will prove useful. These are dry transfers, consisting of letters, in a variety of styles, printed on plastic sheets. The transfer is effected by rubbing with a ball-point pen on to any smooth, dry surface. Spacing and layout are left to the individual, and the sheets are made in various sizes and colours of lettering. Incidentally, the Klemboy Automatic Paper Holder (Terstan) is a self-adhesive clip for diagrams, which may be stuck to a wall, or, in a more elaborate form, will slide along a plastic or metal rail fixed to a wall.

Addresses

Aerofilms Ltd, 4 Albemarle Street, London W.1.
Chatto and Windus, 40-2 William IV Street, London W.C.2.

Educational Supply Association Ltd, P.O. Box 22, Pinnacles, Harlow, Essex.
Invicta Plastics Ltd, Educational Aids Division, Oadby, Leicester.
Letraset Ltd, St George's House, 195-203 Waterloo Road, London S.E.1.
Oxford University Press, Education Department, Oxford.
Pictorial Charts Educational Trust, 181 Uxbridge Road, Hanwell, London W.7.
Platignum, School Division, Six Hills Way, Stevenage, Herts.
Terstan Agencies Ltd, 8-12 Broadwick Street, London W.1.

Duplicating, copying, and printing machines

Essential in an English department is some form of producing copy for a class, or indeed for the whole school. Perhaps the best-known method is by the printing ink duplicator method, where the stencil is cut, either on a typewriter, or by hand using a stylus. Gestetner, Roneo and Ofrex are some of the best-known makers. The Banda and Ofrex spirit duplicators require master-copies which are drawn, written, or typed upon, using coloured carbon papers. Several colour effects may be obtained by this method.

Copying machines are rather more versatile machines. Basically there are two types, heat copiers and photo copiers. The Bandaflex Thermocopying machine will do the following work: 'originals' into spirit master-copy, or into ink stencil, into overhead projector transparency or into black and white office copy. The Fordifax master maker (Ofrex) will make a similar selection of master-copies, including coloured overhead projector transparencies.

The Ofrex Fordicopier makes straightforward photo-copies, but requires chemicals and negative and positive papers. Hellerman have a number of Photoprint machines available and the Bandadevelop does similar work. Another type of machine is the Gakken stencil cutting machine (Fenn), which will reproduce half-tone photographs and line drawings to a high-quality standard. The production of copies for large numbers can be expensive, and, therefore, if copying from an original is necessary, it is cheaper to make a stencil or master-copy to be run off on a duplicating machine, rather than produce finished prints direct from the copying machine.

Typewriters are necessary in the English department. Apart from being useful to members of the English department staff, there is no harm in pupils typing out their projects and other work, thus practising the skills they may have learnt in commercial subjects. Typewriters may be purchased locally or from firms such as Hellerman, or indeed there are many dealers who advertise high discount on typewriter prices.

It is sometimes the duty of the English department to produce form or school magazines. The form magazine may be produced adequately on a duplicator or copying machine. However, the school magazine may be a more polished product, requiring the use of type, blocks and a printing machine. Many local printers will undertake the job of printing, but costs should be calculated beforehand, if the magazine is to sell at a reasonable price. F. S. Moore Ltd is one firm with experience in printing school magazines. For schools which prefer to print their own material, local newspapers and some University presses will supply photo blocks, while Adana Ltd produce type, blocks, accessories, ink and machines. Typesetting is a skilled job, but, with the aid of the teacher, pupils are quite capable of setting up for the magazine. A good knowledge of spelling and grammar is important in this work.

Addresses

Adana (Printing Machines) Ltd, 15-19 Church Street, Twickenham, Middlesex.
Banda, Block and Anderson Ltd, Banda House, Cambridge Grove, Hammersmith, London W.6.
Fenn Import Ltd, 35 Hartshill Road, Stoke-on-Trent, Staffs.
Gestetner Ltd, P.O. Box 23, Gestetner House, 210 Euston Road, London N.W.1.
Esmond Hellerman Ltd, Hellerman House, Windmill Lane, Sunbury-on-Thames, Middlesex, TW16 7EW.
F. S. Moore Ltd, 33-4 Chancery Lane, London W.C.2.
Ofrex Ltd, Fordigraph Division, Ofrex House, Stephen Street, London W.1.
Roneo Ltd, 17 Southampton Row, London W.C.1.

Overhead projectors and episcopes

Overhead projectors (see diagram) are being advertised widely by many manufacturers. Although fairly costly, this machine with its multiplicity of uses recommends itself to the English department, and indeed, the day may come when every classroom has one, as basic equipment.

The basis of the overhead projector is a glass platen, illuminated from beneath, covered by an acetate sheet or roll which may be written upon, and, through lenses, the image projected on to a screen. Usually the projector is placed in front of the teacher, and projected on to a wall or screen behind the teacher. The bright light makes an instant impact on the class; class contact is maintained as the teacher always

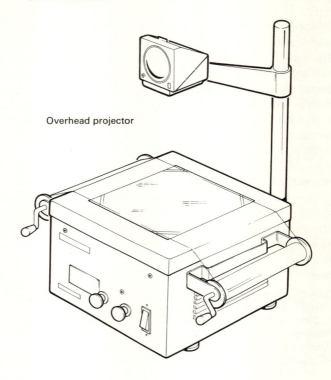

Overhead projector

faces the pupils; a clear picture is shown, even in full daylight, and the teacher is able to write on the platen in his normal handwriting using felt pen or water-based markers. The choice of models is wide and the only difference appears to be in price, light intensity, silence of cooling systems, length of lamp life and number of lamps, whether plastic or metal construction and the types of lenses.

As well as projections of the teacher's direct writing, transparencies, either commercially made or prepared in advance by the teacher, may illustrate the lessons. The original transparencies are then retained for future use or cleaned with a damp cloth. Firms offering overhead projectors include Fenn, Leitz, Modern Educational Aids, Hodgson, Ofrex, Bell and Howell, 3M, E. J. Arnold, and Elite.

The 3M Transparency maker is a machine, which makes overhead-projector transparencies from teachers' own drawings and illustrations. It uses an all-electric Infra-Red method, and may also be used as a copying machine. In connection with the making of transparencies,

Letraset Projectatype-instant lettering, rubbed down with a ball-point, makes for a professional touch, and Lumacolour Mechanical Pencils are useful for writing direct on to the acetate-sheet base. Of the many prepared transparencies, few are suitable for direct use in the English department, although 3M have a set on 'Phonics'.

Where the overhead projector has to be shared with other teachers, a trolley such as the Arnold's Overhead Projection Trolley is useful. Suitable screens for the projector include the 3M Traveller Wall Screen, and Arnold's Tiltmaster Wall Screen.

The I.T.M. Vu-Lyte Episcope is a rather cumbersome, but very effective machine, for the projection of pages from books, including large thick volumes, and of three dimensional objects and photographs. A black-out or Ektalite screen is necessary, but the colour projection is excellent and a movable arrow indicates points of interest, without the necessity of the teacher leaving the machine. Cooling is silent and effective.

Addresses

E. J. Arnold and Son Ltd, Butterley Street, Leeds 10.
Bell and Howell A-V Ltd, Alperton House, Bridgewater Road,
Wembley, Middlesex.
Elite Optics Ltd, 354 Caerphilly Road, Cardiff, CF4 4XJ.
Fenn Import Ltd, Fenn House, Glebe Street, Stoke-on-Trent, ST4 1HR.
Hodgson's Audio Visual Aids Division, Charles Street, Sheffield,
S1 1GT.
I.T.M. International Tutor Machines Ltd, Ashford Road, Ashford,
Middlesex.
E. Leitz (Instruments) Ltd, 30 Mortimer Street, London W.1.
Letraset Ltd, St George's House, 195-203 Waterloo Road, London
S.E.1.
Lumacolour, Education Dept, Royal Sovereign-Staedtler Ltd,
83 Copers Cope Road, Beckenham, Kent.
3M, Minnesota, Mining and Manufacturing Co. Ltd, 3M House, Wigmore
Street, London W.1.
Modern Educational Aids Ltd, 43-5 Queens Road, Bristol, BS8 1QQ.
Ofrex Ltd, Fordigraph Education Aids Division, Ofrex House, Stephen
Street, London W.1.

Radio, radiovision, television and video-tape recording

The B.B.C. presents excellent radio broadcasts to schools, while the I.T.A. and B.B.C. provide first-class services of television programmes for schools. Many of the programmes are designed specifically for

English teaching, specialising in creative writing, drama or poetry; while others are useful in the wider sense of English teaching, such as careers programmes and integrated or liberal studies.

The School Broadcasting Council for the United Kingdom guides and sponsors the B.B.C. school broadcasting service. There are various programme committees, the members of which are head teachers and other educationalists. There is in London a headquarters staff, and education officers in different parts of the country, whose duties include visits to schools to study their needs, and to invite comments from teachers. Similarly, the Independent Television Authority Education Advisory Council is in overall charge of I.T.A. television programmes for schools, aided by the Schools Committee and advisory councils for each producing company, to whom teachers' reports are always welcome. In addition the I.T.A. has a Schoolteacher Fellowship Scheme, whereby teachers are seconded for one term, to study some aspect of educational television, at a university department of education or under a similar educational body. Details may be obtained from the Education Office of I.T.A.

Written and oral criticisms of television programmes could form a useful part of the work of the English department.

Radio

This is an aid in which the stimulus is created through the aural senses, leading perhaps to further application through reading, writing and speaking. Lacking the visual, except in pamphlet form or wall chart, it has been suggested that school radio programmes are outmoded. However, many schools use the programmes provided with great success and the B.B.C. continues its policy of presenting many broadcasts through this medium. Their future plans indicate continued use of schools' radio. For example, in the near future (initially in 1973), all schools' radio programmes will be broadcast on V.H.F. only, giving a higher quality of reproduction, particularly of music. Thus, schools contemplating the purchase of new radios, should ensure that V.H.F. models are selected, or, if the school has an existing 'master' radio, a V.H.F. tuning unit will be required for conversion. The idea of a 'master' radio, with wiring to speakers in each classroom is a feature of many schools, although this means that the same programme is available to all classes, no alternative being possible.

The mains receiver, or more simply the battery transistor receiver, proves more successful in classroom use. Some schools allow children to bring their own personal receivers to make the audition more intimate.

ʹThe 'master' radio may serve other useful purposes in the English department, apart from receiving B.B.C. broadcasts. Tape recorders may be connected to record programmes, and through microphone attachments, announcements may be made to classrooms. Some schools broadcast their own local news bulletins and music programmes during breaks and at lunchtimes, whilst the problems of accommodating large numbers in one room, for the system of team teaching, can be partially solved by internal broadcasts.

Local radio stations, which have been and are being set up throughout the country, often have their own education officers, and special programmes can be arranged and broadcast to schools in the area; for example a talk by a well-known personality. With the development of this medium, teachers and pupils will become involved in the preparation of local programmes.

One of the problems of using radio broadcasts is being able to listen at an allotted time. Experience shows that, in some schools, programmes cut into two lessons or the programmes are not suited to the class being taught. This is partially solved by programmes being repeated, but a better solution is to tape record the required programmes, to be used as and when the teacher wishes. The B.B.C. offers various copyright concessions to permit the tape recording of schools programmes, the principal conditions being that the recordings are to be used for instructional purposes only in the premises where they are made, and that the recordings be destroyed within twelve months of their being made. It is possible to purchase schools radio broadcasts on tape from Stagesound Ltd, thus eliminating the chore of taping one's own. B.B.C. Radio Enterprises sell 12-inch L.P. records, including poetry and Drama Workshop broadcasts. At Leeds Teachers' Centre, a monitoring service tape records schools broadcasts. The facility might well be extended to other teachers' centres.

Excellent pamphlets are supplied by the B.B.C. for use by teachers and pupils in connection with schools radio programmes. However, these have to be ordered in the summer term previous to the school year of broadcasting, often before the headmaster has been able to plan the timetable for the following year. It is often a problem to timetable lessons to coincide with broadcasts, although the increasing use of computers for timetabling should help to ease the burden. No doubt the B.B.C. has good reasons for the early orders, but the purchase of pamphlets, particularly if they are not going to be used, can be expensive and wasteful, so great care must be taken in their selection. The use of the tape-recorded broadcast sometimes reduces the number of pamphlets required.

Radio programmes should not be used without preparation and teachers' pamphlets help the teacher to share authority with unseen producers and writers from outside. In the pamphlets, the producers inform the teacher of the content of programmes, preparation required, linking activities, suggested books, tape-recording suggestions and future plans. The pupils' pamphlets, often regarded as essential, illustrate and clarify the broadcasts, adding questions, suggesting future work and giving background information.

Radiovision

This is perhaps one of the finest extensions of the B.B.C. schools radio, as it links the aural with the visual under circumstances entirely in control of the teacher. The basis is a radio broadcast for schools to tape record themselves, providing a commentary for use with a pre-purchased 35mm film-strip. The vividly coloured pictures in a darkened room heighten the experience for the pupils, while the teacher, operating the tape recorder and film-strip projector at the front of the class, has full control.

Radiovision programmes include drama, music, actuality, sound effects and talk. The teacher can prepare the lessons, having seen the strips in advance. The programmes may be used over and over again, continuously or with stop and start, providing they are destroyed, under the special copyright concessions, after three years. The teachers' notes are useful as they show the printed script opposite the numbered picture frames. The film-strips should be ordered from B.B.C. Publications; they may also be viewed at the National Audio-Visual Aids Centre.

Television

This is a device for broadcasting in sound and vision to a vast audience using pictures which usually move. It gives a feeling of confidence and a sense of security to pupils, because it uses a medium which is familiar in the home. Both I.T.A. and B.B.C. provide excellent schools programmes, many of which are useful for the teaching of English, although some non-educational programmes such as sport, travel or drama act as stimuli for discussion or for written work. Television turns ideas into reality, using film extracts, still pictures, charts, models and people. The television camera can concentrate on important detail and magnify it to screen size. The teacher on television is seen in close up − often having a partially hypnotic effect on a class, but a strong personality is required to hold the attention for long periods. However, the presence of the class teacher is necessary as the television teacher cannot see the reaction of the audience, neither can he answer questions or comments.

Both I.T.A. and B.B.C. have commenced to show programmes in colour but producers realise that black and white pictures will be used in many schools, for several years to come, owing to the high cost of colour receivers.

Teachers' and pupils' pamphlets, similar to those mentioned in the radio section (pp. 152-4), are published by both television authorities, again to be ordered well in advance. *I.T.V. Education News* is a stimulating newspaper-magazine drawing the attention of teachers to various aspects of I.T.V. school and adult education broadcasts.

Wall charts are also available for some programmes. Reports from teachers on programmes are always welcome and advisers will visit schools and teachers' centres to discuss programmes and future plans. The selection, by teachers, of useful television programmes is aided greatly by the 'Out of School' programmes shown during the holidays. One wonders if similar programmes could be devised for children's viewing − holiday education programmes.

As with radio, the problem arises of timetabling T.V. programmes − the producers assist by repeating programmes during the week, and twice during the half-term periods. I.T.A. and B.B.C. co-operate in trying to avoid showing programmes for similar age-groups at the same time. One other problem, still unsolved, is the brevity of the school terms on television − most schools have several blank weeks at the beginning and end of each term. The answer to many of these problems is the video-tape recorder, which, after being used for recording T.V. programmes, may then be used to transmit programmes at an appropriate time, such programmes having been vetted by the teacher. Alternatively, some schools television programmes are available for sale or hire through B.B.C. T.V. Enterprises. Television programmes are most useful when providing background material, e.g. application of ideas in everyday life.

There are many television sets useful for schools, but the Radio Rentals and D.E.R. 24-inch Schools Television receiver receives 405/625 monochrome programmes from the off-air channels; takes local closed-circuit programmes e.g. I.L.E.A. 'piped' programmes; will record programmes through video-tape recorders; and act as a video monitor as well. It has a strong wooden case, lockable doors, a hood for daylight viewing and a metal stand with castors.

Video-tape recording

As the tape recorder is used for recording sound, so the video-tape recorder is used to record vision and sound direct from a television receiver, or a closed-circuit camera system. The equipment is, at present, rather expensive, but the Shibaden (General Video System) and Sony (Hodgson) seem adequate for school use. It is legal to record education programmes for further use by schools, under an agreement by which an annual fee is paid by the local education authority.

A recent development by Decca and Telefunken is the video disc, which can be played repeatedly on a special video record player, plugged into and producing sound and pictures through, a normal television receiver. Black and white discs have been perfected and experiment is still going on with colour. It has been stated already that the earliest use of this medium will be for educational programmes.

Closed-circuit television

Some fortunate schools are equipped or wired for closed-circuit television, which may take the form of a school circuit or a local area circuit. The equipment, used initially in industry and for medicine, consists of a control 'console' with a 'vision mixer', at which the director can select pictures from one or more cameras, films, slides or charts. The equipment need not be complicated. In schools, pupils are able to take an active part in the teaching process, by acting as camera crew, programme planners and direction assistants.

The programmes viewed may include class drama, talks, discussions, news items and, in the local field, people could be interviewed for a few minutes, who would not be prepared to give a full lecture. The I.L.E.A. already has its own 'piped' programmes, and it will be interesting to study further developments in this field.

Shibaden (General Video Systems) and Sony equipment seem suited to school use.

Addresses

B.B.C., 35 Marylebone High Street, London W1M 4AA.
B.B.C. Publications, London W1A 1AR.
B.B.C. Radio and Television Enterprises, Villiers House, Haven Green, Ealing, London W.5.

Education Officer, I.T.A., 70 Brompton Road, London S.W.3.
    Also Education Officers, Local T.V. Companies – see *T.V. Times* or
    I.T.V. Education News for addresses.
General Video Systems Ltd, 61-3 Watford Way, Hendon, London
    N.W.4.
Hodgson's Audio Visual Aids Division, Charles Street, Sheffield,
    S1 1GT.
National Audio Visual Aids Centre, 254-6 Belsize Road, London N.W.6.
Radio Rentals Contracts Ltd, Relay House, Percy Street, Swindon,
    Wilts.
The School Broadcasting Council for the U.K., The Langham, Portland
    Place, London W1A 1AA.
Sony Ltd, Ascot Road, Bedfont, Feltham, Middlesex.
Stagesound (London) Ltd, 11-22 King Street, London W.C.2.

Tape recording, record players, records, tapes, cassettes

This equipment is essential for the English department because so much
use can be made of the items, both actively and passively. One can
record and play back material written and spoken by pupils, teachers
and others; one can have tapes or cassettes or records of material,
prepared by the teacher, and recorded professionally, and one can
purchase pre-recorded material.

Tape recording

There are many makes of tape recorder on the market, and the choice
of machine is up to the individual; some run from the mains, others are
battery driven, some use tape spools, some cassettes, which in the near
future, may entirely supersede tape spools. Tape recording enables one
to record and erase, or record for posterity. When reheard, the
recordings bring back the original pleasures of the initial recording.
Microphone, record player or radio can be fed into the tape recorder,
providing a multiplicity of uses. In the classroom, tapes enable pupils to
hear their own voices; to create sound effects as background to poetry,
prose readings or drama; to study or correct speech defects and to
cultivate the 'interview' technique. A separate speaker is desirable, for
the normal 2 to 3-inch built-in speaker has a too limited frequency
range for pleasurable listening. Classroom drama may be recorded (see
Chapter 5) and a tape recorder is essential for music and sound effects
during school 'productions'. Some schools have links with other schools
at home or abroad and the 3-inch message tapes are useful for the
exchange of news and other recorded items.

Teachers should prepare themselves in the technique of tape recording, before facing a class. It is important to know the difference between two-track and four-track machines; the speeds of the tapes (speech is satisfactory on all speeds, but music only on the faster speeds); recording levels and magic eyes; which button to press and so on. Careful experiment in the classroom is essential, as many rooms have a resonance unsuitable for recording. A recording booth (E. J. Arnold), or a home-made booth using egg boxes, glued with rubber solution to hardboard, will form a simple base, but other situations for the microphone may include a convenient store room or library, where the echo will be deadened. Pupils, of course, play their parts — self-discipline is essential, as scraping chairs, extraneous voices and noises may ruin the recordings.

Cassette recorders

These have some advantages over the more cumbersome spool tape recorders — they are smaller, portable, some run off the mains, others are battery-powered and they need little technical knowledge. The cassette (see diagram) is a cartridge containing standard recording tape, working on a sealed-in spool-to-spool basis. There is no threading of tape — the cassette just slots into the machine. The tape does not stretch and it is dustproof. One problem with the cassette recorder is the lack of volume for play-back, but E. J. Arnold's Packette range is quite adequate for classroom use.

Cassette recorder

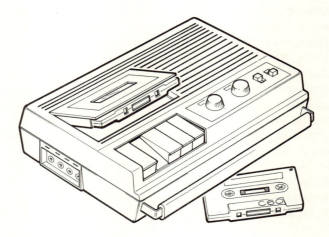

Portable battery cassette recorders are extremely useful for interviews, when pupils could do their own recordings. Philips and the Grundig E.N7 electronic notebook (Hodgson) are ideal for this work. Many schools have tape clubs, when more advanced work, including splicing and editing tapes, might be attempted, and pupils could build their own tape recorders and other audio equipment from Heathkit or similar.

Record players

A 'must' in every English department; there are so many makes available that it would be difficult to specify one particular model, but the Philips 3-speed battery-driven Record Reproducer would be useful in situations where power points were at a premium (Linguaphone Institute). If the volume of the record player were insufficient for the size of the rooms, extension speakers could be used (Heathkit or Hodgson).

Records

So far as the English department is concerned, poetry and drama are both enriched by the use of records. Poetry is better read aloud, and when the professional actor, or indeed the poet himself, gives his interpretation, often a new insight into the poem evolves. In drama, famous actors perform well-known rôles from the theatre and from the classics, assisting pupils in the appreciation of some of the more difficult passages. Music, of course, finds its place in the department as a background to drama, mime or movement, and suitable records should be kept in stock.

The largest and widest selection of records for English department use comes from Caedmon Records (John Murray Ltd). The Linguaphone Institute has several records including 'English through the Centuries'. Some modern short stories are recorded by Longman, E. J. Arnold supply poetry records, and the 'Argo Book of Recorded Verse' covers seven centuries of English poetry. Pergamon produces 'Birth, Marriage and Death', a thematic selection of poetry. Other firms producing records include E.M.I. Records, Macdonald and Evans, Spoken Arts, Jupiter Recordings, Daily Express, Faringdon Records and Guild Sound and Vision Ltd.

Pre-recorded tapes and cassettes

Several firms specialise in pre-recorded tapes suitable for use in the English department. 'Tape books for schools' (Student Recordings Ltd) are produced in close association with educational book publishers. Several tapes cover Spoken English, based on such books as *Speak for Yourself* by David and Audrey Price. English language is well catered for and there is an interesting series of English prose and poetry.

Topic Tapes (Sound and Visual Products) contain material relevant to the interests of adolescents, and form the bases of discussions, e.g.:

(1) personal problems — aspects of human relationships, morals, sex, parents;
(2) society as a whole — race relations, class, social groups;
(3) problems of behaviour — drugs and addiction, jobs, careers;
(4) current affairs;
(5) leisure and arts.

E. J. Arnold produces two interesting tapes 'On Speaking Terms' and 'Jennings at School', while Pergamon have 'Key Phonetics' by P. Sanderson — useful for the study of the language — and tapes based on themes such as 'Justice' and '13 to 16'.

Few pre-recorded cassettes suitable for English teaching have, as yet, been produced. No doubt many more will be produced, as this medium increases in popularity. The 3M company, however, produces 'The Art of Shakespeare' packs.

Perhaps the finest development is the Time, Life and Works series of Educational Audio Visual Ltd, in which records, tapes and filmstrips are combined in a similar way to the B.B.C. Radiovision (q.v.). At present, the series includes 'Chaucer', 'Shakespeare' and 'Poetry', and 'An Audio Visual History of English Literature'.

An excellent service is provided by the Carwal branch of Pergamon, which will provide recordings, tapes, film-strips and slides from teachers' own materials.

Addresses

Argo Record Co. Ltd, 113 Fulham Road, London S.W.3.
E. J. Arnold and Son Ltd, Butterley Street, Leeds 10.
Carwal Audio Visual Aids, 250 Woodcote Road, Wallington, Surrey.
Daily Express (Living Shakespeare), 26 Poppins Court, Fleet Street, London E.C.4.
Educational Audio Visual Ltd, 38 Warren Street, London W1P 5PD.
E.M.I. Records (Laureate Series), E.M.I. House, 20 Manchester Square, London W.1.
Faringdon Records, Greville Street, London E.C.4.
Guild Sound and Vision Ltd, Film Library, Kingston Road, London SW19 3NR.

Heathkit Division, Daystrom Ltd, Bristol Road, Gloucester.
Hodgson's Audio Visual Aids Division, Charles Street, Sheffield, S1 1GT.
Jupiter Recordings, 140 Kensington Church Street, London W.8.
The Linguaphone Institute Ltd, Ed. Department, Linguaphone House,
    207-9 Regent Street, London W.1.
Longman Group Ltd, Pinnacles, Harlow, Essex.
Macdonald and Evans (Educational Recordings) Ltd, 8 John Street,
    London W.C.1.
John Murray Ltd, Caedmon Records, 65 Clerkenwell Road, London
    E.C.1.
Pergamon Press Ltd, Headington Hill Hall, Oxford, OX3 0BW.
Sound and Visual Products Ltd, 16 Howe Street, Edinburgh.
Spoken Arts, School and College Services, 79 Mermin Square, Dublin 2.
Student Recordings Ltd, 15 Devon Square, Newton Abbot, Devon.

Film-strip projectors, slide projectors, film-strips, slides, micro films

This type of equipment provides a purely visual aid for the teacher or
pupil to add his own commentary. A film-strip is literally a strip of
35mm film, containing a different still picture in each frame, whereas a
slide is an individual 35mm frame, placed in glass or, more simply, in a
cardboard or plastic mount. It is possible to make one's own slides
from 35mm film, giving a more original and individual approach than
the commercially-produced strips and slides. Efficient presentation is
essential, as nothing disturbs a class more than watching the teacher
struggling with blackout, wrong type of plug, pictures upside down and
so on.

Film-strip projectors, slide projectors
These are produced as separate individual items, or combined in one
machine. A wide selection is available on the market, but the Rank-
Aldis combined strip and slide projector (Hodgson) has proved
successful in schools. Another interesting machine is the Orlux N24
low-voltage projector, which may be used from either the rear or the
front of the class, using different lenses. It has a quartz iodine lamp,
which affords cooler running and longer life (Modern Educational Aids).
A silent cooling system is important in a projector.

   The Leitz Pradovit Slide-only Projector provides sharp images, pure
colour, even illumination, lamp economy, cooling, remote control
(even from the front of the class), autofocus, automatic interval-timer,
single slide projection or magazine loading, a light pointer and facilities
for tape recorder-slide presentations.

   E. J. Arnold supplies one of the smallest strip-slide projectors, the
AV002, an almost pocket-sized machine, suitable for use with the

Arnold 'Teamscreen' – a daylight-viewing screen (see diagram), in which the projector is worked from the side, giving a clear picture, about the size of a television screen. Similar screens are available from Hodgson. Arnold's Prima Film-strip Projector is designed for rear projection. The Kodak Ektalite Projection Screen Model 2, as reviewed in September 1970 issue of *The A.M.A.* is an ideal curved screen, which eliminates the need for blackout.

Daylight-viewing screen

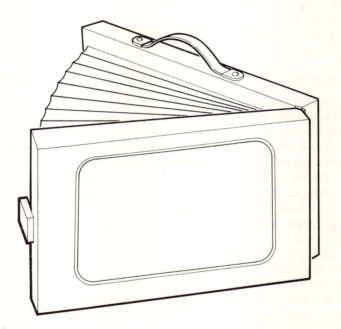

For large pictures, especially those in colour, a good blackout or Ektalite screen is required and a beaded screen, such as the Photax Tripod Screen (E. J. Arnold) gives a far better picture than those projected on the wall. For classroom use, however, one must appreciate that a beaded screen offers a narrow viewing angle to the class (owing to its 'directional' qualities, whereas a matt screen is 'non-directional' and can be viewed from a wider angle.

Film-strips
There are hundreds of different film-strips available. The film-strip projector was one of the first visual aids to be made in early post-war

years, and firms were quick to provide strips on many different subjects, together with excellent teachers' notes.

Interesting from the English viewpoint are 'Great Stories told in Pictures' – Hulton; Educational Productions' strips on 'Shakespeare', 'The Stage', 'Other Plays', 'Prose', 'Dante' and 'Blake'; Educational Audio Visual Ltd's records, tapes and film-strips on 'English Literature and American Literature', 'Shakespeare', 'Wordsworth', 'Chaucer' and 'Dickens'; the B.B.C. Radiovision programme (q.v.) and E. J. Arnold's strips on English literature. The excellent film-strips produced by Common Ground are available through the Educational Supply Association. Some of the strips are in colour, others in black and white; some may be half-frame and others whole-frame.

Slides

Few prepared slides are available, so here is a field for the creative teacher-photographer to prepare his own slides, or for the pupils to bring their own. As with strips, slides have the advantage that they can be shown repeatedly, with stop and start, back reference and so on. Oral work is much more interesting if a pupil is able to illustrate a talk with slides.

Commercially prepared slides suitable for English are available from E. J. Arnold, while the *Encyclopaedia Britannica* Avipaks include slides to stimulate the imagination for creative writing. Film-strips, of course, may be cut up and made into slides, mounted in plastic frames or cardboard, avoiding the problem of the strip being in a teaching order different from that desired by the teacher.

Microfilms and projectors

This is a new visual aid in which microfilm is used to photograph documents, illuminated manuscripts, parish registers, newspapers, technical journals and theses. The Psalms, Gospels and the works of Dante and Blake are filmed, but a special microfilm projector is necessary (Micro Methods).

Addresses

E. J. Arnold and Son Ltd, Butterley Street, Leeds 10.
Bell and Howell A-V Ltd, Alperton House, Bridgewater Road, Wembley, Middlesex.
Educational Audio Visual Ltd, 38 Warren Street, London W1P 5PD.
Educational Productions Ltd, East Ardsley, Wakefield, Yorkshire.
Educational Supply Association Ltd, P.O. Box 22, Pinnacles, Harlow, Essex.

Encyclopaedia Britannica International, Dorland House, 18-20 Regent
Street, London S.W.1.
Hodgson's Audio Visual Aids Division, Charles Street, Sheffield,
S1 1GT.
Hulton Educational Publications Ltd, 55 Saffron Hill, London E.C.1.
E. Leitz (Instruments) Ltd, 30 Mortimer Street, London W.1.
Micro Methods Ltd., East Ardsley, Wakefield, Yorkshire.
Modern Educational Aids Ltd, 43-5 Queens Road, Bristol, BS8 1QQ.

Film projectors, films, film loops

The moving picture has an attraction for pupils, and providing a film is
not too long, maintains their attention. Colour photography is still
reproduced at its best in cine-film and slides, rather than on television,
although of course, there are many good black-and-white films available
too. 16mm films are the best films available for schools, especially
sound films, although 8mm films are suitable for classroom use. Pupils
will sometimes bring their own 8mm films to show.

Bell and Howell make several 16mm filmosound projectors, suitable
for school use. A good blackout and a beaded screen or an Ektalite
screen are essential, together with a machine with quiet running
qualities, clear sound, efficient lighting and facilities for still and
animation.

The teacher must decide the purpose to be served by a particular
film. He has no control over the content of the film and so a follow-up
is essential – discussions, drama, story-telling, poetry, writing, reading
and model making are all possible outlets. Films can help the teacher by
showing practical skills, close-ups, speeded-up or slowed-down
movement, and visual description in either photographic, diagrammatic
or animated cartoon form.

There are many films available for hire, which were originally
produced for the commercial cinema – some of which have become
'screen classics'. The hire of such entertainment films for school use is
to be encouraged, but only after considering the high cost of hire and
the fact that the film may have been seen previously by pupils at the
cinema or on television. Films may be hired from the Rank Film
Library, the British Film Institute and from the Central Film Library.
As much advance notice as possible is required. 'Clips' from films may
be hired quite cheaply and may form the basis of creative writing, of
discussion, of analysis or of criticism.

Guild Sound and Vision Ltd, as well as having films for hire, loan
many industrially sponsored films free of charge to members. Many of
the films are useful for integrated studies and a careful perusal of their

catalogue will suggest a few stimulating films suitable for the English department. Early booking is again essential.

Two bodies assist teachers who use films: the British Film Institute offers corporate membership to schools and education authorities, and their education department provides pamphlets, courses, lectures and advice; the Society for Education in Film and Television aims to help create a discriminating attitude towards mass entertainment media.

Film loops

As in tape recording, the cassette has now come to the film projector. The film-loop cassette eliminates reels, sprockets, threading and rewinding. The films, which are sealed from dust, run for several minutes, and are spliced together in a continuous loop, ready for repeated use. Special film-loop projectors are necessary (see diagram) and these can be used for front or rear projection. An interesting projector is the 'T.H.D. 8mm cassette projector' (Guild Sound and Vision Ltd), and also the 'Technicolor' projector (Ofrex and E. J. Arnold). The I.C.E.M. projector (Macmillan) requires no blackout and, like the others, has a stop-frame device, while Bell and Howell have recently produced a new film-loop projector.

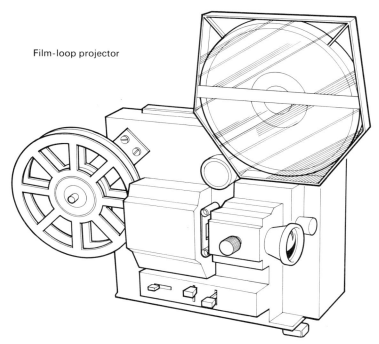

Film-loop projector

Guild Sound and Vision Ltd issue a film-loop catalogue, which includes a section on 'Human Relationships' — ideal for discussions. The loops do not moralise, but present situations in which teenagers might find themselves. 'Stagecraft' is another useful section. Macmillan supply 'Open-Ended Stories' for the stimulation of English composition. Each loop depicts an incomplete situation from which pupils are left to develop their own conclusions in written or oral form. Plot, character and motive may be discussed. Longman supply similar stories.

Addresses

E. J. Arnold and Son Ltd, Butterley Street, Leeds 10.
Bell and Howell A-V Ltd, Alperton House, Bridgewater Road, Wembley, Middlesex.
The British Film Institute, 81 Dean Street, London W.1.
The Central Film Library, Government Buildings, Bromyard Ave, Acton, London W.3.
Longman, Pinnacles, Harlow, Essex.
Macmillan and Co. Ltd, Educational Sales Dept, Houndmills, Basingstoke, Hants.
Ofrex Ltd, Fordigraph Division, Ofrex House, Stephen Street, London W.1.
Rank Film Library, 1 Aintree Road, Perivale, Middlesex.
Sound-Services Film Library, Wilton Crescent, Merton Park, London S.W.19.
Guild Sound and Vision Ltd, Kingston Road, London SW19 3NR.

Film-making

Classroom drama, movement, stage production, theatre in the round, tape-recorded drama and then film-making are natural developments in the teaching of drama. The equipment necessary for film-making includes cine cameras, films, 8mm projector (or 16mm), tape recorders and lighting equipment. The cameras and films should be selected preferably with advice from experts, and may be obtained from Gnome or a local photographic shop. A good tape recorder or battery cassette recorder, with suitable microphones (Grampian) is important and portable studio lighting, such as the Berkey (Hodgson) will be useful. Alternatively, video-tape recordings can be made instead of using cine cameras. Sony equipment (Hodgson) is excellent and projection can be made on to a suitable television screen.

Teachers must prepare themselves well in the technique of film-making preferably before purchasing equipment. The Society for Education in Film and Television publishes a booklet *Film making in*

School, and the National Audio-Visual Aids Centre runs courses in making 8mm films.

Addresses

Gnome Photographic Products Ltd, Gnome Corner, Caerphilly Road, Cardiff, CF4 4XJ.
Grampian Reproducers Ltd, Hanworth Trading Estate, Feltham, Middlesex.
Hodgson Audio Visual Aids Division, Charles Street, Sheffield, S1 1GT.
National Audio-Visual Aids Centre, 254-6 Belsize Road, London, N.W.6.
The Society for Education in Film and Television, 34 Second Ave., London E.17.

Cinema and theatre visits, peripatetic aids

Visits can be the most memorable experiences of school life, whether or not they are educationally successful. The commercial cinema sometimes presents films which have strong links with work in the English department; films of 'set books'; films based on books by the same authors as 'set books'; filmed classics and so forth. (My own school had the interesting experience of being used in the film *Kes*, based on the novel *Kestrel for a Knave*, by Barry Hines, a former colleague of mine. The culmination of this was a visit to the local cinema to see the finished product, followed by interesting written and oral criticisms of the children's own performances, and those of the teachers and the professional cast.) Some education authorities sponsor special showings of films in local cinemas, thus eliminating the financial burden of hiring films for showing in schools.

Theatre visits, similarly, bring realism to drama. It is good in these days for pupils to see a 'live' show, and to study acting methods, stage and costume design and voice production. Visits to Stratford-upon-Avon and London theatres may prove fruitful, but costly. The professional theatre in the provinces is by no means as dead as some critics would have it. Touring companies provide opportunities to see first class 'London-type' productions, but there are some excellent repertory theatres, e.g. Nottingham Playhouse, Exeter Northcott, Sheffield Crucible, Manchester Library Theatre and Birmingham Rep. to mention just a few. Smaller reps. put on good performances. The standard of rep. and the boldness of choice of play have risen considerably in the last decade. Many new theatres have been built since the war, and are worthy of visits, e.g. Chichester, Bolton, Coventry, Leeds and Guildford.

Many theatres arrange 'Theatre Days' when school parties can actually experience working with the professionals, e.g. 'Theatregoround' at Stratford-upon-Avon, 'Out Theatre' at Worcester, Bristol Old Vic and Oxford Playhouse.

School parties may be interested in the Regional Arts Association's transport subsidy for parties of ten or more visiting provincial theatres, when half the transport costs are paid. Details are usually available from the theatres.

Where pupils like to perform themselves, the National Youth Theatre is a pinnacle at which they should aim. One must not omit or decry good amateur productions and pupils should visit and, indeed, be encouraged to take part in local amateur productions. The South Yorkshire Theatre for Youth is an excellent example of a body which concerns itself with performances by young people. The existence of Theatre, in the future, depends on our present pupils and their interest in it.

Theatre, of course, can be brought to the schools. Several small professional companies tour schools and small halls, providing programmes suitable (and sometimes unsuitable) for pupils. Individual artistes visit schools giving talks, dramatic performances, mime, verse, puppetry, etc.

More recent developments have been visits by groups of professional actors, usually part of a local repertory company, to perform to and with children. Movement, mime and drama are performed and costumes are supplied for the pupils to 'dress up'. Vanguard Theatre of Sheffield is a good example, together with Brian Way and the London Children's Theatre Centre; the Northcott, Exeter; the Welsh National Theatre; and the Swan, Worcester.

Universities and colleges of education, particularly those which specialise in drama, e.g. Bretton Hall, near Wakefield, are often willing to co-operate with schools by performances in schools or in their home bases. In addition, several amateur 'Children's Theatre' groups pay regular visits to schools.

Some local authorities employ pianists, who, apart from assisting in the music departments, will improvise music for drama, movement and mime. Lectures by visiting novelists, poets and playwrights may prove interesting. These can be arranged locally, but there is a scheme, financed half by the local education authority and half by the Arts Council to enable such talks to be given in schools. D.E.S.

Administrative Memorandum 17/69 as amended in February 1971, includes a list of speakers.

Stage equipment and the school production

Facilities for a school production vary from school building to school building. Some schools have large halls, some even have theatres; others have to make do with classrooms divided by partitions, and some have to borrow halls or perform out of doors. Given the necessary space for production, the next consideration is the acting area. Is a stage provided? Has it a proscenium arch? Is there an apron? Is a portable stage necessary? Would rostrum blocks help? Is the production to be 'in the round'? Has the stage any fly space? What lighting and amplification are necessary? Is the law being broken, in any way, by the production?

To deal with the last question first — several regulations have to be obeyed. Firstly, the hall must be licensed for occasional stage plays (if a safety curtain is fitted, an annual play licence is usual), and for music, singing and dancing. Licences are issued by the local council. Royalties must be paid for each performance to the author of the script, unless the author is long since dead, payment being made usually through an agent named in the script. The local fire-chief must be informed in advance, and local regulations covering fire exits, width of aisles and fireproofing of scenery and props, must be obeyed. In addition, a royalty is paid to the Phonographic Performance Ltd, for the use of gramophone records during a performance and during the intervals. Finally the Performing Rights Society charges a fee for sheet music and scores used in a show but many local authorities already hold licences to cover this. It is as well, also, to see that adequate insurance coverage is made.

Where portable stage equipment is required, the woodwork department may prove helpful, but Byfleet produce a remarkably varied selection of equipment, rostra, steps, blocks, screens, and platforms. A study of their catalogue is extremely rewarding. Another useful material for portable stages, scene-building and storage (usually a problem in schools) is Dexion — life-size Meccano, which is quickly bolted together. A newer development than the standard Dexion is Speedframe, with tap-together components.

Stage lighting is best purchased or hired from the two principal dealers — Furse and Rank Strand. Both firms offer advice freely. Amplification, although still a dirty word with some stage directors, needs expert advice and both Grampian and Reslosound will give help. Records of sound effects may be borrowed from some public libraries, or may be purchased from E. J. Arnold, Stage-Sound Ltd, E.M.I. or the B.B.C. Costumes, properties and scenery are best made in school or hired locally. Brodie and Middleton supply materials for making and painting scenery, while the publication *Tabs* by Furse is a useful source of information.

Addresses

E. J. Arnold and Son Ltd, Butterley Street, Leeds 10.
B.B.C. Radio and Television Enterprises, Villiers House, Haven Green, Ealing, London W.5.
Brodie and Middleton Ltd, 79 Long Acre, London W.C.2.
Byfleet Furniture Ltd, York Road, Byfleet, Surrey.
Dexion Ltd, Dexion House, Empire Way, Wembley, Middlesex.
E.M.I. Records, E.M.I. House, 20 Manchester Square, London W.1.
W. J. Furse and Co. Ltd, 20 Traffic Street, Nottingham.
Grampian Reproducers Ltd, Hanworth Trading Estate, Feltham, Middlesex.
The Performing Rights Society, Copyright House, 33 Margaret Street, London W.1.
Phonographic Performance Ltd, Avon House, 356-66 Oxford Street, London W.1.
Rank Strand Electric Ltd, 29 King Street, Covent Garden, London W.C.2.
Reslosound Ltd, 24 Upper Brook Street, London W.1.
Stagesound (London) Ltd, 11-22 King Street, London W.C.2.

Intercom and language laboratories

It is extremely useful (in fact in the large comprehensive school it is essential) for the head of a school to be able to contact staff, without the time-wasting of a personal visit or of the loss of classtime by a pupil being sent with a message. Similarly, the head of an English department might wish to consult colleagues in his department. Intercom, or an internal telephone system provide the answer. With intercom, the voice is heard over a speaker, and this would also be a way of addressing a class; useful too, for team teaching. On the other hand the telephone system lends itself to more private conversation. Centrum supplies and advises on both systems. The Mini-Page is a radio-controlled system of intercom, where a miniature radio receiver is kept inside a pocket, and the wearer can be quickly and discreetly contacted (Shipton).

Where a school is fortunate enough to have a language laboratory (and we would not, at present, recommend the purchase of one for the

English department's sole use), there seems to be no reason why, at suitable times, the lab. should not be used for remedial work in English, or for reading skills, grammatical training or comprehension. Pupils sit at booths with a tape recorder (or teaching machine) and work at their own speeds, responding to work set on tape or on film. The teacher sits at a console, monitoring, offering advice and conversing with individuals or with the entire group. Details of language laboratories and their use may be obtained from Modern Educational Aids and Cybernetic.

Addresses

Centrum Electronics Ltd, Terminal House, Grosvenor Gardens, London
    S.W.1.
Cybernetic Developments Ltd, Chertsey Road, Byfleet, Surrey.
Modern Educational Aids Ltd, 43-5 Queens Road, Bristol, BS8 1QQ.
Shipton Group, Modern Telephones Ltd, Shipton Group House, Oval
    Road, London N.W.1.

Teaching machines

Are teaching machines expensive 'gimmicks', or do they actually motivate effective learning? There are many and varied teaching machines on the market, but they are essentially for individual work and so one machine for every pupil in a class is necessary.

    The simplest machines are those flat box-like ones designed for linear programming (see diagram), enabling the pupil to proceed from

Linear teaching machine

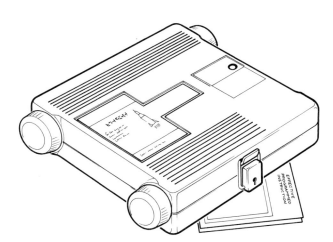

the known to the unknown, by a series of small graduated steps. At each step, the student gives a response and is then shown the correct answer. Flushed with success, the pupil proceeds, at his own pace, or within a specified time, to master new knowledge. The programmes may be purchased ready prepared, or in the form of blanks for the teacher to programme himself. The machines are virtually cheat-proof.

Fully-branching teaching machine.

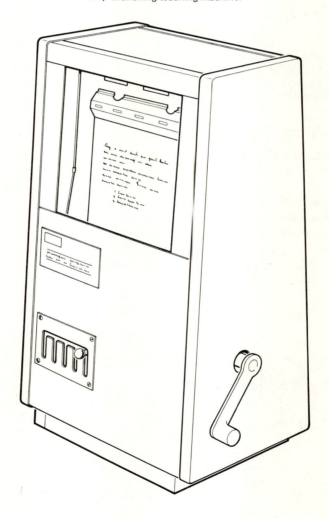

I.T.M.'s Grundymaster is one such machine and they produce a programme 'Spelling Difficulties', suitable for secondary schools. Taskmaster produce the Tutorpack Teaching Machine and programmes, while E. J. Arnold has the low-priced Bingley Tutor and the Airedale Programmes, which fit the machine, including 'What's in a Word', 'Sentence building' and 'General English'. They also provide a service for teachers to make their own programmes. The E.S.A. Esatutor Teaching Machine requires written answers and their programmes cover 'English skills' and 'Punctuation'.

A much more complex teaching aid is the 'television-cabinet'-type fully-branching teaching machine (see diagram opposite). In this type, alternative answers may be given; repetition, in case of errors, is necessary, remedial work is covered, and programmes may include printed, diagrammatic and other visual material.

The E.S.A. Canterbury Teaching Machine is one of the simplest of these machines, and the Grundytutor (I.T.M.), one of the more sophisticated, uses a 35mm back projector. Push buttons are used for the responses.

Other varieties of teaching machine are available. For example, the Bell and Howell Language Master System consists of a machine and special 'talking cards'. These cards carry visual information, words, illustrations and a two-track magnetic strip. One track is for the teacher to pre-record verbal information, and the other is for the child to record his response to what he sees and hears. Cards available include 'Reading Skills Development' and 'Word Study Kits'.

The Stillitron Teaching Aid uses conventionally printed and bound books; the pupil uses 'responding books', choosing from several possible responses. A green or red light indicates correctness or otherwise. 'English Basic Comprehension Tests' are available.

E. J. Arnold's Readmaster Reading Trainer is aimed at developing reading speed with a high level of comprehension. It is designed to increase the number of words and phrases read at a time, and to eliminate the habit of 'speaking the words', while reading. Arnold's Synchrofax Audio Page synchronizes the written and spoken word. The machine uses writing paper on which typing, handwriting, diagrams and photographs may be placed. The reverse side of the paper has a magnetic recording surface and teachers' instructions may be recorded on the Synchrofax recorder. The playback machine enables, by means of earphones, several pupils to hear the commentary, and to study the visual material at the same time.

We are not convinced that the results from using teaching machines will compensate for the financial outlay, and indeed for the storage problems. We think, however, that there is a strong case for using them with small groups of slow learners.

Addresses

E. J. Arnold and Son Ltd, Butterley Street, Leeds 10.
Bell and Howell A-V Ltd, Alperton House, Bridgewater Road, Wembley, Middlesex.
Educational Supply Association Ltd, School Materials Division, P.O. Box 22, Pinnacles, Harlow, Essex.
I.T.M. International Tutor Machines Ltd, Ashford Road, Ashford, Middlesex.
Stillitron, Stillit Books Ltd, 72 New Bond Street, London W.1.
Taskmaster Ltd, Clarendon Park, Leicester.

Library-book processing

In order to lengthen the lives of library books and to keep the covers in a clean state, a certain amount of processing is required, in addition to the formalities of Accession, Classification and Cataloguing.

In my school library, accessions are made in an Accessions register, the library book is stamped, twice only, with the school stamp, the Dewey classification number is stuck on the spine with Dymo tape (Dymo label-printer), the paper jacket edges are bound with coloured tapes and a polythene cover is put on.

Catalogue cards are typed, and any lending library papers are pasted in. Some schools are fortunate enough to receive books ready processed. There are many firms dealing with processing materials and charging equipment. Selection is up to the teacher's choice, but ancillary help in a school library would benefit teachers and pupils.

Addresses

E. J. Arnold and Son Ltd, Butterley Street, Leeds 10.
Don Gresswell Ltd, Bridge House, Grange Park, London N.21.
Esmond Hellerman Ltd, Hellerman House, Windmill Lane, Sunbury-on-Thames, Middlesex, TW16 7EW.
Thomas Hope and Sankey Hudson Ltd, Ashton Mills, Chapeltown Street, Manchester, M1 2NH.
Invicta Plastics Ltd, Oadby, Leicester.
Librex Educational Co., Meadow Lane, London Road, Nottingham, NG2 3HS.
M. D. Morrison Ltd, 34-6 Royal College Street, London N.W.1.
Ofrex Ltd, Fordigraph Division, Ofrex House, Stephen Street, London W.1.
Speedry Products Ltd, 83 Copers Cope Road, Beckenham, Kent.

Magazines, paperbacks and newspapers

The English department often has the responsibility of ordering daily newspapers, weekly and monthly magazines. Guidance will be offered in the selection, by other heads of departments, but the pupils' own wishes should not be ignored. Such newspapers and magazines are usually displayed, in the first instance, in the school library, but old copies may be dispersed to the appropriate school departments.

The selling of paperback books is often handled in the English department, although Scholastic Publications suggest the formation of Scoop Clubs, where the pupils deal with the ordering, dispensing and the formation of discussion groups (see Chapter 7).

Scholastic Publications and W. H. Smith also supply bulk orders of paperbacks on a sale or return basis, the profits made being either passed on to pupils or into the schools funds. Similarly, 'Books for Students' provide book exhibitions for schools, and the titles may be ordered in advance (see Chapter 6).

Teaching-aid newspapers, for classroom use, have made their appearance in recent years. They are small, but well-prepared and deal with topics which appeal to adolescents. *Everyweek*, suitable for ages ten to twelve years and the new *Now*, ages thirteen to fourteen are two of the publications of *Everyweek* Educational Press. *Project 70*, a magazine suitable for Liberal Studies, is published by *Encyclopaedia Britannica*, while the provocative *You* for fifteen- and sixteen-year-olds is published by the National Marriage Guidance Council.

Addresses

Books for Students, Godalming, Surrey.
Encyclopaedia Britannica International, Dorland House, 18-20 Regent Street, London S.W.1.
Everyweek Educational Press Ltd, High Street, Rickmansworth, Herts, WD3 1EU.
National Marriage Guidance Council, 58 Queen Anne Street, London W1M 0BT.
Scholastic Publications, Brookhampton Lane, Kineton, Warwickshire.

Useful addresses for teachers of English

(1) The National Committee for Audio-Visual Aids in Education, 33 Queen Anne Street, London W.1, incorporates several bodies, including E.F.V.A. and V.E.N.I.S.S.

E.F.V.A. – the Educational Foundation for Visual Aids supplies catalogues and literature on films, film-strips, slides, transparencies suitable for English teaching, cassettes, wall charts, tapes and records. It also issues a monthly magazine *Visual Education.*

V.E.N.I.S.S. – the Visual Education National Information Service for Schools, also provides information and catalogues on visual aids. *Ava*, a magazine, is published at 250 Woodcote Road, Wallington, Surrey.

Linked with the National Committee for Audio-Visual Aids in Education is the National Audio-Visual Aids Centre at 254-6 Belsize Road, London N.W.6. This is a show room, with every type of audio-visual aid displayed and for sale, including B.B.C. Radiovision strips. They also run courses for teachers, put on special displays and give training and technical advice.

The National Audio-Visual Aids Library is at Paxton Place, Gipsy Road, London S.E.27, and their catalogue contains films and film-strips suitable for teaching English language and literature.

(2) The National Association for the Teaching of English, 5 Imperial Road, Edgerton, Huddersfield, promotes a knowledge and appreciation of English language and literature and upholds the standard of English writing and speech. Publications are produced and lectures and conferences are held both nationally and locally.

(3) The Royal Society of Literature, 1 Hyde Park Gardens, London W.2, promotes lectures, poetry readings and discussions.

(4) The Poetry Society, 21 Earls Court Square, London S.W.5, encourages the writing of poetry and verse reading in schools. Auditions and examinations are held and there is a library.

(5) The Society for Italic Handwriting, c/o The City Literary Institute, Stukely Street, Drury Lane, London W.C.2.

(6) The School Library Association, Premier House, 150 Southampton Row, London W.C.1. Membership is open to individual school libraries or schools. There are local branches.

(7) The National Book League, 7 Albemarle Street, London W.1. Members are sent book lists, readers' guides and bibliographies. Touring exhibitions are available and there is an education department.

(8) The Children's Book Centre, 140 Kensington Church Street, London W.8, publishes criticisms of recent books for children in *Children's Book News.*

(9) National Operatic and Dramatic Society, 1 Crestfield Street, London W.C.1, permits the use of their library of plays and operatic scripts by affiliated schools and societies.

(10) The British Drama League, 9-10 Fitzroy Square, London W.1, runs summer schools on drama, and provides adjudicators for festivals and training courses.

(11) The Educational Puppetry Association, 23a Southampton Place, London W.C.1, supplies leaflets on puppetry, runs courses and has a lending library.

(12) The English Speaking Board (director Christabel Burniston), 32 Roe Lane, Southport, Lancs, develops teaching techniques, where speech is central to the learning situation; conducts a series of examinations in Spoken English, organises training courses and

conferences; publishes books and a journal, *Spoken English.*

(13) The Schools Council, 160 Great Portland Street, London W1N 6LL, whose publication *Dialogue* contains up-to-date information on the various projects in action, and also stimulating articles by leading educationists.

(14) The Society of Teachers of Speech and Drama, 82 St John's Road, Sevenoaks, Kent, which publishes the magazine *Speech and Drama.*

Book list

Abrahall, C. H. *Amateur Dramatics* (Collins, 1963).

Allen, J. *Going to the Theatre* (Dent, 1962).

Buchanan, A. and Reed, S. *Going to the Cinema* (rev. ed., Dent, 1957).

Burgess, C. V. *Discovering the Theatre* (U.L.P., 1960).

Chilver, P. *Staging a School Play* (Batsford, 1967).

Courtney, R. *The School Play* (Cassell, 1966).

Film making in School (S.E.F.T.).

Hamilton, P. *Amateur Stage Handbook* (Pitman, 1957).

Oughton, F. *Tape Recording and Hi-fi* (Collins, 1964).

Peters, K. *Your Book of Tape Recording* (Faber, 1966).

Schultz, M. J. *The Teacher and Overhead Projection* (Prentice-Hall, 1965).

Teaching Liberal Studies, ed. M. P. Jones and R. N. G. Warburton (Longman, 1967).

The Use of English (quarterly journal), ed. F. Whitehead (Chatto and Windus).

10 The internal assessment of English

Anthony Pike

The statistics of marking are frightening. The teacher looking back over the year's work in a pupil's English book will marvel at the time he has spent reading all that manuscript. Let him then multiply it by the number of children in the class and then the number of classes he teaches; the total of offerings that he has read and evaluated is in the thousands. It is a marking load that has been one of the greatest in the staff-room, one, moreover, that has not dealt with the reiteration of facts or practice in a new skill. It has been suggested that only a sample should be read and marked, but this is dishonouring the contract made with the child: the pupil writes and the teacher reads.

It was impossible to write the opening paragraph without using different parts of the verb 'to mark', with all the emotional overtones of 'to make unclean' and 'to scar'. 'Evaluate' is also unsatisfactory as it implies order of merit and some acknowledgement of a fixed standard that some can never hope to achieve. Yet the teacher will read well over a hundred pieces of written work every week and he must make some judgement: this is one of the things he was trained to do and in doing so he demonstrates one of his more important functions. This is to decide whether the work with which he is presented is the best that the child can do, and to give him some indication when he has or has not achieved the grade of which he, individually, is capable.

Perhaps to over-simplify, the marking of individual pieces of written work gives the teacher two tasks: the making of a value judgement and the correction of mistakes. The approach to correction is not as simple as it may appear to the colleague looking over your shoulder and pointing out the spelling mistake that you have missed. In a selective school, it should be possible to work from an absolute standard and correct quite severely anything that does not reach the norm. As time passes, the majority of teachers will be dealing with pupils covering the whole ability range, perhaps even in the same class, so it will be impossible to apply a rigid standard openly. To illustrate the difficulties, read this story written by a fourth-year boy. It is a definite improvement on his earlier work.

178

House wife and her nieghbours

One day A women was hanging her washing up and when she had done it the next doors boy had gone and frew some a mud balls all over her washing. And she came out and caught him red handed and gave him some fist. He went into the house crying and fetched his mother out and she said what

have you hit my John for cant you love him alone this his the second time this happened. And she hit her in the nose and made hit bleed and the other women hit

here back ana nocked
her filang to the floor.
and She got up and there
was a fight and the a
police man came along and
stoped it ana said who
started it ana the women
whith the washing said
her son started it by
throwing mud ball ate my
washing. So I hit
him and he went in
crying and fetched his
mother out and she hit
me so I hit her back ana
it started a fight. So
the police man said well
boy why dont you make freinds
and no more fighting And
he said Ill let you of this
time but next time I wont.

The immediate reaction might be to correct every mistake. If so, the opening would look like this:

<u>House wife and her neighbours</u>

One day a woman was hanging her washing up. ~~and~~ When she had done it, the next-door boy ~~had gone and~~ threw some ~~a~~ mud balls all over ~~her~~ washing *it*. And she came out and caught him red-handed and gave him some fist. He went into the house crying and fetched his mother out and she said,"What

Continue in this way and the boy will be unable to read anything constructive in your comments, with the likely result that he will be discouraged from making much effort next time. Yet we are bound to ask ourselves if the conversation should be set out correctly, if he should be able to spell 'it', 'stopped', and 'with'? Some time must surely be spent on these simpler mistakes, writing them neatly in the child's book. A lesson could be spent on the punctuation of conversation, but, as this is a skill that can defeat even the most able, is it necessary to belabour a technique that is certainly not going to be used by this particular pupil after he has left school? For the younger ones, simple remedial work-cards could be devised so that those who need the practice can be given one to work through. To help the pupil who is shaky on punctuation, he could be given some lines of conversation correctly set out, and then the continuation of the conversation with some marks missing. There is a danger that whatever skill is learnt in this way may not transfer to the next story that the child writes. To help with the spelling of the more obvious words, many, including David Holbrook in *English for Maturity*, have advocated lists to be learned by rote.

The purpose of correction is to help the pupil do better next time he puts pen to paper. This must be said loudly and clearly so that we can avoid a battlefield of red ink. The next stage is evaluation of the piece. If we return to the story of the woman and her neighbour, we see that the defects are obvious; we must look for the qualities so that we can give a fair grading, and, what is our immediate concern, a fair comment. It was better than his previous work, so we could write 'Better'. This is unhelpful, as the boy can only really be better if he has repeated an identical assignment, and shown in the second version a greater grasp of punctuation, vocabulary and spelling. While we can praise the economy of the writing, the vividness of the expression and the convincing dialogue, we cannot forget that this barely literate boy was due to leave school at the end of the next term. It is likely that the comment will be 'You have written an interesting story' and then the teacher can sit back with an uneasy feeling of hypocrisy, because it is not very interesting and could have been treated more competently by an able first-former. But this boy was not able, we are not going to emblazon this on his book, so we fall back on the comment that was put at the end of the story, 'You have tried really hard with this. Well done'.

To make this problem of fair comment and accurate grading a little more real, look at the extract from another fourth-year story. It was written by a girl in a large comprehensive school, so the experience of boarding-school life is Blyton + Brent-Dyer, not real. Clearly there is little to correct and the dialogue is generally accurately punctuated and fairly convincing, albeit derivative.

My younger sister had been looking forward to this day for months. She did not realize that she would soon be serving time at the school I had entered four years previous. My mother, Anne and myself were standing on the platform of the station waiting for the train to Little Hampton. Anne was very proud of herself in her new uniform, just as I had been four years before her.

    'You will look after Anne, won't you Jane?', said mother, an anxious ring to her voice.

    'Mmmme,' I said answering the same question for the fourth time that morning.

The train pulled in, and a voice said loud and clear
'The train now arriving on platform six is the eight thirty to Little Hampton.'
We climbed on the train and seated ourselves in one of the compartments. My mother carried Anne's largest case as it was too heavy for her.
'You've got everything haven't you?'
'Yes,' I said carmly. After all the times I had made this trip she always asked the same questions.
The whistle blew and my mother kissed us, and said she hoped Anne would like her new school. We leaned out of the window and waved to my mother as she stood and the platform, soon she was behind us and we sat down at the beginning of our journey.
Anne looked out of the window but I sat and thought. My mother had warned me that I hadn't to say anything that would worry Anne, but I knew even then before we reached the school she would know everything about it.

I expect most will agree that the second example is not a brilliant piece of writing for a fourteen-year-old, but it is clearly better than the first piece, so there is no problem of grading it in relation to the first. The clear 'highs' and 'lows' are not the cause of the difficulties in working out an order of merit; they occur in the central portion of the list, an area that may produce disagreements amongst colleagues when engaged in continuous assessment.

Although it is a question that most teachers would be reluctant to answer, as no clear guide can be given to the beginner, what do we look for when we sit, pen poised, over a child's book? We should have some idea about what we are expecting if our preparation has been carefully done. Therefore, what are our criteria for awarding a high or a low grade? We shall no doubt take into account spelling, punctuation, handwriting, relevance, imaginative power, but are we going to give each of our sub-headings a mark out of ten, or perhaps vary the loading so that we can present ourselves with a shattering mathematical formula that has then to be reduced to a manageable sum, or even a letter grade? In the Schools Council Bulletin No. 12, *Multiple Marking of English Compositions*, three broad criteria were evolved: 'involvement', 'organisation' and 'mechanical accuracy'. The usual response from a teacher of English when asked how he marks is 'general impression', but can this term help a beginner? It may be taking refuge behind a mask of authority to say that the teacher has specialised in English at college or university, or it has been his second love. If not, why is he teaching English? Assuming, then, we have a teacher who has demonstrated his sensitivity to language and has weighed the mind of a

Campbell against that of a Keats, surely he can make some judgement on the achievement of John Smith of 3J? So, firstly, ask yourself 'Did that interest me?', 'Did he bring some new light on to the topic?', 'Did I enjoy it?'. If the answer to all three is 'Yes', then that book should go to the top section of the pile. And so, by reading all the offerings, if possible at one sitting and not as an accompaniment to learned or not-so-learned discussion, some blocked order of merit can be found, possibly extending as far as five sections. This is no flippant remark about concentration; you are reading something seriously and you did make it plain that you wanted the pupil to give all his mind to the task in hand. There will be the child whose spelling is poor and expression awkward. Both these are a hindrance to your interest and enjoyment and so, whatever the quality of the imagination shown, a mis-spelt, clumsily-expressed piece cannot be given the same credit as one that does not show these defects. On the other hand, the carefully-written, neat piece of sterile imagination does not receive a firm 'Yes' either.

I am not suggesting that when we mark we should work out an order of merit each time. In time, it is sufficient to go through a pile of books and award a grade for each piece according to a particular standard. I know the problem of maintaining a fixed standard is not easy for the beginner. It is of little use for the old hands to say glibly that they can tell at once what grade an essay deserves. The usual fault of the young marker is that he is too severe; he would be well-advised to search for good points rather than express horror at the mistakes. An interesting example of the severity of the young marker can be shown in a school by giving a fifth or sixth form some work to mark that has been done by younger pupils. Such markers can be ruthless.

With the disappearance of narrow streaming from our schools, and the tendency to unstream altogether, the overall standard may be difficult to assess, and the grading that the child himself sees may be inaccurate, unhelpful or discouraging. In view of the practices outlined above, the teacher would be advised to keep a record that reflects the child's performance on an absolute scale, A to E or as a percentage, restricting himself to the much more difficult task of putting full comments on the books. Therefore, assuming that our two examples printed earlier appeared in the same group, one would clearly be A and the other E. But on the books these gradings would not be shown. The teacher is naturally going to be asked how a child is doing, and the only satisfactory solution is for the school to devise a system of grading that suits all departments, satisfies the parents and gives the pupils the necessary encouragement.

Lest anyone feels that the foregoing remarks indicate a slackness of approach or approval of mistakes, it is necessary to say that in trying to help the weaker ones and encourage them as much as possible, the able ones are not to be allowed to be careless. In their report on the 1968 examinations, the Joint Matriculation Board said:

The enjoyment of much of the candidates' work was seriously marred by a wretched inability to write a page or two of good English; not only were spelling and punctuation erratic, but words were misused, clichés abounded, sentences were formless and essays amorphous . . .

a sentiment that is repeated by other boards. If any feel that this is an exaggeration, let them look at notices on the staff-room notice-board or even at letters of application for the post of teacher of English. Can one remain unmoved when one such applicant stated that he had the degree of 'Batchelor of Education'? While admitting that we all make mistakes in our written work, it can surely be assumed that anything intended for perusal by a third party should be subject to rigorous checking beforehand.

It is to be hoped that the head of department will have arranged that consistency of standards is maintained in his department, if necessary by arranging trial assessments and discussing the results at a meeting. Continuous assessment cannot be conducted in a vacuum, and it does mean that the teacher's traditional privacy and independence are going to be affected. At the same time every year, possibly the early part of the summer term, the class's teacher should be able to arrange his children into five or six blocks according to their progress in English. Here it is necessary to make a plea for the careful keeping of records. As no value grade is to be placed in the child's book. a list must be kept. We are all too familiar with the change of teacher in mid-year, or, even worse, mid-term. The class has become used to him and he can estimate their achievement. The one who takes over has no time to come to the same conclusion before assessments are called for; how helpful it is to have the careful details that can be passed on. Is there perhaps a case here for the abolition of the mark-book and the introduction of record-cards? The teacher can give a sample of perhaps three books, chosen at random, to an independent assessor. An overall sample for the year, perhaps forty books from a ten-form entry school, will be graded on a single standard by this assessor. The results of his assessment would then be compared with the grades awarded by the class's teacher.

The assessor for each year could be an experienced member of the department, or the whole task could be taken on by the head of department alone. It can then provide him with an insight into what is going on in the lessons of his department, especially those who are non-specialists, without having to snoop in piles of books or invent excuses for calling in samples. In a large school, it might be advisable for one member of the department to take charge of one year's English and call the necessary meetings.

Many heads of English departments are quite satisfied that continuous assessment, with sufficient safeguards employed by experienced teachers, is sufficient to estimate a child's development and progress in English. They claim that an examination that confirms an assessment is unnecessary, and one that is the only acceptable guide is unfair. These statements are quite sound, and there are surely few teachers of any subject who would not subscribe to the second. But there is a case for a yearly examination in English, even though some of the reasons for holding it may not seem to be specifically 'English' ones. For the school it does provide an identical piece of work done under similar conditions, one piece of 'common core' work that is very useful in a large school. For the pupil, it does give him a foretaste of 'examination conditions', an atmosphere that has in the past spurred many on to greater efforts. The mark obtained would be on a single standard for the whole year, as the purpose in conducting the test is to establish a comparison. If any teachers feel that disappointment can arise from publishing the results these could remain unpublished, and the children told that the mark is part of their final grade, a statement that is, after all, quite true.

If the form of the examination is poor then the whole idea is ludicrous. Many of the past objections to tests have been directed against those worthless questions that appear to have been set for the ease of marking. Teachers wish to find how well their pupils understand and appreciate, and how well they can communicate, not whether they can:

Replace the italicized groups of words in each of seven of the following sentences with a verb corresponding to the whole of the original expression and ending in 'ate'. Use no verb twice and do not write out the sentences.

This would seem to be either a party game or training for doing *The Times* crossword puzzle. Most examining boards have discontinued using this type of question, so one need not be included in a school examination paper for 'practice'. Suitable questions that inspire worthwhile work under examination conditions are readily available. Many of the enlightened books, like *Encounters* and *Reflections* contain examples of a set piece that combines questions on the passage with an opportunity to write continuously on a similar theme. As the purpose of the examination is to compare achievement over the whole ability range, the questions will have to be devised so that all the pupils feel that they can have a go. So their school must decide exactly why it is having an English examination and then what is the best form it can take for all the pupils. As an example the following well-known passage from *Portrait of the Artist as a Young Man* could be used for a third or fourth year.

The door opened quietly and closed. A quick whisper ran through the class: the prefect of studies. There was an instant of dead silence and then the loud crack of a pandybat on the last desk. Stephen's heart leapt up in fear.
-Any boys want flogging here, Father Arnall? cried the prefect of studies. Any lazy idle loafers that want flogging in the class?
He came to the middle of the class and saw Fleming on his knees.
-Hoho! he cried. Who is this boy? Why is he on his knees? What is your name, boy?
-Fleming, sir.
-Hoho, Fleming! An idler of course. I can see it in your eye. Why is he on his knees, Father Arnall?
-He wrote a bad Latin theme, Father Arnall said, and he missed all the questions in grammar.
-Of course he did! cried the prefect of studies, of course he did! A born idler! I can see that in the corner of his eye.
He banged his pandybat down on the desk and cried:
-Up Fleming! Up, my boy!
Fleming stood up slowly.
-Hold out! cried the prefect of studies.
Fleming held out his hand. The pandybat came down on it with a loud smacking sound: one, two, three, four, five, six.
-Other hand!
The pandybat came down again in six loud quick smacks.
-Kneel down! cried the prefect of studies.
Fleming knelt down, squeezing his hands under his armpits, his face contorted with pain; but Stephen knew how hard his hands were because Fleming was always rubbing rosin into them. But perhaps he was in great pain for the noise of the pandybat was terrible. Stephen's heart was beating and fluttering.
-At your work, all of you! shouted the prefect of studies. We want no lazy idle loafers here, lazy idle little schemers. At your work I tell you. Father Dolan will be in to see you every day. Father Dolan will be in tomorrow.
He poked one of the boys in the side with his pandybat, saying:
-You, boy! When will Father Dolan be in again?
-Tomorrow, sir, said Tom Furlong's voice.
-Tomorrow and tomorrow and tomorrow, said the prefect of studies. Make up your minds for that. Every day Father Dolan. Write away.

You, boy, who are you?

   Stephen's heart jumped suddenly.

-Dedalus, sir.

-Why are you not writing like the others?

-I . . . my . . .

   He could not speak with fright.

-Why is he not writing, Father Arnall?

-He broke his glasses, said Father Arnall, and I exempted him from work.

-Broke? What is this I hear? What is this your name is! said the prefect of studies.

-Dedalus, sir.

-Out here, Dedalus. Lazy little schemer. I see schemer in your face. Where did you break your glasses?

   Stephen stumbled into the middle of the class, blinded by fear and haste.

-Where did you break your glasses? repeated the prefect of studies.

-The cinder-path, sir.

-Hoho! The cinder-path! cried the prefect of studies. I know that trick.

   Stephen lifted his eyes in wonder and saw for a moment Father Dolan's whitegrey not young face, his baldy whitegrey head with fluff at the sides of it, the steel rims of his spectacles and his nocoloured eyes looking through the glasses. Why did he say he knew that trick?

-Lazy idle little loafer! cried the prefect of studies. Broke my glasses! An old schoolboy trick! Out with your hand this moment!

   (x)   Stephen closed his eyes and held out in the air his trembling hand with the palm upwards. He felt the prefect of studies touch it for a moment at the fingers to straighten it and then the swish of the sleeve of the soutane as the pandybat was lifted to strike. A hot burning stinging tingling blow like the loud crack of a broken stick made his trembling hand crumple together like a leaf in the fire: and at the sound and the pain scalding tears were driven into his eyes. His whole body was shaking with fright, his arm was shaking and his crumpled burning livid hand shook like a loose leaf in the air. A cry sprang to his lips, a prayer to be let off. But though the tears scalded his eyes and his limbs trembled with pain and fright he held back the hot tears and the cry that scalded his throat.

-Other hand! shouted the prefect of studies.

   (y)   Stephen drew back his maimed and quivering right arm and held out his left hand. The soutane sleeve swished again as the pandybat was lifted and a loud crashing sound and a fierce maddening tingling burning pain made his hand shrink together with the palms and fingers in a livid quivering mass. The scalding water burst forth from his eyes and, burning with shame and agony and fear, he drew back his shaking arm in terror and burst out into a whine of pain. His body shook with a palsy of fright and in shame and rage he felt the scalding cry come from his throat and the scalding tears falling out of his eyes and down his flaming cheeks.

-Kneel down, cried the prefect of studies.

Stephen knelt down quickly pressing his beaten hands to his sides. To think of them beaten and swollen with pain all in a moment made him feel so sorry for them as if they were not his own but someone else's that he was sorry for. And as he knelt, calming the last sobs in his throat and feeling the burning tingling pain pressed into his sides, he thought of the hands which he had held out in the air with the palms up and the firm touch of the prefect of studies when he had steadied the shaking fingers and of the beaten swollen reddened mass of palm and fingers that shook helplessly in the air.

-Get to your work, all of you, cried the prefect of studies from the door. Father Dolan will be in every day to see if any boy, any lazy idle little loafer wants flogging. Every day. Every day.

The door closed behind him.

James Joyce, *A Portrait of the Artist as a Young Man*

The questions that could be set on this are likely to be under these headings: simple understanding of the story; deeper questions on characterisation; a follow-up question. Here are some suggestions.

(1) Who was the first boy to be punished? What had he done wrong?

(2) Why were this boy's hands always hard?

(3) What did the prefect of studies say was the reason for Stephen's breaking his glasses?

(4) What do you think about the prefect of studies? Is he doing his job well, or is he being cruel?

(5) The paragraphs marked x and y describe the pain that Stephen felt when he was caned. Read them again carefully, and, remembering some time when you have been hurt, though not as a punishment, say what your suffering was like.

(6) What is your opinion of Stephen? Is he behaving as you would, or is he being a coward?

(7) Was Stephen punished unjustly or not? Do not say 'Yes' or 'No', but explain carefully what you think.

(8) You can probably remember some time when you were punished unjustly for something that you knew was not wrong, even though you may not have been caned. Tell what happened to you.

Many examining boards are now using multiple-choice for dealing with factual questions. These, though easy to mark, are difficult to write and do not give the pupil a chance to write continuous English. There is a chance, too, that the clumsily-written item may help the inspired guesser. As an example for you to criticise, take question 2 above: 'Why were this boy's hands always hard?'

    A. He was always being punished.

    B. He did a great deal of gardening.

C. He was always rubbing rosin into them.

D. He was older than Stephen.

E. He put something on them to make them hard.

Two are obviously wrong (B and D), one a correct statement but not the right answer (A), one nearly right (a distractor − E), and one correct (C). Is it worth going to all the trouble?

'General impression' is not a reliable way of marking the above answers, so some numerical weighting will have to be used.

The continuous writing that comes at the end of the comprehension is of a personal nature. The opportunity should be given, once again to the whole ability range, to write impersonally. We have all met, set, marked but probably not attempted ourselves such titles as 'The Value of Discipline' or 'The Charm of Birds', thereby facing the child with a difficult topic and depriving him at the same time of any helpful material. Therefore, to help the pupil as much as possible, and still retain the advantages of a common piece of work done under identical conditions, all children concerned could be given varied documents and asked to write on a topic relevant to all this material. The topic chosen will be one suitable to the area and school, but a suggestion could be that the theme is one of the local interest like the construction of a new airport. All the children would be given a map of the area concerned, the plans of the airport, photographs of the countryside, especially that part that would be destroyed, details of speeches and statements made by both sides − reported in 'tabloid' rather than *Times* manner to give the weaker pupils a chance of following the arguments, and exposing them to the bigotry and prejudice of both sides. The continuous writing would be for the pupils to write a report on their conclusions. By this method all are given enough material to work from, so they should not be at a loss for something to write. Rather more difficult to organise, but of greater stimulus, would be to have recordings of 'speeches' giving the two points of view.

For those who would like to see a 'literature' content in a common examination, it is as well to remind them that in the first three years any questions would be 'memory tests'. Discussion on books and poetry is largely an oral exercise. By the fourth year, some pupils are likely to be intended for 'O' Level English literature in the fifth year, and the C.S.E. requirements include evidence of books read. The fairest scheme, and not in this case for the whole ability range, would be for certain fourth-year pupils to be given a prose passage with questions on the author's style. They could also be given two poems on a similar theme to compare. Questions on books read during the year, either as part of the English course or on their own, could be set provided broad hints were given on the nature of the exercise.

Any final assessment should take into account oral English, especially as many children express themselves better in this way. It is possibly more difficult to grade them as a general impression cannot be reinforced by a second hearing. Chapter 2 on 'Spoken English' deals with this matter fully.

The purpose of this chapter is internal assessment of English, and so is not intended to cover the fifth year. With the extension of Mode 3 examinations in G.C.E. as well as C.S.E., the abilities of teachers to assess their pupils accurately is tested to the full. The Joint Matriculation Board some years ago inaugurated a scheme whereby the 'O'-Level grade for English language was awarded as a result of continuous assessment moderated at the end of the course by other teachers. Schemes like this, as well as Mode 3 C.S.E., will stand or fall on the credibility that can be placed in them by the world. Already, bitter attacks have been made by the Press on the G.C.E. assessment scheme. But the main problem is not how we assessed the fifth formers who had chosen to stay on an extra year, but how we now assess the fifth formers who have been obliged to stay on following the raising of the school-leaving age. Newsom did mention this:

All pupils who remain at school till the age of sixteen should receive some form of internal leaving certificate. This need not follow a uniform pattern but local consultation between schools, the youth employment service, further education and employers would be helpful at arriving at a form most likely to be useful to the pupil . . . schools should look ahead to a situation in which all pupils will be in full-time education to sixteen. (Recommendations (a) and (b), p. 85.)

The anomaly of two examinations at 16+ must go, and steps are being taken in this direction. Until then, it would seem to be confusing the issue to have a system of three examinations in one school: G.C.E., C.S.E. and a Leaving Certificate. What credence are employers going to place in the third of these as it proclaims that the candidate was not good enough for the other two? The only answer at the moment is to assume that those who cannot tackle G.C.E. will be candidates for C.S.E., and the latter course must be devised to help the weaker pupils realise their potential. Certainly, these will not show as many high grades, but a look at the G.C.E. results will show that the majority of passes are grades 4, 5 and 6, so C.S.E. would not be out of step in having the majority of passes there in grades 4 and 5.

So far, with the emphasis on class-work and examinations, it has been taken for granted that work is done in school time. The day-school pupil spends the greater part of his time at home, or certainly off the school premises. Many parents attach great importance to homework, feeling that the full satchel indicates hard work. Most schools must hear sometime in the year the complaint that a particular child is not being given enough homework. It is perhaps too cynical to suggest that the value placed on homework is in proportion to the amount it keeps the children quiet in the evening. A suggestion that the best homework would be for the parents to encourage the children to read, have intelligent conversations with them, take them out to the cinema or theatre, might be considered impertinence. From interviews at parents' evenings we have all learned that it is a great point in the child's favour that he does his homework regularly (see Chapter 6).

Homework, in the form remembered from the days of the selective schools, does not really fit in with modern educational thinking. Newsom gives some advice on homework, using the term with reluctance, but feeling that 'extra-curricular' is not suitable:

We are strongly of the opinion that all boys and girls would profit from undertaking some work for themselves outside what is done in lessons; we also think this work could, and for many of our pupils, especially, should, take more various forms than what is conventionally recognised now as homework. (Paragraph 125.)

The question is how we can extend the school life beyond school in a particularly 'English' way. The traditional, and often useful, idea of finishing work started in class has its place, but it does create an artificial break that we as teachers do not find very congenial when we are engaged in some work of our own. We too have met the pupils whose idea of finishing off is to add a sentence, or cannot or will not do any more unsupervised. What can be more profitable is preparation for future work, with a generous time-allowance given. A homework timetable should be flexible so that the teacher can set work for a deadline and leave the pupils to decide on which night they will actually do the preparation. It must be said that work must not be created artificially for entry in the class record-book; most teachers have the ingenuity to create a description that will allay the suspicions of authority. As most of our pupils are likely to be working on some topic that stretches over a period of time, there are often tasks that cannot be done except out of school hours: interviewing old people for 'The Family', looking at the local housing for 'Homes', collecting advertisements or newspapers for various topics, or, on a simpler level, from looking at animals and noting their behaviour, to playing with water.

And then there is reading. We all know the reluctant reader, or the home where reading is not encouraged. The compilation of a reading-list, or even a viewing-and-listening list will ensure that a little work is done at home. What we must avoid is the charge that too much written homework prevented the children from reading (see Chapter 6).

The examination candidates will have little difficulty in finding something to do at home, but so often, the demands of other subjects push English into the background. Pupils need to be convinced that all their reading, speaking and thinking is helping them become more mature and this, strangely enough, will help them with their English examination. Those who are lucky to be working on continuous assessment in the fifth year may have a different problem: as the boards expect most of the work to be done in class, parents may wonder why so little is done at home. Once again, the answer is to use out-of-school time for preparation and reading.

Both the school day and the staff attitude to extra-curricular activities are in need of review. It would seem to be beneficial to regard the extra-curricular activities that are supposed to interfere with homework as homework. A school should provide, after a break for tea (provided by the school kitchen?) opportunity for drama, poetry-reading, play rehearsals, debates, discussions, lectures, tape recording, magazine preparation, and, of course, for matters not specifically 'English'. The library would remain open, and there would be places provided for quiet, academic work. The whole would be supervised by the school staff. With the inevitable increase in the number of neighbourhood schools this would not seem to be an impossible task; in fact, many new schools are working along these lines. The general idea is not an evening class but a continuation and extension of the school day, with sufficient variety to ensure that the children do not imagine that it is more of the same. The questions of staffing, free time and salaries are outside the scope of this chapter.

This chapter has attempted to cope with the thorny and controversial matters of assessment, examinations and homework. As long as we remember that what we are doing is for the benefit of the child and to make us better able to understand his needs and progress, we can retain what of the old ideas are worth-while and what of the new represent a genuine progression. We do have that great advantage that we are teaching that subject 'English', the one subject that brings the pupils into contact with all forms of fine experience and one that, in Frank Whitehead's words 'will enable them to see through and reject the cheap, the slipshod and the debilitating' (*Directions in the Teaching of English*).

Book list

An Experimental Scheme of School Assessment in English Language.
Joint Matriculation Board: first report, 1965; second report, 1967; third report, 1970.

Crocker, A. C. *Statistics for the Teacher* (Penguin, 1970).

Green, John A. *Teacher-made Tests* (Harper and Row, 1963).

Jackson, Brian. *English versus Examinations* (Chatto and Windus, 1965).

Multiple Marking of English Compositions (Examinations Bulletin No. 12; Schools Council, H.M.S.O., 1966).

Stevens, Frances. *English and Examinations* (Hutchinson, 1970).

A thematic approach to English teaching

11

Michael Woods

This method of English teaching has become increasingly in vogue over the last few years, and well may remain so; on the other hand, it may be replaced by what might seem to some yet another 'trendy' system, with precious little to recommend it to the old hands. Be that as it may, the following few pages are appended not as an idealised guide to what this method of teaching the subject should be, but rather as a record of an Odyssey. It is an Odyssey which is by no means finally accomplished; indeed, in many senses it is only just beginning.

Let us not confuse this method of teaching English with the 'interest folder' or some such — though that activity may, in modified form, comprise a part or aspect of a theme to be studied. We are all too familiar with the kind of thing undertaken in some junior schools — 'Find out all you can about the Atlantic Ocean by next Tuesday' — and, if this was what I meant by the term 'thematic approach', I would be the first to condemn it. A true thematic approach to the teaching of English is subtler, more demanding, and ultimately more rewarding, as we shall see.

It involves, at the outset, the 'traditional' aims of the teacher of English: it is centred on wide reading; it provides opportunities for writing of various kinds; it allows plenty of scope for oral work . . . and so on. And you need not neglect drama, poetry, reference work in the library, language work and spelling activity either in the pursuit of your chosen theme.

'But,' it may be asked, 'if this so-called thematic approach has all the avenues open to it of the old-style approach to English teaching — aims upon which we are all agreed — why should we bother to pursue it at all? Isn't it just another lot of extra work for nothing?'

My answer to this is twofold. I must confess I had been searching for some years for a means of unifying the diverse elements of English teaching — those very aims we are all intent on pursuing — into some sort of coherent entity. I had experienced both the rigid formal syllabus and the 'Take what you want from the cupboard' approach. I don't think either is very helpful to a young teacher, though the former probably just wins by a nose. A young teacher needs not only guidance, but encouragement: he needs not only to know where he is going, but also to have something definite to aim at, something which stimulates him to give of his best, something which makes the very act of teaching itself a progress and an adventure.

I was therefore searching for something which would fulfil these aims. Moreover, I wanted a scheme of work in which the creative aspects of English became paramount: and the kind of syllabus which proceeded on the lines of 'Third year is précis year' and similar dicta didn't seem to me to satisfy any of them.

It was after experimenting with various schemes, and numerous half-baked 'projects', therefore, that I hit upon Geoffrey Summerfield's excellent book *Topics in English* (Batsford, 1965), *q.v.*, and the scales were lifted from my eyes. Anyone who wishes to pursue a thematic approach seriously, or anyone just mildly interested, should read this outstanding volume. Therein you will find Summerfield's own experiment with themes, and a wealth of data and material. My own debt to this book is immense; and perhaps my main justification for proceeding with this section now is that my experiment was different from Summerfield's. His fluency and expertise are certainly greater than mine.

However, armed with the Summerfieldian Bible, I set about producing my first 'topic' or theme: Monsters. This would have been more successful if we had had any books — at least any which were about monsters. However, inspired by my (relative) success, I persevered. And this experience has provided me with the second part of my answer to the question, 'Why teach English this way?'

A thematic approach to English teaching seems to me to have several built-in advantages *per se*. First, it fuses all those diverse elements of English teaching — reading, writing, and what have you — into a coherent and continuous whole. Second, it is open-ended: that is to say that, subject to certain provisions mentioned later, you can go where you will and how you will, guided (it is to be hoped) as much by the interest of the children as by your own inclinations. Third, it is essentially creative. Although one might have a 'scheme of work', this can be seen often as no more than suggestions for activity: the process of pursuing a theme is basically a *participation* between teacher and taught. Fourth, it enables a study in depth to be made over a period of time — not necessarily of the factual aspects or elements of the theme, but of its emotional development: as the theme 'unwinds', it is hoped pupils' reactions and feelings will undergo some kind of similar development. Fifth, there is the linguistic aspect. Various sections of the theme interact, and can be self-reinforcing. What was mentioned last Tuesday can be recalled Thursday fortnight without too much effort, *because* you are dealing with a commonly developing theme, in which the pupils and teacher *share*. Moreover, you will have plenty of opportunity for collecting material for language study from the diversity of the pupils' work; and this diversity itself may necessitate the teaching of various language skills or techniques. Or you may wish to use the time at your disposal in a continuous or meaningful application of a certain aspect of language study or technique – the writing of different kinds of dialogue, say, or an examination of the language of preference and prejudice. And last, but by no means least, I have found that pupils' interest in you and your 'subject' is stimulated and maintained more readily by this method than any other I have tried.

Let us suppose, therefore, that you have overcome your scruples and reservations and wish to set up, or organise, your teaching on 'thematic' lines. How do you go about it? Well, there are some general considerations to be borne in mind first.

To be successful, a topic must offer wide variety within a given field. Subjects like 'Youth' or 'Nature' are much too wide and ambiguous, yet 'Friends and relations' or 'Autumn' can be quite productive. Summerfield is even more explicit sometimes. He has things like 'Horses and donkeys', 'The American Civil War', as well as more generalised ones such as 'Night and dreams' or 'The sea'. But the more delineated ones are not hamstrung by lack of material and the more generalised are sharpened by a viewpoint. The choosing of a given theme may at first seem confusing, but perhaps what follows may help to make the position clearer.

For your topic or theme, whatever it is, must offer scope for a wide variety of different kinds of writing, especially, as far as I am concerned, those requiring some sort of emotional response. (I daresay it would be possible to construct a theme whose responses were purely factual, but this seems to me to be a thematic approach of quite the wrong kind.) Thus the responses conditioned by 'Youth' or 'Nature' are likely to be wild and woolly – unless you limit them – but with a theme like 'Friends and relations' you are limited before you start. Or if not limited, circumscribed. You could perhaps see opportunities to evoke a friendly response for one, and a hostile for the other. This is the sort of thing you should be looking for. Take another theme, like 'Outsiders'.

There are many people in our society today who are 'outside' – and not just the conventional outcasts, either. How are we to respond to them? Does it vary with each differing circumstance? There is a wealth of opportunity here for requiring your pupils to respond emotionally – and getting them to supply the circumstances, too.

You will perhaps already begin to realise that topics or themes do not and cannot exist in watertight compartments. In considering the above, for instance, we began by considering which situations were most likely to produce an emotional response in our pupils, and a written one at that. Yet, in the case of outsiders, there is no need to confine the response to the written word: it is more likely, if anything, to be spoken. You can use it for dramatic work if you wish. Or have a debate. Or make up a tape. You could perhaps find a poem on the subject – certainly a piece of prose. Notice how this one example can serve a multiplicity of purposes, if you so wish. Indeed, this is the third aspect of the thematic approach that I wish to emphasise: that provision for many different kinds of written work is not enough; your chosen theme must also offer ample scope for as many other aims ('traditional' aims, if you like) of English teaching as possible.

Try and make a rough estimate of how long your particular theme is going to last. Summerfield favours a diverse number of short themes, ultimately hoping that each child will choose its own: for practical purposes I have found one term a useful duration for a well-running theme (and even that is sometimes too short). Alternatively, you could devise schemes whereby two (or more) shorter themes are presented during one term, or something extra (say three or four 'linked' poems or a couple of short stories) is offered as a contrast to the main theme.

When you have considered the above, you can get down to mapping out some assignments. Always have more material than you need: there is no point in 'drying up' halfway through and, in any case, the more you have to choose from, the easier you can organise things like group work, if you want to. Some assignments will need treatment over two to three weeks, or longer (for example, a dramatic sequence, or the rehearsing and polishing of a set of tape recordings, or a library assignment): some can be dealt with in an afternoon, maybe (the first draft of a piece of writing, for instance). But the proper development of a theme needs tight control by the teacher if it is not to wander or degenerate into an excuse for doing nothing. The same rules that apply to other modes of teaching also apply here, except that approaches must seem more flexible, formality must be sacrificed sometimes, and a lot of the onus for clarifying and criticising the work is placed on the

pupils themselves. As far as the teacher is concerned, it is better to walk
than to run: the object of the exercise is not to finish your scheme of
work in record time, but to pursue several different kinds of activity in
a meaningful way to the ultimate benefit of your pupils' abilities.

It is, of course, assumed from the outset that in considering your
theme you will have had some reading matter in mind. Summerfield has
various classifications. I have found it helpful to build extended work
(that lasting a term, say) round one or two central works of literature,
say a novel, or a long poem like *Reynard the Fox.* Supplementary
sources are also considered. This may be an extract from something
which everyone ought to read, or something which will only be read by
a few: a poem readily available in anthology or one which you have to
choose between duplicating or reading aloud from one copy. All these
considerations have relevance, and you must satisfy yourself where to
lay your hands on this stuff if it's not readily available. An investigation
of the library resources is also advisable.

Perhaps now, after weighing all the pros and cons, after sniffing
round the stock cupboards and having ransacked your attic, you are
ready to start. At the outset of any enterprise we have to consider what
equipment we need. Our equipment for this approach to English
teaching is divisible into three main classes.

Equipment

The first is the pupils themselves. This is not a poor attempt at an even
worse joke. They are the stuff out of which the end product comes —
the poem, the discussion, or whatever. It is their reactions you are
dealing with, as well as their expanding knowledge: their feelings and
thoughts, anything that amuses or intrigues them, anything that 'sets
off sparks'. You will be quite unscrupulous and use all this. You will
design your lessons to nurse and encourage it. But it is to be hoped you
will always treat your charges with respect. Not only do they provide
the golden egg, but the 'knowledge' which they are gaining as the theme
unfolds may well be knowledge of themselves.

The second most important item is books. Summerfield divides
books roughly into two main classes: to be read aloud by the teacher
(short extracts, poems), to be read alone by the pupil (longer works).
He also mentions background reading — works of reference, finding
out where to find it out, and so on. For our purposes, as I have already
said, themes revolve around one or two main works. These are usually
prose, but not exclusively: some of the longer poems of Masefield are

used, for instance, as well as such things as *Beowulf* (Serraillier version, and very popular), *Macbeth, The Royal Hunt of the Sun* and so on. If you can afford it and have the space, a wide variety of reading available in each English room (single copies, or half sets) is a good idea. I have tried to provide 'class libraries' of small sets in some cases: thus 'The Gang' (a first-year theme) has a class library of *One Hundred and One Dalmatians, Emil and the Detectives, A Hundred Million Francs* and *The Otterbury Incident* (soon to be replaced by *The Children's Crusade*). These can be read quite quickly, discussed, compared, written about, or what you will. Anthologies of poems and short stories are freely exchanged between groups: sometimes particular anthologies which are particularly useful are specifically sent with the various themes.

Generally speaking, you need books which will not merely provoke work *on* them ('What did so-and-so do next?') but *from* them ('Look at the description of Shane's first appearance. Now write a piece called simply "The stranger".'). The distinction is an important one. It is all too easy for a book to fall into the first category – the category into which it has too often been condemned. G.C.E. examinations in literature are only just breaking free of it now. But the idea of using books not merely as fodder for comprehension questions but as springboards for further development puts quite a different value on them. Of course, one must *comprehend* the details of the story, characters and so on if one is to talk about them meaningfully: that nobody would deny. But to get a *response* from a work of literature is to go beyond this, and this is the aspect which a thematic approach should encourage.

Sometimes you will find a book 'sticks': very little can be got from it, and few people like it. Dickens, sorrowfully enough, often 'sticks' – especially with junior forms. *Beowulf* never does. Nor does the Book of Exodus (see later).

Beware of the spurious 'text books' and 'courses'. The market is being increasingly flooded with them, and they are generally of little value to anybody. (A similar situation occurred some years ago when C.S.E. was first introduced: many old texts were hastily tarted up and offered to an unsuspecting public as 'brand new' C.S.E. material.) It is not just idealism to say that you should not need a 'course book' of any kind: your chosen theme is your course, and the texts involved in its execution should give you all the material you need.

The last 'general' word about books must, of course, concern the use of the school library. It should be obvious what sort of rôle the library can play in thematic work. It is, above all things, a source for 'finding out': but it is wise to ascertain beforehand just what there is to find out and, when you have done that, to make sure that each member of the class is not finding out about the same thing at the same time. More will be said about this when a detailed scheme is considered later, but it may be worth-while stressing that each library assignment need not take the same pattern. Indeed, it is undesirable that it should do so: boredom will quickly set in, and your library lessons will be scuppered. The commonest form of library assignment is to compile a booklet or monograph on a set topic. This is a procedure followed increasingly by other teachers in other disciplines, so be wary. There are other things you can do. For instance, the compilation of 'Dictionaries' is a useful thing to do. These are of course about a chosen topic – say, 'Predators' – but entries are limited to certain basic information, illustrations are allowed (great credit to those who attempt their own), and the finished product must be arranged in alphabetical order. The library lesson can also be used for the collection and collation of notes by groups or individuals prior to the giving of talks, or the compilation of a 'book' to which everybody contributes. Simple exercises in the art of note-making are useful – indeed, necessary. You can also help your pupils explore the shelves of the library by pointing out certain books or authors you may think it worth-while for them to read. And here you can include fiction in your ambit. Not only is this useful from the point of view of your theme (there is a wealth of information about whaling, say, in *Moby Dick*) but it is a valuable activity in its own right. It will often be the teacher of English who opens new avenues for literary exploration, or who provides links between one type of book and another.

Quite apart from books, there is quite a lot of ancillary equipment you will find useful for your work with themes. See if you can meaningfully include some music, for instance: this can set the mood or scene for a piece of writing (or reading), or it can be used for 'music and movement'. Pictures are a great asset – a box full of bits from old colour magazines is a veritable gold mine. A tape recorder is a help. Some may consider it an essential (ideally, of course, it should be) but it is possible to do without it. For your oral and dramatic work is often improvised, then and there, on situations and ideas which have arisen, and unless the tape recorder is set up and available when you want it, the impetus may well be lost. This is not to say, however, that situations for taping cannot be 'arranged': but as the work gathers its own impetus, you may well find it damaging to spend too much time treading on the toes of spontaneous enthusiasm.

Sometimes you need more specific items which the pupils themselves can bring or collect — for example, a collection of the *minutest* objects they can find in the school grounds (which they can then, of course, write about!). You may need to co-operate with other departments. A friendly art department is certainly a help when making masks or puppets, or just giving the pupils a chance to illustrate what they've done: and co-operation with historians or scientists or geographers on particular points ought to be to everyone's mutual benefit.

Examples of themes

Perhaps it is best now to move to concrete examples, and see how all this is put into practical use.

A third-year theme which always goes down well is 'Plagues'. (This is also treated in *Topics in English*, but in a different way.) The main literary sources for our work are: The Plagues of Egypt from the Book of Exodus (beginning at chapter seven); the diaries of Samuel Pepys (a useful edition, published by Nelson, is *A Shorter Pepys*); and *The Day of the Triffids*. There is also subsidiary material, which you might or might not use: Doris Lessing's story 'A Mild Attack of Locusts', for instance (available in *Good Stories*, published by Arnold), or an extract from *The Decameron* (First Day) in which Boccaccio describes a plague which hits Florence, and talks about the reactions of the inhabitants. There is Philip Larkin's poem 'Myxomatosis'. One of the choruses from Christopher Fry's *The Boy With A Cart* (often reprinted as 'Rain on Dry Ground') tells of the ending of drought. Lawrence's 'Walk Warily' (available in the Penguin edition) deals with more Puritan blightings. 'Binsey Poplars' shows Hopkins's feelings at the human destruction of nature. There are other examples of this same attitude, but you might like to offer some poems in contrast, to show things in their pristine state, before they were blighted or twisted or stricken. 'Welsh Incident' is an obvious example, too — perhaps over-obvious — of a visitation by alien creatures. Further prose material can be found in *A Journal of the Plague Year*, other Wyndham books, and science fiction generally.

However, one of the methods of 'presenting' this theme is to begin and end with Exodus. There is plenty of opportunity here for free writing as well as general discussion, mime and vocabulary work. The Doris Lessing story will supplement the study of the plague of locusts; *The Triffids* has links with the plagues of darkness and also with Boccaccio's story, which shows men's selfishness in the face of adversity. It is possible also to get a religious discussion going on the topic of God's purposes (why was Pharaoh's heart so often hardened?). If you have a taste for the familiar, then Browning's 'The Pied Piper' has links with the death of the firstborn. The death of the cattle (what was 'a murrain'?) has a connection too with fairly recent events in this country and elsewhere.

A lot of the children's writing is read and enjoyed, discussed and evaluated; but it is always written with some definite purpose in mind, one which is, moreover, easily appreciable by the class because they are in continuous contact with the kinds of stimulus from which it springs. Judgements are constantly at work, reactions are continually being assessed. The progress of a theme is an ever-present activity in which the whole class is engaged, including the leader, the teacher. Many writing situations and discussion points will thus arise *ad hoc*. Not every work will have specific assignments allocated to it — the Boccaccio, for instance, might be kept 'in reserve' as a kind of touchstone for commenting on the behaviour of characters in *The Triffids* and Pepys's accounts.

If you start with the Book of Exodus, therefore, you will obviously begin by reading the relevant sections. Perhaps you will be asking too much if you try to take them all at a time: it may be better to tackle them separately, commenting on and asking for comments as you go. This may spark off some debate or discussion (a possible line of enquiry has already been indicated): or you may adopt another treatment. You may, for instance, wish to present some of the episodes in dramatic form. There is certainly scope here: there is plenty of pleading with Pharaoh and plenty of Pharaoh saying no. There are also situations from the point of view of those whose children die, cattle are slaughtered, and generally suffer. Pharaoh is surely their enemy, although he is their liege lord (are there mumblings of a revolution here?). Or are the real enemies the Jews? One group tackling this once did a series of 'interviews' in which they sent their on-the-spot reporter to talk to the Egyptians and the Israelites. The idea is not as fanciful as it sounds: some of the interviews uncovered ancient hatreds, and went a long way to explain some of the present conflict.

This particular sequence of situations is also rich in providing plenty of mime work: seeing a cloud of locusts in the distance; rescuing a sheep or baby during a locust attack; feeling one's way in the darkness; the *smell* of the river of blood; attitudes of mourning and grief; dodging hailstones . . . almost any one of these will suggest means of branching off into some other activity or developing the activity already in hand.

The situations given in the Book of Exodus also provide plenty of opportunities for creative writing. Here are two examples of free-verse writing by fourteen-year-olds, descriptive of two of the Plagues of Egypt: lice and the river of blood.

The lice

Aaron
stretched out
his hand
with his rod;

and Lo!

Lice all over
the land of Egypt.

Creeping.
Crawling.
Contaminating.
Corrupting
every home.

Itching.
Irritating.
Inhabiting
every one.

Distressing.
Disturbing
everything.

Lice!

The river of blood

The river runs,
Soothing!
Gurgling!
Thick and sticky
Red as an artery
Cut in half.

Fish die, birds too,
Frogs dry up . . .
Death on the beach
Like an ancient D-Day!
People thirst for water, not blood . . .

The stench is sickening,
A smell of evil,
A smell no-one can escape from.

Crocodiles no more menace the riverside,
Which is engulfed in great clots of
Blood,
Like scabs, ripely picked,
Placed on the banks for inspection.

These items are offered to illustrate what can be done with a given theme. The class concerned had, prior to this, little or no experience of this kind of writing: their attempts at composition had been confined to such topics as 'A day by the seaside'.

It is also possible to transpose directly from these Biblical situations. Having reacted to the one, it should not be too difficult to extend one's reactions to the realms of imagination. Hence it is possible to obtain some good writing on such subjects as: 'Imagine what it would be like to have a plague of one of the following: earwigs, caterpillars, bats' or, again: 'Imagine some plague or other attacks the place where you live. Write, in diary form, a day-by-day account of what happens to a group of people you know'.

This is working *from* source material. If work *on* a book is required, then here are some specific questions which might be fruitfully asked about *The Day of the Triffids*:

(1) Describe how they attempted to cope with things at Tynsham Manor. Do you think this is/was a sensible way of dealing with the problem? (This is especially interesting because Tynsham Manor was run on quasi-religious lines.)

(2) Examine some of the ways in which the blind people are made use of. Does anyone try to help them? How?

(3) Look at Bill's explanation of the disaster (Chapter fifteen). Do you think, perhaps, this may be the book's message?

(4) Summarise Torrence's suggestions to Bill and Josella in the last chapter of the book. Comment on (i) the suggestions; and (ii) Bill's way of dealing with Torrence and his crew.

and a link up:

(5) Do you find any connection between the way people behave in this story and the way people behave in the story by Boccaccio? Could you summarise it in so many words? What are your reactions to this?

There are many more questions which could be asked, but it will perhaps be worth noting that the form in which they appear above allows for oral as well as written questioning.

Not all of the work undertaken need be of this nature, either. One of the most popular assignments is the designing of one's own 'vegetable monster'. The working parts must be labelled like any diagram in the science book. If you have a tape recorder (or even if you haven't) you might like to attempt a treatment of some of the scenes described by Pepys in his account of the Fire of London. These can either be in the form of dramatised episodes from the book, or an individually written treatment by the child (a long descriptive piece, say, arranged for several voices). Sound effects can be included for verisimilitude.

Documentary 'programmes' can also be written using information collected on a library scavenge. The causes and effects of almost any well-known disease – smallpox, scurvy, malaria, T.B. – will provide the material, and the programme could trace, perhaps, the attempts of science to deal with the phenomenon. It need not be comprehensive: if the resultant product is to be judged by literary rather than encyclopaedic standards then it is perhaps best to limit oneself to a specific moment in the disease's history – say Jenner's initial attempts at vaccination.

Other library assignments can fall into a more conventional mode. It is easy to compile monographs or booklets on such things as the causes of the Great Plague of 1665, or the spread of the Fire of 1666, and the attempts to stop it spreading. Indeed, the pupils may have already done something like this in their history lessons. In which case, the common cold may be more instructive – our attempts to combat it (including a survey and study of cold 'cures' and their advertisement) – or the locust (a biological link-up here) – or parasites. Individual plague carriers or means of combating disease often provide plenty of material for booklets, talks, and so on.

The spread of infection might well lead us on to some interesting word work. Apart from a general list of words to be discussed and studied – disinfectant, pesticide, vermin, scour(ge), dearth are only a few – some time can well be spent on deciding differences. How does a *plague* differ from an *epidemic*? In what ways can something be said to be *infectious* but not *contagious*? Roget will furnish many more examples. You could also talk about cleanliness and hygiene – personal and public. Lists might be compiled of things which can help *prevent* infection from spreading. Word lists can also be compiled from specific plagues or incidents.

There are other attitudes and avenues to explore. How does an authority – say, a town council or a government – give warning of extreme danger without being too alarmist? The natural reaction to words like cholera, typhoid, and so on, is emotive, to say the least.

Florence Nightingale's experience at Scutari might provide the other side of the coin: here she encountered appalling filth and disease, but met nothing but apathy. How does one present a case? How does one educate public opinion to accept things like vaccination? These are tasks which might well be attempted.

A theme which is very popular in the second year is one which we call 'Little people'. This one is especially interesting to me in that it gives a practical demonstration of textual cross-reference. The two main sources are the first two books of *Gulliver's Travels* and T. H. White's charming story, *Mistress Masham's Repose.* There is a lot of useful work which may be done on and from the *Travels* themselves: but in a sense they are subsidiary to the other book, and must be tackled first.

For there are definite references to *Gulliver* in the T. H. White novel which must be elucidated if complete comprehension is to be obtained. You must know, for instance, of the controversies of the heels and the eggs, the character of Flimnap, and Gulliver's arrival home from Lilliput, to mention only three. This last is especially important, as it introduces Captain Biddel and the sheep, as well as the Emperor of Blefuscu's picture, all necessary adjuncts to the life of the People on the Island, and Maria's adventures with them.

But there are other links, too, which it is useful to observe. The sequence where Maria helps (hinders?) the People hunt a pike is reminiscent of Gulliver's encounters with Brobdingnagian bees. (It might even lead to an examination of passages of White's masterpiece, *The Sword in the Stone*, where Wart goes to visit the old pike or flies out hunting at night.) Indeed, in many respects, Maria *is* Gulliver, but in a more recognisable form perhaps: she is referred to as the 'Child Mountain', and her encounters with the People have the more recognisable flavour of a human predicament. Well-intentioned but clumsy, her attempts to come to terms with the diminutive residents of the Island have a more authentic ring than those of her famous predecessor.

However, the situations in which Gulliver finds himself can provide many useful starting points. Encounters with giant insects can easily be written about, especially if you can obtain some real insects and imagine what they would be like blown up to giant size. Pictures can be helpful here, or work with a microscope, but the child's imagination will usually supply the requisite catalyst. Again, the inventory of Gulliver's possessions taken by the courtiers of Lilliput has provided the basis of many a guessing game: we take several well-known items, like a comb, or a bootlace, or a hair slide, and describe them without saying what they are. Posters can be devised advertising the performances Gulliver is going to give in Brobdingnag: the performances themselves can afterwards be enacted if we wish. Gulliver's flight through the cornfield, too, or his encounter with the bee, or Gulliver in Lilliput stepping over things or trying to pick them up can provide interesting and useful mime work.

Nor must we forget the human aspect. Gulliver in Lilliput, like Maria, finds himself in a position of great power. On the whole, he uses it wisely. During his second voyage, however, he becomes a victim. Maria, likewise, is a victim of Miss Brown and Mr Hater. One's sympathies here can be employed in many directions. Girls of this age especially like to write pieces about cruel stepmothers or vindictive orphanages and the like. Or you could use the situation for dramatic work or compose a piece of verse about captivity.

Mention of Miss Brown and Mr Hater leads you on quite naturally to a general discussion of character. Perhaps these two have parallels in *Gulliver*. Certainly there are unscrupulous characters there. Opposites can also be found. There is Gulliver's 'little nurse' Glumdalclitch, for instance. She shows the little man (which is what he has now become) great kindness and concern. Yet it is to be hoped that your discussion would take you beyond the bounds of establishing which characters are merely 'nice' or 'nasty'. Miss Brown and Mr Hater, for instance, are villains, but rather ludicrously presented: perhaps pupils know they should never take them seriously, that they are bound to come to a sticky end. Likewise the Professor, who seems to be some kind of absent-minded nitwit, displays, as the story reaches its climax, reserves of native cunning and tenacity. By contrast, many of the characters in *Gulliver* may be found somewhat two-dimensional. The Lilliputians seem much more alive on Maria's Island than they do in the pages of Swift's satire.

Yet perhaps the most important link between the two books is a linguistic one. Throughout *Mistress Masham's Repose* there are constant references to Lilliputian language. Moreover, in the original the Emperor of Lilliput has extravagant Christian names, Gulliver has to swear a Lilliputian oath, and the names and measurements of his possessions are all given in Lilliputian. This is your starting point. It is not much of a step from this to compile your own Lilliputian dictionaries, each part of the class taking a section at a time: words of measurement, for instance, is an obvious starter here. You may even experiment, if you wish, with parts of speech, or idiom. Some people like to try and build up simple sentences.

But this is a game which all can play and it takes very little encouragement to get it going. Soon the dictionaries (English ones) are out, and the groups are eagerly discussing among themselves. Lists have to be compiled and co-ordinated. Some standard pronunciation must be agreed on. Duplication is to be avoided, so frequent interchange of material has to be arranged. The claims of rival words must be adjudicated. A certain simplicity is perhaps the keynote. It is useless having a language nobody can pronounce, or one whose orthography is so bizarre it can never be written down. Initial phonic units may be simple and basic, in which case they can be added to, or over complicated, in which case they must be watered down. Either way, it will readily be seen that what you are trying to do is experiment with the roots of language itself: how it derives, from a simple unity of sound and symbol, into the complicated structure in use today; how it expands and grows, according to different needs and pressures; how it lives and develops, amoeba-like, as new demands are made on it and new contingencies have to be met.

This is really the purpose of the exercise. Its purpose is not necessarily to strengthen our pupils' knowledge of any particular part of written or spoken English (though it should do this): nor to provide scope merely in extra-curricular work in other languages (the formation of irregular verbs, for instance). It is a practical demonstration, at grass roots level, of how a language originates, and how it can be seen to develop.

Of course, it is an artificial exercise. That is why it is treated as a game. It takes no notice, for example, of the *need* which is behind most communication in the first instance: the baby needs food, or warmth, or attention, so it cries. This need, if you like, is assumed, and you experiment one stage further along the line. That is one reason why an existing language has not been chosen for this task. Any existing language is overlaid with habits, attitudes and difficulties which it is too cumbersome to get involved with and which would take too long to circumvent. You are playing a game. You can make up your own rules as you go along. You don't have to adopt anyone else's.

Since you are making up your own rules, you can follow them wherever they lead you. You can, if you like, examine structures. You might do this when you attempt to make up a few sentences. This may sound simple enough, but you might wonder whether they have to obey certain rules. If so, are these the rules of your own sentences (such as you know them) or are they the rules sentences have in German, say, or

Italian, which is a much different kettle of fish? Or is it best to dispense
with rules altogether? What prevents your saying 'I in the up got
morning' — and hoping to be understood? Well, perhaps you are more
used to saying certain things in certain ways. Certainly the 'rules' which
are supposed to govern English can be seen largely as a matter of
convention, beyond certain limits. This may sound a rather highfalutin'
thing to do with twelve- or thirteen-year-olds, but a line of enquiry can
be started in this way and, if not pursued too relentlessly, can have
beneficial effects.

Or take word work. When you are compiling your initial lists, you
have to get down to basic quantities. You have all heard about a 'basic
vocabulary' in English, but this is an all-purpose one. Your basic
vocabularies, you find, have to be tailored to basic needs, jobs,
requirements of all kind. You must try and concentrate on essentials.
But trying to decide what is essential and what is not is a tricky business
sometimes. The resultant discussion is often highly vocal, as representatives
from the various groups try and justify the words they have chosen.

There is a further bonus, too, in oral work. Just as the wearing of a
mask in a drama lesson may serve to release the inhibitions of a shy
child, so operating within the limits of your new-found 'language' can
lead to much blossoming forth of inflection and delivery. Meaning, you
find, is usage. It is quite possible, for instance, to determine the
meaning or intention of what is being said without necessarily knowing
what the words may mean: the tone of voice, the attitude of the
speaker, the expression on his face — all these things give colour and
substance to the words he uses. Moreover, there will obviously be a
rhythm and lilt to your new 'language' when it is spoken, just as there
is to any other. Here is a first-rate opportunity to examine this problem
in situ, as it were, without running any risk of offending anybody or
being embarrassed yourselves by groping about with your own language.
If what you are teaching here is skill, then there is much to be said for
attempting to do just that. Indeed, I have even found this method to
work with tongue-tied seniors who need a little verbal uplift: whereas
their own language can be seen as a stumbling block, they are often
quite happy to jigger about with 'nonsense' vocabularies, threatening or
cajoling or persuading each other in terms which are literally
unintelligible, but which are given meaning purely by the intention of
the communications. 'Nonsense' poetry, of course, provides a classic
example of this. But the ice will have been well and truly broken: and
when they return to using their own language again, it is as beings
refreshed.

Unless the foregoing sounds too pompous, let me again emphasise that the whole of this aspect of the work is to be seen as a linguistic *game* playable with pupils of twelve or thirteen years old. It is the teacher who directs the various enquiries. Perhaps you will only have time for one or two: almost certainly you will not have time for them all. But if you can keep your enquiries within the bounds of the game that is being played, and not grow too obsessed with your native tendency to label and catalogue the various entities discovered, then you have a chance to see at first hand with your pupils various aspects of language at work. Much enjoyment will be had; and the 'language' you so construct between you will be capable of jumping through any particular hoop you care to concoct for it.

Other virtues of themes

This, however, is not the only avenue which can be explored by means of this particular theme. There are other, more conventional, modes of development. Yet perhaps this is a good point to stop and emphasise that one of the virtues of this method of teaching English is its flexibility. Horses can be adapted for courses, and vice versa. If you find you are pursuing something particularly interesting, you carry on pursuing it. If you discover that what you are trying to do definitely doesn't come across, it may rest in peace. If your pupils aren't yet quite ready for something you wish to do, it can either be modified to suit present requirements, or kept on ice until the millennium arrives.

The real success of this particular type of English teaching lies not so much in the bundles of stimulating and exciting material you may have, but in what you do with it. If you see it as an opportunity for skimming through vast quantities of print, so that you can say you have 'read' *Gulliver* or 'done' *Reynard the Fox*, then you are bound to fail. It is, above all, an opportunity to *teach*: and just as the pupils in your care learn, as it were, by doing, then you find out more about yourself and your subject in like manner.

For this is a method which really tests a person's ability to teach. Nothing shows up sooner than failure. You must, for example, always have your objectives constantly in view: whatever you design for your pupils to undertake must be both purposeful and relevant to the development of a particular skill or discipline. Your 'discipline', too, needs to be of quite a high order: it is worse than useless to undertake some of the things I have outlined above if the pupils only see it as a chance to swing from the lights. Your knowledge of your subject needs

to be extensive yet capable of adaptation and enlargement: in time, you
learn to remember the things that 'went well' so that you may be able
to whisk them out again for future encounters. The resources (and
limitations) of your local libraries must be known to you.

In the classroom, your function may be seen, like that of Queen
Victoria, to 'encourage and warn'. You must develop an awareness of
when to build up the steam, and when to apply the brake. But I have
generally found there is less reluctance among pupils to participate in a
system which gives them plenty of books to read, which sends them out
on surveys, which brings them face to face with nature and themselves,
than one which keeps them exclusively bound behind a desk. As far as
the teacher is concerned, the process is best seen as a partnership: not
only must Sir be prepared to initiate, he must also be willing to share.
If there is research to be done, he must roll up his sleeves and do his bit
when needed. If people are going out and about examining objects or
collecting specimens, then he must be by their side. If there is writing
or acting to be done, the teacher must participate. This is not a system
where you can put your feet up on the desk with *The Times
Educational Supplement* and let them 'get on with it'.

Nor is it a panacea for all ills in English. It may well cure a good
many of them, but I have already hinted that it will only work if the
people behind it make it work. And what of these people? Must they
not be 'super teachers', gifted like the gods? Is not the system
unworkable because it is too complex?

The simple answer is, of course, that any teacher worth his (or her)
salt ought to be able to perform any of the tasks I have mentioned
without too much difficulty. You may find, like the rest of us, that you
are better at some things than others. But this is no drawback. A class
which had Mr *X* last year (who was especially good on creative writing
but not so hot on drama) will have Miss *Y* next year (and she's very
good at drama though, perhaps, not so hot on research). The fact that
Miss *Y* may be new, or young, or unproven in her abilities as a teacher
is no real drawback, either. New teachers, as well as part-time teachers,
can easily fit into this system if their steps are well directed from above.
The only real misfit is the teacher who does not want to change.

One of the most popular themes with first-year pupils is the resurrected
'Monsters'. (As you see, we try to provide some kind of continuity.)
Here the main sources are the Serraillier version of *Beowulf* (available in
The Windmill Book of Ballads) and *Macbeth.* There is plenty of
supplementary material, ranging from David and Goliath in the Book of

Samuel to Ray Bradbury's story 'The Fog Horn'. You can also pick up several Greek myths on the way, if you wish, or pay a visit to Giant Despair in Doubting Castle: but, as is usual with your scheme, you find you have a surplus of material rather than a dearth, so it is best to be selective.

You will probably find that pupils come up to secondary school with widely differing levels of achievement, and are naturally nervous at starting this new life. Something like the epic of *Beowulf* which, in this translation at any rate, cries out to be read aloud, is a godsend here. The story is gripping enough in itself, and you soon find the timid and hesitant swept along by it. Nor have I yet found any child suffer from nightmares or grisly consequences as a result of the reading: they accept it as a fiction, and some even complain that its grim bloodthirstiness is just too improbable. But when you explain about myth and legend, and pick up a few of your own (Robin Hood, Dick Turpin are easy examples) the thing attains a kind of perspective.

Beowulf is useful for reading aloud, by Sir in the first instance, and by his charges later. Some passages, Grendel's first appearance, say, or the fight with the Fire Dragon, are especially good for practice. The style definitely needs to be declamatory. Once the rolling, ringing swing of the thing is attained, all is usually well. *Beowulf* is definitely not suited to a throwaway style of delivery. Indeed, many of the most gripping passages call for special effects: not only in grasping the drama of the fights, but in the passages (say) where Hrothgar, giver of treasure, mourns the supposed death of the hero.

Practice in reading aloud is very useful at this stage. It is an eye-opener to those who can and those who can't. Those who can't often transpire to be the victims of some badly-taught system of reading, inflicted on them in their earliest years. The English teacher should, of course, be aware of these things now. The 'eleven-plus', if your locality still has it, is no guarantee against bad reading habits, nor bad writing ones either.

But *Beowulf* is on an epic plane, and you must not belittle it too much by introducing too many considerations of this sort, important though they are. Beowulf is the archetypal epic hero, and he fights with monsters. What is more, he is successful, and performs feats no man can equal. Whether this is Christian allegory or not need not concern you here. What does concern you is that you have an enthralling story, of a pristine simplicity, yet told (in this translation at least) with such exuberance of style that it leaps off the page and hits you. What better introduction to the world of books for an eleven-year-old? Perhaps he has come from a school which makes no bones about books and their value. Perhaps he hasn't. Either way, you will be doing him a service. And you will also have implanted in his mind the idea that, like them or not as the case may be (and there are some who genuinely can't take *Beowulf*), books are things at this new school which cannot be ignored. And this is a point well worth making.

What else has *Beowulf* to offer you? You can read aloud from it in various ways, singly and in groups. Some parts are ideal for choral speaking. It also offers us plenty of scope for dramatic work. Try the opening bars of *Finlandia*, for instance, while miming something creeping, menacingly, through the mist. Or be the thanes of Hrothgar, asleep on the ground, when Grendel first comes. Or consider the monsters Beowulf sees swimming in the lake, the lake which is the home of Grendel's mother. These offer many chances for inspired mime work, both singly and in groups. Groups, in fact, can produce some excellent 'monsters': hands and feet are synchronised, bodies writhe in unison, locomotion can even be provided.

Discussion there will certainly be, about the poem and its hero, even about its style. I do not think this is too early to bring to a child's notice that such a thing as style exists. In this Serraillier version, for instance, you will find many examples of alliteration as well as inversion. The alliteration is interesting. This can lead, quite easily and naturally to work on tongue-twisters, always a useful bit of speaking practice. But they will find, from the work that you have done, that some of the examples they uncover are not really tongue-twisters at all, but only alliterations ('My mother's mate makes macs' is one recent example). A true tongue-twister has more to it than just a ubiquitous first letter.

As far as written work is concerned, readers of this chapter will by now have grasped the idea that there is a distinction between work *on* a text, and work *from* it. Thus, an attempt to find out what is learnt of the daily life of people at the time the poem was written belongs to the former category: imagining you are one of Hrothgar's thanes telling what happened when Grendel first came upon you belongs to the latter. Many opportunities arise for either approach: one which combines the two, to a certain extent, is to attempt to describe what happened as you waited by the lake for Beowulf to re-emerge. Here you give the child a chance to combine his grasp of fact with an attempt to use his descriptive powers.

It is well to make your first acquaintance with the library, too, during the early weeks. And this is not to mean just going to the building called the library and sitting there: too many of our children, it seems, have spent their early years doing just that. Either they have been allowed to go to the library, but have not been allowed to borrow from it, or they have had no library at all. Some have been lucky, of course. But the examples quoted above are recent ones within our own intake, and only point to the folly of assuming anything about such people. Even if they have had anything approaching a reference section, it seems they have often not been taught how to use it. We all know, of course, what an encyclopaedia is: it's something Daddy bought from that man at the door in the hope that it would help us pass the 'eleven-plus'.

One of the ways to break this particular iceberg is to give out simple assignments, using the resources of your own library and any others you can lay your hands on. This particular theme offers some useful opportunities for doing this. Like 'Little people', it is concerned basically with size: here, with super-sizes. Thus, some famous buildings or structures which come into this category are things like the Eiffel Tower, the Sphinx, the Colossus of Rhodes, the Giant's Causeway, the Empire State Building, the Jumbo Jet, and so on. It is not too much trouble to ask your young charges to write perhaps a couple of pages on one of these items. A similar thing may be attempted with creatures and people: characters like the Cyclops, Atlas, the Minotaur, Tarzan, King Kong. The object of the exercise is simply to find out who they were, and then transform the information into a personal account, but the experience gained in looking things up (and knowing where to do it) is invaluable. Maps can also be compiled indicating the whereabouts of some of today's 'monsters' of the animal kingdom, or forays made into the past. A dinosaur or two always goes down well. It is also possible to have groups working on each of the labours of Hercules, for instance, the result being presented as a continuous booklet, or a radio programme.

There are other 'general' things which might be attempted. Newspaper accounts can be compiled of the night a 'monster' attacked a local town or village. Legends featuring monsters (like St George and the Dragon) can be enacted, written about, or adapted. The story of Jonah and the Whale is full of possibilities. A favourite one is to read the Biblical account first (just a few verses) then enact the scene. A table or something suitable can represent the whale. Somebody is swallowed. He writhes about, and is then regurgitated. Others follow suit. The experience can then be written about:

> I feel sick
> In all that slime!
> Ribs all around me,
> Flesh and bones . . .
> Ugh!

was how one account began. Indeed, the whale itself provides a fascinating example of a monster nearing extinction. We hunt these fascinating creatures ruthlessly. An American researcher has recently made a record of whales singing, and communicating generally, though I do not think it is available in this country yet.

Dictionaries of 'size' words can be compiled, as well as lists of words showing the qualities of monsters: words like 'ghoulish', 'macabre', 'sinister', 'fiendish'. When discussing *Beowulf* you will have dealt with words like 'epic', 'adventure', 'hero' and so on, as well as words which describe the quality of Beowulf's adventures: many of these may well reappear when you deal with *Macbeth*.

It is best to jump in straight away and start acting the Witch scenes. It is as well to have the class on your side from the word go. Dispel the idea that these are funny old women in pointed hats:

> So wither'd, and so wild in their attire,
> That look not like th'inhabitants o' th' earth,
> And yet are on't . . .

From enacting the scenes with just the witches themselves, you will soon be able to introduce other characters — like Banquo and Macbeth. I always try and stick to the text wherever possible, yet there is no harm in trying to paraphrase, as it were, the substance of a scene, providing the textual details are accurately understood beforehand.

As for the meaning of the play, a good point to start with is motive. Macbeth is the 'hero', yet surely not in the same way as Beowulf: they both perform grisly deeds, but the intentions are different. Was Macbeth simply a good man corrupted by the witches? It is likely that your charges will see the issues in terms as black and white as these, and indeed good that they should do so: that they should realise there are issues at all at this stage, is all most of us ask for, and that they should be able to support what they say with at least some reference to the text. We do not expect to have a clutch of embryo Bradleys on our hands. All we demand is intelligent interest.

And this there usually is. The struggle between good and evil, the ghastly crimes, Macbeth's decline and his wife's slide into madness (not to mention the supernatural solicitings) provide a galvanic sequence.

Lady Macbeth is often the character who inspires least sympathy: she was at least partly to blame for the downfall of an upright man, and young audiences generally tend to feel she deserved all she got. Some may even see her as the true 'monster' of the piece.

An attempt is always made to refer to the text wherever it is important to do so. Thus Birnam Wood is robbed of its full significance unless great play is made of the Witches' promises (and their seeming impossibility) early on. The speech of the bleeding Captain tells us much about Macbeth's character, his loyalty and valour. His letter to his wife indicates another side of this: they had obviously talked of the matter before. Indeed, one class insisted on holding a 'court of enquiry' after Duncan had been killed: there was a tribunal, and everyone had a rôle — a servant, a groom, and so on. People had to justify their actions and account for their movements. Much play was made with details from the scene with Ross and the Old Man, which emphasised the uniqueness of the event: 'What do you mean you heard nothing? The King's horses broke out of their stalls and fought each other' — and so on. This 'cross-examination' lasted for two days, and though it eventually got nowhere, everyone seemed engrossed by it.

Mention should perhaps be made at this point of recorded Shakespeare. Once a text is known, a recording becomes easy to follow: and my own preference is for shortened versions rather than full texts, which have a high boredom quotient and in any case are of variable quality. We have used recordings published by Spoken Arts Recordings (formerly available from McGraw Hill, Maidenhead). These are abridged versions by mainly Irish companies, including people like the legendary Anew MacMaster. They are strongly spoken, though perhaps too melodramatic for some tastes, and the sound effects and evocative rather than completely realistic.

There are other records one might use to reinforce or set a mood. Sibelius has already been mentioned: I have also used Berlioz' *Symphonie Fantastique*, and I would like to conclude this section with a piece written after hearing (more than once) the 'Witches' Sabbath' movement. I find this especially interesting because it is an example of an extended piece of writing sparked off entirely by listening to music.

The witches' sabbath

It was the still of night. I saw them fly away from their home which was a dark wispy cobweb. I watched these dark figments which were running in the sky. They landed in the church graveyard over the road. I quickly got dressed and followed them just in time to see three curled up shadows hobbling along, with the aid of a stick. They passed many grave stones which groaned as they went by.

But it seemed they did not hear them. Now they were going through the church door, past the rows of chairs and up the steps to the altar. Past the altar and through the door behind it, which I had never seen before. There they stopped. Through the cracks in the door I could see them arranging candles about, moving all from the table. That is, the hymn books, a Bible, and piles of papers.

They turned the pictures on the wall the other way round, these cloaked midgets. Their large hoods covered their faces, so they looked all black. So did the room. That also had a large shadow thrown over it. Their three pet cats followed them about, rubbing their mangy fur against their mistresses. Then, all of a sudden, they pulled their hoods back and looked straight into a glaring light, which I could not look at.

A voice called and muttered something in a strange language. They stood very silent and seemed interested.

Then the light vanished and I saw the most hideous faces there ever were to see. They started to chant and scream and hiss at each other. And then they stopped. The church bells had started to ring. Was this some warning? For they started to change all the things back, and ran out of the door like a streak of lightning, cats and all. They took the shadow they threw over the church with them.

I saw them running in the sky. And behind the dawn chasing them. Suddenly light overtook them and they vanished.

In the foregoing pages, an attempt has been made to show some of the things it is possible to do with this approach to English teaching during the first three years of secondary schooling (from eleven onwards). The list does not pretend to be exhaustive. As I have mentioned before, one of the beauties of this particular approach is that it allows the teacher a certain freedom to pick and choose.

It is also possible to carry on this approach beyond the third year. Nowadays more and more examining boards are willing to listen to the schools' requirements: there has long been a Mode 3 C.S.E. examination, and it is also possible to have a Mode 3 G.C.E. (language and literature) at 'O' Level. Some boards, of course, are more co-operative than others. But even if you do not wish to run the gauntlet of Mode 3 exams, I would suggest that the method outlined above offers enough flexibility and scope to equip anybody with the skills necessary for securing a pass at G.C.E., or C.S.E.

For the method (which is basically what it is) is capable of adaptation and extension to suit all manner of tastes and temperaments, both of teacher and taught. The schemes I have outlined are merely some which we have tried and which have, by and large, 'worked'. It is not for me to pretend, however, that they have all worked with equal success. No teaching situation is ideal a hundred per cent of the time: some have not had the success they deserved through inadequate preparation, some have not met with the response we thought they merited, sometimes we have bitten off more than we could chew.

But, as teachers, we have learnt to adapt and adjust ourselves to meet these situations. By and large, the children have been enthusiastic, seldom bored, always responsive, and often stimulated to great heights of endeavour. Indeed, they often comment that it makes the English lesson 'more interesting'; that it is a 'better way of learning English' (notice how the old terminology still clings!); that there's 'always something to do'.

Indeed, there is. As I have tried to emphasise before, it is not so much 'teaching' the subject as 'sharing' it. This is a more accurate description of the activity which goes on. The teacher is basically there to *participate*. He must initiate schemes; share the common stock of experience, dilute it perhaps to make it go further, add to it maybe with some extra knowledge of his own. And although it is true that after a certain while the topics generate their own impetus, he must still be there to guide them along, to introduce new approaches, to try again what hasn't gone so well before. It's an education for him, too.

12 Sixth-form studies

Henry Lawrence

General studies

The form and content of general studies in the sixth form is entirely dependent upon the aims and attitudes of individual schools. This term is subject to many interpretations and may variously be employed to cover, for example, the desire to bring snippets of culture to those 'that sit in darkness' in the science sixth, and the realities of scientific progress into the remote world of the arts pupil, or the plan to outwit Satan by occupying idle hands with extra lessons, or even the period(s) devoted to preparing pupils for the Use of English examination. Some schools, on the other hand, plan general studies on the grand scale and operate schemes which utilise the members and resources of many departments and offer a wide choice of subjects.

There is so wide a variation in the amount of time devoted to this subject, the number of staff employed, the content of the course, and the scale of operations, that it is impossible to provide a clear account of the state of general studies in schools at the present time.

Nevertheless, one factor in this uncertain situation remains remarkably constant, namely, that however widely general studies may be interpreted, the English department is invariably involved. Yet despite this general recognition of English as a subject which has an important part to play in meeting the wider needs of the sixth-form pupil, the English department seems rarely to be called upon to create its own course of general studies. The section on 'General English' which follows seeks to show how effective such a course could be, and offers suggestions on its content, presentation and organisation.

General English

In recent years there has been a radical change in the nature of the sixth form. Increasingly larger numbers of pupils are no longer following the conventional pattern of study leading to an examination in three 'A' levels, and recognition of this fact has led to many re-appraisals of the 'A'-Level system, culminating in the School

Council's recent proposals for 'Q'- and 'F'-Level examinations. However, we are not here concerned with the academic sixth-former whose course, whatever the examination system, will be straightforward, but with the growing numbers of those who will be preparing, perhaps, for only one external examination or even none at all, and many of the latter will spend, often, only one year in the sixth form.

In the last five years the total of sixth-form pupils has increased by 50%, and with the raising of the statutory leaving age this upward trend will become more marked. But this need not be a grave problem, provided, and this is an essential condition, teachers of English are available in adequate numbers to deal with this situation. If this condition is met then an invaluable opportunity will be provided to escape from the confines of an examination-dominated system and to provide a course of general English studies for these pupils, many of whom would formerly have never entered the sixth form at all.

What are the characteristics of these pupils? I suggest they share many of the following qualities:

(1) They are ruthlessly logical, critical of authority, and question traditional values and beliefs.

(2) They have a lively interest in the present and its implications for the future, rather than in the past.

(3) They are independent, self-centred and unwilling to conform.

(4) Many are acutely aware of the problems presented by our society e.g. racial prejudice, the effects of science and technology, law and order, the pollution of our environment.

(5) They are interested in the affairs of their community and are often active in service to that community, e.g. care of old people, play centres.

(6) They are politically aware, especially of 'power politics' and its implications in terms of war.

(7) They are vitally concerned with the problem of human relationships and especially as expressed in terms of love and hate, sex and violence, involvement in or total withdrawal from society. In addition to this, many are much more adult in terms of experience of life than in the past.

Assuming this is accurate, what guide can these qualities be to the sixth-form teacher of English?

Firstly, it is imperative that we avoid creating a watered-down 'A'-Level pattern course. We should base our approach firmly on contemporary writers, but, as I shall hope to show, this does not mean we exclude the great writers of the past. We must, however, avoid any suggestion that they should read certain of the latter 'because it is good for them'.

The course should not be built around a number of set books; perhaps, at first, not around books at all. The starting point might well be a discussion on some aspect of human relationships leading in turn to the treatment of this same theme by various writers. Our aim should be to demonstrate that literature is concerned with life, and that many of the problems which seem so vital and so new to the pupil, are the basic human problems which have confronted every age, and because they are of fundamental importance in any society they find their way into literature. Many writers possess a deep insight into human nature, and though they do not provide answers to our questions they can help us to see our difficulties in detachment, and so to take a more balanced attitude. Thus we can enable our pupils, many of whose homes will be culturally poor, to develop breadth of vision, a critical understanding of their world and a sense of values.

But an English course can do more than this. It can make them aware of the influences which tend to affect their taste, moral values and political and religious attitudes and provide them with the opportunity of acquiring confidence in their own judgement.

It is clear, then, I am making a bold claim for the study of English, namely that more than any other subject it can assist young people in the difficult task of growing to maturity.

Although the teacher of English is provided with the opportunity of creating the type of course he believes will cater for the needs of his pupils, it cannot be denied that he will be confronted with considerable problems. Among these are:

(1) Since there is no obvious attainable goal such as an examination certificate, the amount of response and enthusiasm will depend entirely on the skill and zeal of the teacher. Such a course will increase the already heavy demands on him, and it must be recognised that not all teachers are temperamentally equipped to work in this way with young adults.

(2) Written work will be an essential part of this course, for a growing maturity in the individual should be evident also in his power of communication. The pupil must not only be encouraged to write, but should feel the need to express his views because he is stimulated by the work he is doing. Since forms may be large there will be an equally large volume of marking.

(3) The provision of texts will also provide problems. If, as I have

suggested, we avoid the 'set book' approach, then a large variety of texts will have to be available, or duplicated copies of poems or relevant extracts from the book under discussion.

(4) Such a course could make heavy demands on the school's supply of 'hardware'. There will have to be careful planning to avoid clashes of demand for the same item of equipment.

With the warning then that enthusiasm at the prospect of such a course is no substitute for careful planning, and may be destroyed by the unforeseen problems created, let us look at some factors which may contribute to the successful planning of such a course.

The basic approach

The thematic approach (see Chapter 11) may be the most likely method of interesting and involving our pupils, for the chosen theme could reflect the immediate concerns of the pupils themselves, and be explored through the work of a variety of writers. Many sixth-formers will consider the literature of the past as having nothing relevant to say to the present. It must be our aim to dispel this illusion not only because it is false, but also because we will wish to free them from prejudice and encourage breadth of vision.

To illustrate this point let us assume our general theme is 'Human relationships' and we are examining in particular the effect of very close relationships on the individuals concerned in a family or similar setting. We could explore this situation in its various aspects through such a pattern of works as the following:

(1) The poems 'Mother and Son' and 'Sorry' by R. S. Thomas; 'My Father in the Night Commanding No' by Louis Simpson; 'Letter to a Young Mother' by Paul Roche; or 'Domestic Dramas' by Elizabeth Jennings.

(2) The plays *Look Back in Anger* by John Osborne; *Death of a Salesman* by Arthur Miller; *She Stoops to Conquer* by Oliver Goldsmith and Shakespeare's *King Lear*.

(3) Novels could include *Billy Liar* by Keith Waterhouse; *Sons and Lovers* by D. H. Lawrence; *Victory* by Conrad (the father's advice to Heyst), and the effect of Miss Havisham's teaching on Estella in *Great Expectations* by Dickens.

In this way our approach can cover a wide range of literature and treatment.

The suggested approach outlined in the previous paragraph indicates why a 'set book' pattern is not a sound basis for planning. A relevant extract from Shakespeare's play may be entirely effective, but a reading of the whole play could merely serve to convince pupils that 'good' literature is a deadly bore.

Another fruitful approach is to view a theme through many and different eyes. Not only could we employ literature, but also experts in other fields. For example, the theme of 'War' could be seen in the work of the artist and historian. The same battle could be seen through the eyes of a general, an ordinary soldier and an enemy soldier, or a British, French and German soldier. A factual military account and a novelist's description of the same battle could be compared and contrasted. In these ways we will enable our students to appreciate the necessity for a balanced judgement and an open mind.

By the use of these and other methods, we shall be giving our pupils a deeper insight into life, and demanding a more mature and reflective response from them. They will be enabled to acquire a sense of values, and a better understanding of people and human relationships.

Writing

It should be the aim of our course so to stimulate and involve the pupil that he will want to express his views in writing, and acquire a style which will enable him to communicate fluently and effectively. But we must not be content only with the traditional sixth-form essay, and should encourage poetry writing, creative prose, the composition of one-act plays, in fact any medium of expression which acts as an incentive.

As teachers of English we are interested in reading and discussing language in all its forms, and we will want our students to develop a critical attitude towards the work of others and also to acquire a confidence in their own judgements. As an aid to developing an independent approach we might employ the Topic Folder approach. A central theme is set and each pupil over a prescribed period produces a selection of written work related to this theme which can take a variety of forms, e.g. poetry, essays both creative and factual, criticism, comment, etc. The preparation, reading and written work must be entirely his own. Such a folder could provide the less academic student with a satisfying outlet for his individuality. Here is a piece of work which is entirely personal in opinions, choice of reading and research, form and presentation. It is something which he has created by himself and for himself, concrete evidence of his own industry, enthusiasm and ingenuity.

Sufficient has been said to indicate that there is ample scope for a great variety in written work, and we should seek to employ as many methods as possible to create and maintain the enthusiasm of our pupils.

Drama

I have said that the majority of these sixth-formers will be intensely interested in people and human relationships. This is an excellent starting point for our work in drama, because as John Hodgson, principal lecturer in drama, Bretton College of Education has so well said, 'Its primary focus is upon the growth and development of the individual through the understanding of himself in relationships with other people — an imaginative recreation of aspects of human situations. It is a means of enquiry into the nature of man as a living and responding being.'

Obviously drama will play a major part in our course because it explores those relationships which are of such concern to our pupils at this stage of their development. The forms of drama work which can be attempted depend on many factors which will vary from school to school. It is clear, however, that it offers a rich opportunity for teachers to exploit in as full a measure as conditions, skill and enthusiasm permit. The possibilities of this form of literature will be limited only by the availability of suitable texts, and as the resources of any department of English are restricted, and the demands on them heavy, perhaps some suggestions can be made on means of overcoming this problem.

Sets of texts can be obtained from the British Drama League (see Chapter 5), and, in some areas, from local drama leagues and public libraries. The main drawback is, of course, that only sufficient texts for an actual production will be available.

Paperback editions are valuable because they often contain several plays by different authors, or a selection of plays by a single playwright. Small sets, enough for one copy to be shared by two pupils, can thus make a wide variety of plays available for large forms.

Obviously every opportunity will be taken of seeing plays, films, television presentations, etc., and of hearing performances on tape or records.

Poetry

Though drama may provide problems of making an adequate number of texts available, poetry certainly should not. Good anthologies are plentiful, and all schools have duplicating machines if the poems chosen are not easily available in any text. B.B.C. publications are also a good source of texts built around the thematic approach.

It is important that we as teachers should avoid the analytical approach typical of 'A'-Level appreciation exercises. The poem must be allowed to speak for itself, and must not be weighed down by a load of technical and background information which can become more important than the poem itself. We should also avoid any treatment which stresses the written version at the expense of the spoken. A good reading by the teacher, or a recording, can create a noticeable impact on pupils, and we should not destroy this effect by intruding critical comment. This impact not only often produces an enthusiastic oral response but also results in some of their best writing.

We should also try to instil the idea that poetry is not a way of using language set apart from all others. It may be a highly personal means of communication, but it is a way of sharing an experience and seeking to ensure the maximum response from others. We seek to do the same when we are talking to others with a similar intention, but, unlike the poet, having at our disposal audible voices, facial expression and gesture. Poetry is vivid talk in a memorable form, and in the same way people will listen intently and appreciatively to a skilled and experienced speaker, so they will respond to the poet's voice if only they will listen to him. Both activities should be regarded as completely natural.

Speech

At all times we shall be encouraging our pupils to express themselves orally. For many of them, spoken communication will so far outweigh written communication after they leave school, as to be virtually their sole method of expression.

Naturally the lessons themselves must offer opportunities for students to express their opinions and reactions. But we are all aware that in every class there is the vocal minority which, given the chance, will dominate such lessons. The answer to this situation could be for each pupil to give a short talk on some topic related to the themes of our lessons, and to be prepared to answer questions from the other members of his form. Using this method, we ensure that he has to get away from his prepared talk, and express himself naturally, freely and spontaneously in replying to questions. Group discussions are also especially relevant here.

Speech is the supremely important factor in the development of personality, and has a decisive effect on human happiness and well-being. This means of communication conditions our intellectual and social growth, and we must do our utmost to ensure that our pupils achieve as high a standard as possible. The Newsom Report makes the development of the power of spoken language a central concern of education, 'There is no gift like the gift of speech; and the level at which people have learned to use it determines the level of their companionship and the level at which their life is lived'.

The English room

In the preceding sections the emphasis has rightly been on what we should aim to do for our students at this important stage of their school careers. But it is equally important that some mention should be made of the surroundings in which we carry out this task.

There are undeniable advantages in having one room specifically set aside for sixth-form lessons. These are:

(1) All the reference books and sets of texts could be stored here, and be readily available for use.

(2) Aids such as tape recorders, record players, the library of tapes and records, and a radio could be permanently housed here, and again be readily accessible.

(3) Pictures, photographs, illustrations, charts, etc. could be displayed around the room.

(4) If easily-stacked tables were provided, these could be set aside when not required and a more informal seating pattern created for discussion, listening to recordings, etc., or for providing space for drama activity.

Such a room would create a greater sense of community, of belonging to a group with a distinct purpose meeting in a room which is their own, and is completely unlike the setting for any of their other lessons. It could encourage a greater sense of involvement and stimulate a desire to contribute to the facilities of this room, as for example, in the offer of books, photographs, pictures.

In conclusion, then, however many changes may take place in the nature of the sixth form, English will always have a vital and important rôle to play. As Denys Thompson has said, 'Words are not an adjunct to living. They are part of life itself. They supply the indispensable moulds for the shaping of our thoughts and feeling – our distinctive humanity cannot continue without literature. The reason for the centrality of literature is that it stands for humanity. Literature upholds the human values.'

'A'-Level papers

Although we have been concerned with the changes which are taking
place in the sixth form, many pupils will still wish to prepare for the
'A'-Level Examination.

It should be assumed that the new sixth-former's initial reaction will
be shocked surprise. He will be rather overwhelmed by the number of
texts he is expected to study and their difficulty, and somewhat
alarmed by the new methods of work and the higher standards
demanded. This first reaction is valuable for it serves to impress on a
pupil at the outset that he has entered on a course of study quite
different from anything he has experienced before, and one which will
make considerable demands on him. We must therefore give him time
to adjust himself to this new set of factors.

It should be emphasised at the beginning that as senior pupils they
must now be prepared to act like students. They must adopt a
responsible attitude to their work, and expect to do a considerable
amount of unsupervised study. Although there will not be a homework
timetable as there was in the lower school, they should be using this
time for wide reading, since the work done in the classroom is not
enough to prepare them for their examination.

It should also be made clear at this stage that the aim of English
studies is not merely preparation for an examination. After two years'
intensive study pupils should have had experience of a wide range of
literature, an insight into the historical background of the writers
selected, and should be able to make a critical assessment of a piece of
writing in a clear, concise style.

The most difficult task confronting the teacher is that of training
pupils to read critically and to have confidence in their own critical
judgement. We can only achieve this by providing them with frequent
opportunities of reading and discussing a wide variety of literary forms.
Opinions and interpretation must be supported by close analysis and
reasoned argument. No pupil should ever be allowed to indulge in vague
generalisations but must be prepared to submit his judgement to the
critical examination of other members of his group, and to defend it.
The teacher's rôle is to encourage, stimulate and suggest lines of
approach, and if he offers a critical verdict he should support it with
clear reasons, and be prepared to argue his case. A teacher may be
tempted because of his wider knowledge and experience to push a
discussion the way he feels it ought to go, on the reasonable grounds
that it will produce more fruitful results. But we should be chary of

taking away the responsibility of students to reach a decision, even if it eventually is wrong. What matters is a whole-hearted response rather than a critical verdict.

The books set for study are intended to represent the basic minimum, and other related texts by the chosen authors should be introduced. To many teachers this remark will seem so obvious as hardly to be worth making. Yet some 'A'-Level examiners' reports still contain criticism of pupils whose knowledge is confined to the set books. By providing a wider experience of each author's work we are enriching our pupils' knowledge of literature, which is our main purpose, and, at the same time, providing them with wider material for examination purposes. The treatment of jealousy in *Othello*, for example, could be compared with that in the portrait of Leontes in *The Winter's Tale*; and any study of Wordsworth is inadequate unless a pupil has a firm grasp of eighteenth-century literary theory and practice as supremely represented in the poetry of Pope.

Texts must also be placed firmly in their historical background. Literature grows from life, so the close connection between art and the life of the artist should be made abundantly evident. Yet examiners' comments reveal that candidates' answers often display very inadequate background knowledge.

One of the major problems facing beginners is that of presenting their written work in an appropriately mature manner. They discover with dismay that the techniques and methods which were acceptable at 'O' Level are now inadequate, and they find themselves struggling not only with more difficult material but also a more effective style to express their opinions. At this stage they need considerable help and encouragement and time must be devoted in class to the preparatory work required for an essay. Such a lesson should include suggestions as to the major points to be considered, and the titles of suitable reference books. Returned essays should be accompanied by detailed and helpful comments, and these are far more important than a grade. A teacher must be prepared to discuss his comments with a particular pupil, and though this takes time, in the first-year sixth this is time well spent. Praise as well as criticism is very important, for it is extremely difficult to restore the confidence of a pupil who has been discouraged early in his career, and the insecure pupil is an almost certain failure.

We are all acutely aware as teachers that our classroom, analytical approach to literature can result in a pupil 'knowing' a play, but in the process losing its impact as a vital, living dramatic creation. For this reason every opportunity should be grasped of seeing a live production;

this term embraces theatre, cinema and television performances. Use should also be made of radio productions, which it is permissible to record on tape, and televised serial versions both on normal programmes and schools television. Films may also be hired for school performances.

Even with such means available, it is still possible that the particular play set for study cannot be seen, and the recorded version is then the best alternative. In many ways it is of greater value for the purpose of study, since the emphasis will be on the text, and the distortions which may result from a stage producer's 'interpretation' will be absent. The other great advantages of the recorded version are that it can be used for illustrating a point, serve as a basis for discussion, and, after a play has been studied in great detail, it can enable a pupil to hear it with a new critical awareness and thus with a heightened appreciation.

Sixth-form students must learn to make their own notes for future reference. We should never employ dictated or printed notes, not even when we feel that a rather weak group would benefit from this type of assistance. The oft-repeated warning by examiners that less able candidates fail because they cannot adapt their memorised notes to the demands of a question, reveals the great weakness of this method. If assistance is felt to be necessary, it is better to dictate a brief summary of the main points covered at the end of a lesson. It should be emphasised repeatedly that notes serve only as a guide, not as a complete record. They are not intended to relieve pupils from the responsibility of making their own critical judgements, or to be a substitute for their own reading and research.

The first-year sixth former is used to the 'O' Level type of question which tells him precisely what he has to do, and we, at first, should also set straightforward questions, for our aim at this stage is to enable a pupil to learn to select relevant material and to present it effectively. When, however, we are satisfied that they are becoming proficient we must introduce them to the more complex 'A' Level type of question. Past papers should be used to demonstrate the absolute necessity of weighing every word in a question before deciding on a line of approach, particularly when it opens with a quotation and ends with such words as 'Discuss', 'Comment' or 'Do you agree?' It must be emphasised that these quotations are intended not to be proved but to provoke discussion. A candidate may well have to begin his answer with a clear statement of his own interpretation, and then to support this with a closely-argued, logical answer based solidly on a thorough knowledge of the text involved.

Many students are at first somewhat alarmed by the responsibility this approach places on them, and frequent practice in answering such questions is essential, which must be followed by careful and detailed criticism of their answers in the classroom. Though some students dislike their faults and follies being made public, it should be emphasised that the aim is not to embarrass but to help others to avoid committing the same mistakes. In this connection it is important we should pass on to the students, particularly those in the second year, the criticisms contained in the examiners' reports. They are intended to be made known, for the examiners hope that by detailing the most common faults, many of which appear with increasing regularity, they can improve the prospects of those sitting the current examination. Many teachers with long experience in the sixth form will know of these faults, and will have warned their pupils, but the fact that the examiners themselves also refer to them often has a most salutary effect. It is unfortunately true that teachers of English as well as prophets lack honour in their own country!

Use of English paper

In 1962 a sub-committee of the Committee of Vice-Chancellors and Principals reported that far too many undergraduates in their first year 'find undue difficulty in expressing themselves clearly and accurately in their own language'. They asserted that a pass in English at 'O' Level was inadequate for university studies, and they proposed a Use of English paper to ensure that sixth-formers continued their studies, and could produce a certificate of competence. Few teachers of English would challenge the findings of the committee, but many would challenge the belief that this examination can achieve the desired aim.

Can any external examination in English, it is argued, bring about a general raising of standards, if those same standards are not demanded by the other specialist subjects taken by a candidate? Are we not implying that in papers other than English, it is *what* you say not *how* you say it which is of primary importance? Standards throughout the country would be improved tremendously, if every subject demanded an appropriate skill in expression as a qualification in deciding the level of grade to be awarded.

Many universities accept students who have either failed or not even entered for this examination. The qualifying standard is still the 'O' Level pass condemned in 1962, and even this is not required by London University. If the universities themselves do not demand evidence of a standard they asserted was essential, it is small wonder that the value and function of this examination is questioned, not only by teachers but by pupils, as well. It is regrettable that the authority of the Use of English examination should be weakened by those who have most to gain from it.

Many would like this to become a compulsory examination for all those who have spent two years studying in the sixth form. It is wrong, they argue, to apply it only to intending university candidates. The pupil who enters industry, business or one of the professions direct from school surely requires a similar qualification, not only as an aid to his future studies, though this is important, but as evidence of a standard which ought to be expected from all pupils who reach this stage in their secondary education.

Support for the contention contained in the previous paragraph is to be found in the examiners' comments on the results in many parts of the country. In the Welsh Joint Education Committee Examiners' Report for 1970, for example, there are references to the 'poverty of expression', 'faulty sentence-structure', 'poverty of punctuation' and 'appalling weakness in vocabulary' found in the work of many candidates. This situation is not unique to Wales, and if these are the weaknesses of those who intend to enter universities can we feel complacent about those sixth-form pupils whose standard of English is untested and unknown?

Whatever its shortcomings, this examination has created a national standard of sixth-form English, and many pupils have benefited from the preparation required and from the wider discussion of the uses of language such preparation involves.

Consideration of this examination has raised certain important questions, not the least of which is the attitude of the universities themselves. We also support the remark in the Eighth Report of the S.S.E.C. 1964 *The Examining of English Language* that further study should be given to schemes which take into account a candidate's performance in English in all his advanced level subjects.

Finally, perhaps it is time to review this examination in the light of our experience over the last few years, and our assessment of the nature of the sixth form of the future.

Team teaching

Henry Lawrence

13

The introduction of the comprehensive system of secondary education
has resulted in many teachers questioning the teaching approach typical
of the grammar school, based on what has been called 'the two by four
curriculum', i.e. the two covers of a textbook and the four walls of a
classroom, because it no longer seemed to meet the needs of those
less academic pupils who would never have attended a grammar
school.

The detailed English syllabus, course book, strict and heavy
homework timetable, and examination-dominated system seemed
entirely irrelevant in this new situation where pupils could no longer be
thought of in terms of homogeneous groups, and therefore many
teachers were forced to examine and re-assess their material and its
presentation. As they could not any longer assume a static situation, a
more flexible approach was sought which could be tailored to fit the
changing needs of their pupils.

American educationists have for some years been experimenting
with new teaching techniques, and after examining their methods
Dr Lovell in his book *Team Teaching* provided the following broad
definition, 'A form of teaching organization in which two or more
teachers have the responsibility, working together, for all the teaching
of a given group of pupils in some specified area of the curriculum'.
But it should be stressed that this definition seeks to cover a very wide
variety of practice. It will, however, serve as a starting-point for an
examination of this method.

The teaching team can vary from two teachers sharing the
presentation of lessons in a single subject, to a large group of teachers
from different disciplines, combining to present a theme to which each
subject makes its own specialist contribution.

The advantages claimed for the team-teaching method are:

(1) It can be adapted to suit a wide variety of school situations,
because it is highly flexible.

(2) It lends itself to alteration and modification in the light of
changing needs, new ideas and past experience.

(3) The varied abilities of a greater number of teachers are made available to pupils than under the subject specialist system of one teacher for each subject.

(4) Variety and interest are added to the pupils' lessons.

(5) It obviates the criticism that the less able pupils are never taught by the best teachers.

(6) It relieves the situation where the relationship between teacher and class is such that it adversely affects the learning situation.

(7) The teacher is forced to emerge from the isolation of his classroom, re-think his lessons, his material and his approach and be prepared to submit himself to the scrutiny of his colleagues.

(8) He can compare his own methods with those of his colleagues, and is put back in a learning situation which could benefit both himself and his pupils.

(9) It relieves the considerable strain on the energy, patience and ingenuity of the teacher who is solely responsible for creating and sustaining interest and enthusiasm week by week in a class of less able pupils.

(10) Where a teacher has a particular interest, skill or hobby it can be made available to a wider range of pupils, e.g. a teacher who is expert in improvised drama.

(11) It provides help with hardware, e.g. setting up a film, preparing the projector, etc.

(12) Because teachers are enabled to meet and know a greater number of pupils, the staff-pupil relationship is improved.

(13) When a teacher is absent, pupils do not lose their lessons.

This is an impressive list of advantages, but can these claims be justified? Those like Anthony Adams in *Team Teaching and the Teaching of English*, and the authors of *Teaching from Strength*, both of whom have employed this method successfully, would say they can be entirely substantiated. Others, like Dr Denis Lawton and Dr Lovell, who have studied experiments both in America and this country, would have reservations about some of these claims. However, it would be fair to comment that since virtually no school employs exactly the same form of team teaching as another, it would be surprising if there were no divergences of opinion.

But we are here concerned with examining the system itself rather than with passing judgement upon it. However, it can be said that the following factors will make a major contribution toward the ultimate success of any scheme:

(1) It must be clearly established what the employment of this method is intended to achieve.

(2) The teachers involved in the introduction of such a scheme must be whole-hearted in their support, enthusiastic, and keen to ensure its success. Staff should not arbitrarily be selected to take part, for they may soon become discontented passengers and destroy the essential unity of the team.

(3) Very careful and detailed planning must be undertaken well before the commencement of any scheme, and the team of teachers must be involved in every stage of this preparation.

(4) Parents of the pupils involved, when any scheme is introduced, should be kept fully informed, to allay any fears that the experiment may adversely affect future academic success.

(5) Careful consideration must be given to the means by which the progress of the pupils and the success of a course may be evaluated. A record card or sheet for each pupil is suggested, printed in such a manner that it will enable the members of the team to enter a full description of the particular item of work carried out, a mark or grade, and remarks concerning such factors as attitude to work, originality, initiative and progress. Since such varied tasks as model-making, drawing and painting, collecting information, preparing reports and the writing of compositions and poems may have been undertaken, then a fairly detailed picture of a pupil's abilities, potentialities, progress and personality should gradually emerge.

Each member of the team should keep a careful record of his experiences in presenting that section of the work for which he is responsible. At a later date this will enable the team to assess, for example, whether they achieved their objective, what items, methods or approaches require re-thinking, what material might be omitted or expanded, or what extra equipment or material should be introduced in future. If this process is carried out after each programme of work is completed, then a library of projects which have proved successful in practice can be created for future use.

(6) Adequate accommodation must be available. This should include one room, which can be blacked out, of sufficient size to hold several groups of children for such activities as introductory talks, films, talks by outside speakers, etc. In addition there must be smaller neighbouring rooms for independent group activities. Where a scheme involves large numbers, suitable accommodation is vital, for crowded conditions will create serious difficulties. The rooms should be concentrated in one area of the school so as to avoid problems of communication and movement of pupils.

(7) Long-term planning should include consideration of the examinations for which many pupils will be entered at the age of sixteen. It is possible for a scheme for an Integrated Studies C.S.E. Examination Mode 3 to be submitted to the appropriate authority, and this enables a school to plan its work accordingly. Even if this suggestion is not adopted, the programme of work should be of such an academic standard that it will enable a pupil to prepare for such examinations.

These factors indicate the amount of careful and detailed planning which must precede any programme of team teaching. Where this method is employed on a large scale it will involve additional items for consideration. For example, there will be a considerable amount of secretarial work arising from typing and duplicating material prepared by teachers, copying such items as articles, records, poems, etc., typing reports and keeping records. Also someone should be responsible for checking and maintaining all the hardware to be used, and another person should be able to produce such items as charts, maps, slides, etc. It has been found that, in practice, teachers can only deal with such work at the expense of their availability for teaching. This means that secretarial and technical services must be provided.

The duration of each project will, of course, depend to a great extent on such factors as the number of lessons allotted to this form of teaching, the age of the pupils involved and the type and complexity of the theme, but as a general guide it is convenient to adopt the normal divisions of the school year and use a half-term as a working basis. This period of time allows a theme to be treated in some depth, and helps to maintain interest and enthusiasm. Also the forward-planning of such items as outside visits, invitations to visiting speakers and ordering of films is facilitated, and should a theme prove less successful than was anticipated, it is easier to improvise additional material for a shorter period of time.

An example of two projects which covered the period of half a term is given in the Appendix.

An English department is large and therefore lends itself to the team-teaching method, either operating it within the department or acting as a member of an integrated studies approach with other subjects.

Where any department carries out its own scheme, certain additional problems may arise from the fact that not all the members of the department may be willing to be involved. Thus a departmental head may well be faced with the problem of a senior colleague who may be either reluctant or even positively unwilling to change his methods at this late stage in his career. Such a situation would demand very careful and tactful treatment, for, as has already been emphasised, the success of any scheme largely depends on the whole-hearted response of those involved in it.

Finally, the team-teaching approach may well be a means of providing for those pupils remaining in school when the leaving age is raised. In the words of Schools Council Working Paper No. 2,

> The task facing the schools is to work out the large purposes for the curriculum as a whole, and then to probe by experiments of many different kinds — the improvement of content and treatment within traditional subject areas, team teaching over a number of subject areas, the introduction of new topics or even subjects — how best to give the teaching relevance to students' experience so far, and to human needs and purposes in the adult world which they will soon be joining.

It is not intended in this section to provide an exhaustive account of the team teaching method, but rather an introduction containing sufficient information to enable a teacher to decide whether he wishes to pursue the matter further and to read more widely on the subject. To this end, a book list is appended.

Book list

Books

Adams, A. *Team Teaching and the Teaching of English* (Pergamon, 1970).

Bair, M. and Woodward, R. G. *Team Teaching in Action* (New York: Houghton Mifflin, 1964).

An Experiment in Team Teaching (University of Exeter Institute of Education, 1968).

Jones, E. and Adams, A. *A Desk Book for Teachers of English and the Humanities* (Pergamon, 1964).

Lovell, K. *Team Teaching* (University of Leeds Institute of Education, 1967).

Polos, N. *The Dynamics of Team Teaching* (Dubuque, Iowa: William C. Brown, 1965).

Rance, P. *Teaching by Topics* (Ward Lock, 1968).

Shaplin, J. T. and Olds, H. F. *Team Teaching* (New York: Harper and Row, 1964).

Summerfield, G. *Topics in English* (Batsford, 1965).

Teaching in Unstreamed Schools (University of Exeter Institute of Education, 1967).

Trump, J. L. and Baynham, D. *Focus on Change. Guide to Better Schools* (New York: Rand McNally, 1961).

Worrall, P. *et al. Teaching from Strength: An Introduction to Team Teaching* (Hamilton, 1970).

Articles

Bland, H. W. 'Aspects of Team Teaching'. *Educational Development* (Summer, 1967).

'Team Teaching – The Wybourn Plan'. *Educational Development* (Autumn, 1967).

Church, D. P., Garritty, H. J. and James, G. 'Team Teaching'. *Forum* (Autumn, 1965).

Grant, R. 'Team and Theme'. *New Education* (June, 1966).

Hannam, C. 'Experiences of Team Teaching'. *New Era* (February, 1968).

'Team Teaching – Who Leads the Team?' *New Era* (January, 1969).

Lawton, D. 'Team Teaching', *Journal of Joint Association of Classical Teachers* (annual: 1970).

Waterhouse, R. 'Team Teaching'. *Higher Education Journal* (Spring, 1967).

H.M.S.O. Publications

Another Year – to endure or enjoy (Schools Council Welsh Committee, 1967).

Curriculum Innovation in Practice (Schools Council, 1968).

Humanities for the Young School Leaver – Approach through English (Schools Council, 1968).

The New Curriculum (Schools Council, 1967).

Raising the School Leaving Age (Schools Council Working Paper No. 2, 1965).

Society and the Young School Leaver (Schools Council Working Paper No. 11, 1967).

Appendix

The projects here described were part of a larger scheme of work entitled 'Our town', which aimed to trace the growth of the present large industrial centre and docks of Newport from Roman times. They were carried out with a group of seventy pupils from the fourth year for six periods a week, two full afternoons.

The two projects, each designed to cover a half a term's work, covered the Roman and medieval periods, and three teachers were involved from the classics, art and English departments.

Each pupil was provided with a loose-leaf folder and a large-page drawing book.

The Roman period provided an excellent start for there was an important site nearby which had been a legionary fort and town. In addition there were three museums available for visits, and an abundance of material: film-strips, slides, charts, illustrations and maps.

The classics master planned the Roman project as follows:

Roman beginnings

(1) Life in Roman Britain – social, military and religious.

(2) Visits: (i) to Roman site; (ii) to site museum; (iii) to local museum; (iv) to National Museum of Wales.

(3) Show how the town grew at a place on an important Roman route where a tidal river could be forded.

(4) Show how the town is linked with other Roman centres by land and water.

Assignments

(1) Individual — (i) Write out accounts of talks and illustrate them.

(ii) Describe visits to Roman site and museums.

(2) Group — (i) Draw a plan of a typical legionary fort.

(ii) Draw a Roman soldier, name his equipment and draw a chart showing the organisation of the Roman army.

(iii) Describe a Roman villa, draw a picture and make a model.

(iv) Describe and illustrate Roman dress, pottery and household utensils.

Medieval period

This was planned by the members of the English and art departments. The scheme was based on a study of two particular buildings, the castle and the cathedral, which had been specially studied by the art department as part of its architecture course. This fact, together with the resources of the town museum, meant that again an ample supply of material was available.

Castle

(1) Layout, construction and position. All dependent on its function of guarding first the ford, and later the wooden bridge across the river.

(2) Show how the town grew up around the castle, and how this period of its history is reflected in the names of areas and streets.

Church

(1) Construction and position.

(2) Show how the church is on an ancient road route, and why it is built on a mound.

Visits

(i) To cathedral; (ii) to castle; (iii) to museum.

Assignments

Individual — Write accounts of each of the visits mentioned.

Group — (i) Draw a plan of the castle.

(ii) Draw a plan of the church.

(iii) Draw a plan of the town at this period, making a special point of naming those areas and streets which still retain these names.

Throughout this scheme both the classics and English teachers supervised all written work and helped to arrange visits, prepare equipment, order films and so on, while the art teacher provided the · material collected during the special studies of the castle and cathedral.

14 Organisation, or, in place of the syllabus

Raymond Hemington

It was not at first envisaged that we should say much about the syllabus. The old style, rigid syllabus, which detailed what work was to be done each week, with each form, beginning with 'Nouns, kinds of' and ending with '*Hamlet*, final revision of', is obviously a thing of the past. (Was it, indeed ever more than a yellowing document in a desk, kept because THEY might want to see it?) Nevertheless, syllabuses of a sort — work schemes, 'Tentative suggestions for new members of the department', etc. are still drawn up by many heads of departments (we have examined several, including some of our own).

What, if anything, can be usefully said about them here? As is stated in the introduction, the whole of this book is, in a very important sense, a syllabus. English consists of skills to be acquired and awareness to be developed; it is not a body of information to be learnt. The work done each succeeding year is largely repetition, but deepening, widening and increasing in sophistication all the time. However, this generalisation is of little use in practice to the head of department faced with the task of ensuring that all the English taught in school is purposive and worth-while. Neither does it help to be told that we must 'structure the learning situation as an on-going process, involving teachers and taught in a meaningful dialogue, and bringing all the department into the decision-making process'.

The Edwardian miss who threw away her stays had to develop her abdominal muscles. If we abandon the constriction of a rigid syllabus we must strengthen our organisation. The English department staff must meet regularly. If the school is very large it may not be convenient to hold a meeting of all in the department more than once a term, so they must meet in groups more frequently. In one ideal case that has come to our notice, a head has arranged the timetable so that all the members of the English department can meet weekly.

Each teacher should be free to use his own method of teaching, but the head of department must make certain that all the different skills involved in writing and speaking English are going to be covered at some time during the year in each class. He will be wise to keep the distribution of books firmly in his grasp, so that a form can always be assured of a set of books right for it at a given time. In this way the head of department can insure against lop-sided literature teaching — the over-zealous drama enthusiast, the frustrated poet, or the teacher whose literature course consists only of novels.

Deals must be arranged as to who shall have the tape recorder at a given time (there are seldom enough of these things in working order at the same time!), yet an attempt should be made to keep one in hand for the keen but unsystematic colleague who has a sudden inspiration. (A *quid pro quo* with another department?) Other items of hardware need to be similarly apportioned. Suitable places for oral or dramatic work must be allocated. Competition for these will be keen, and will probably involve consultation with other departments. In our crowded schools it is by no means certain that any classroom will have six feet clear in the front for any special purpose; it is even less certain that it will be reasonably sound proof.

Find out well in advance what each one in the department wants in the way of special stationery. It is also necessary to keep in mind the *sort* of form that will be using books and equipment. For example, reinforce paperbacks with plastic covers, and use discretion in surrendering precious books into the hands of individual pupils. Be realistic: budget for generous replacements in sets of popular books in junior forms.

In case of illness, each member of the department should keep a record of what has been done with a form, so that a replacement teacher can build on his own ideas without duplication.

Most English departments have their quota of 'light skirmishers' — victims, willy-nilly, of timetable exigencies, who are 'filling in' by taking six periods a week with 3C, or, even more difficult, doing one period a week with each of six forms, because the parallel forms are engaged in engineering and technical drawing, or Going To The Baths. The good head of department will go out of his way to help these auxiliaries by suggesting things to do, taking advantage of special interests which can enrich the total English experience of the class. That 'one period a week' *can* be made something to look forward to.

In planning ahead, watch 'public relations' with other departments. Find out what classes 5A, B, and C will miss when they go to see *Julius Caesar*, or how it will affect others if you want to use the small hall for a talk by a well-known author. It is tactful not only yourself to see the colleagues involved, but to train pupils to ask permission to miss lessons — well in advance. If you are painstaking as a general rule, you may be forgiven the odd emergency arrangement, when the secretary of the local literary society rings to say that X is talking to them about his work this evening, and would you like him to talk to the sixth this afternoon? (All this may seem like stating the obvious, but one has seen so many enthusiasts come to grief over such little points, that it is worth saying.)

Formal internal examinations in English are obsolescent. The continuous assessment that is taking their place needs to be carefully organised, so that it really *is* continuous, and so that it covers the whole range of work in English over a period of time. Here it is necessary to be realistic. Even the most conscientious will find it impossible to cope with marking one set of written work per week from every form on his personal timetable. It is therefore important not to begin over-ambitiously, and so leave oneself with periods during which one sweats over huge arrears of work, while other work piles up, and meanwhile pupils lose interest in the first work set. Full assessment must be restricted to a limited and carefully selected variety of work. We would suggest, per term, one specimen of each of the following for assessment. (Other things may well be marked, but not exhaustively.)

(1) Personal writing.

(2) Impersonal writing.

(3) Narrative.

(4) Oral work.

(5) Comprehension.

(6) A piece of 1, 2 or 3 assessed purely for technical competence.

(7) Check-up on reading. (In lower forms, simply short questions on details that will indicate whether a book has been read or not.)

(8) A. N. Other. (There is always something that will not fit any category.)

The order in which these things are done will depend on the individual teacher's plan. *The bent of that particular teacher and the needs of his particular classes must over-ride any such scheme.*

Index